IMAGES
of America

NORTH PROVIDENCE

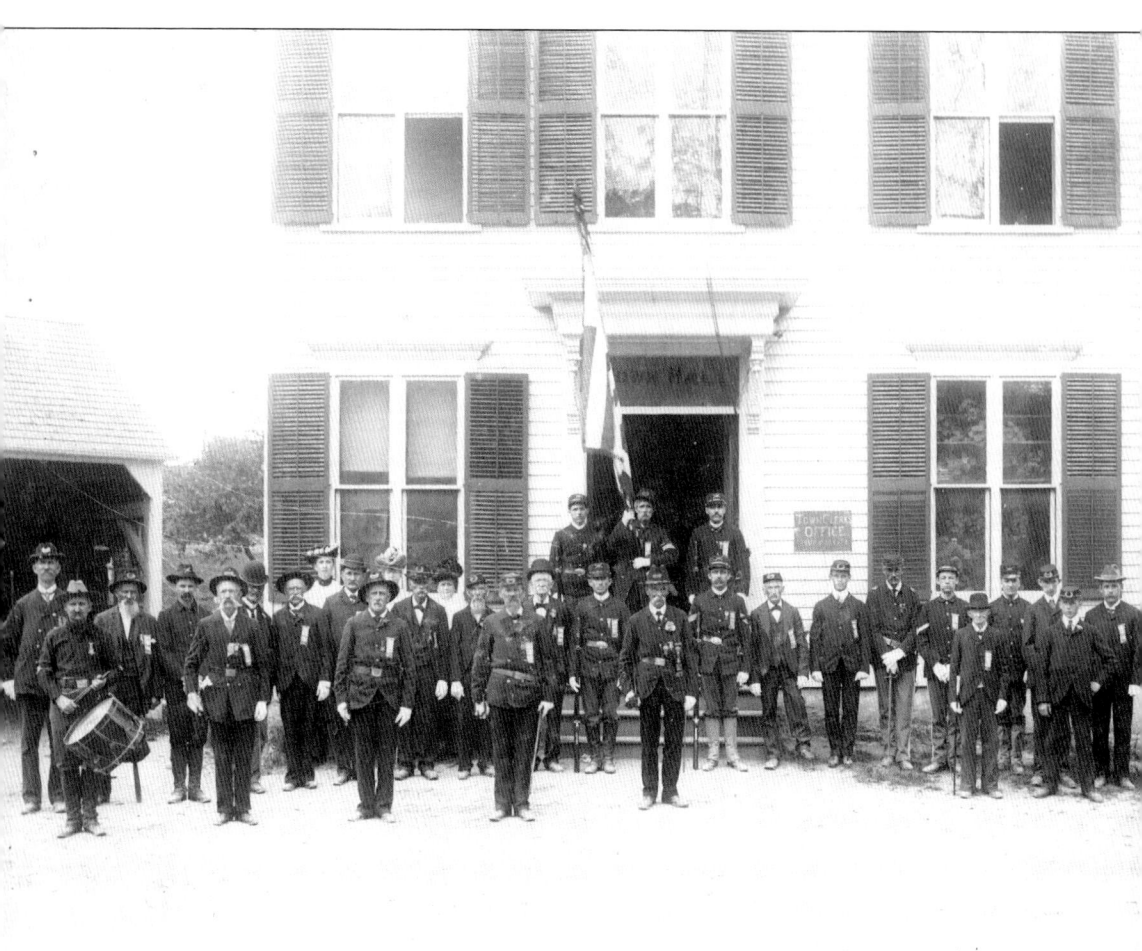

Veterans and sons of veterans are pictured in front of the old 1879 town hall. This picture was taken c. 1901/02. Both Civil War and Spanish American War veterans are pictured. The person in the front row second in line beside the drummer is William F. Allison, a Civil War veteran who died at age ninety-four in 1925.

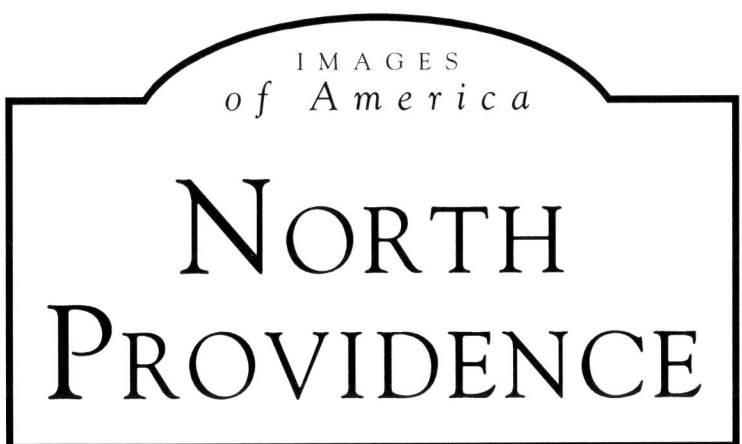

IMAGES of America

NORTH PROVIDENCE

Thomas E. and Barbara A. Greene

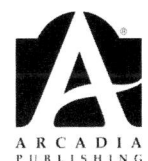

Copyright © 1996 by Thomas E. and Barbara A. Greene
ISBN 978-0-7385-8706-6

Published by Arcadia Publishing
Charleston, South Carolina

Printed in the United States of America

Library of Congress Catalog Card Number: Applied for

For all general information contact Arcadia Publishing at:
Telephone 843-853-2070
Fax 843-853-0044
E-mail sales@arcadiapublishing.com
For customer service and orders:
Toll-Free 1-888-313-2665

Visit us on the Internet at www.arcadiapublishing.com

This book is dedicated to our good friend Vincent Dexter, the first North Providence town historian who unselfishly dedicated his life to town history. Here he is pictured with the first mayor, Sal Mancini, at the old town hall.

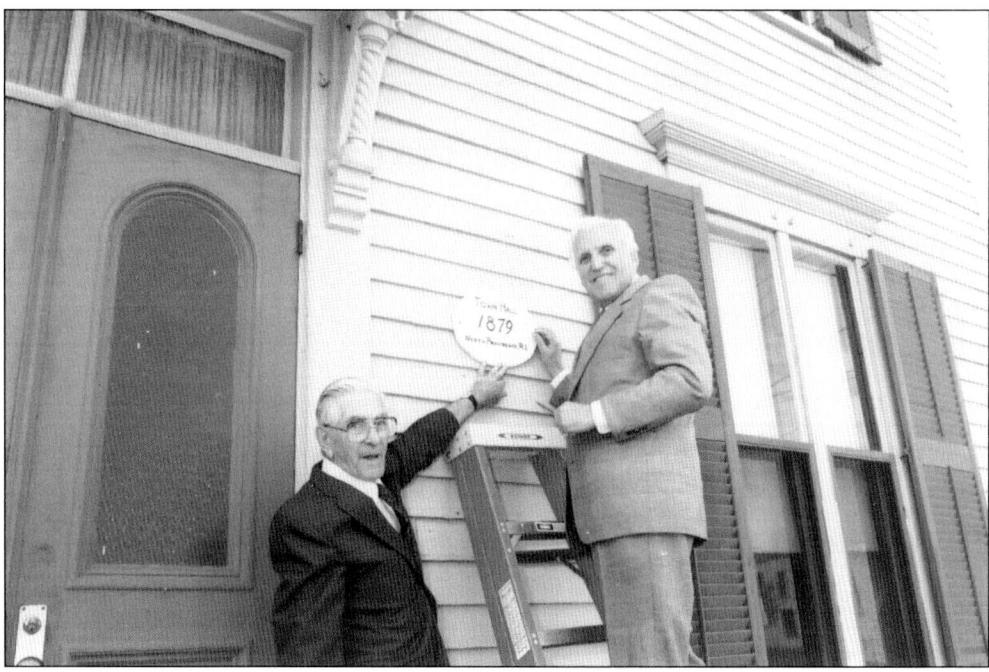

Contents

Introduction		7
1.	Allendale	9
2.	Centerdale	17
3.	Fruit Hill	55
4.	Greystone	71
5.	Lymansville	83
6.	Marieville	97
7.	Woodville/Geneva	109
Acknowledgments		128

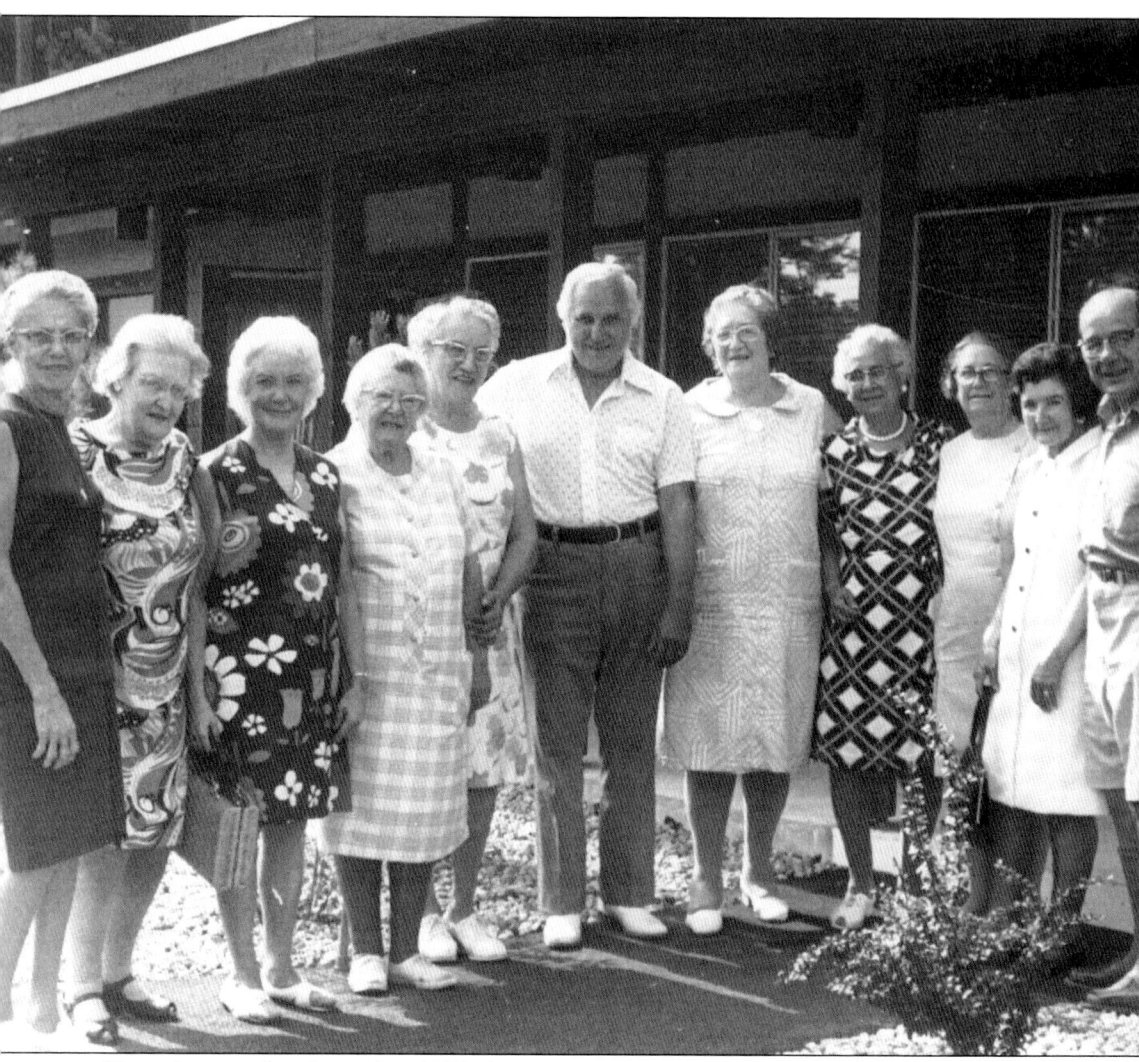

This photograph taken after 1975 shows senior citizens at the Sunset Terrace Apartments. From left to right are: Bernice Mitchell, Hope Spearman, Eva Leach, unknown, unknown, Mayor Sal Mancini, Theresa Paolantonio, Elsie Isles, Anna M. Greene, Betty Caccia, and Henry Belanger.

Introduction

During the mid-eighteenth century, a group of farmers from the northern section of Providence petitioned the general assembly to allow them to become a separate town. They were unhappy with the government of Providence because they felt it did not meet their particular needs as farmers, as it was more concerned with the merchants and businessmen of the time. On June 13, 1765, the general assembly passed the request. Over the next one hundred years, the boundaries of North Providence changed as parts of the town were reunited with Providence in 1767, 1873, and 1874. In addition, in 1874, a large part of the town was annexed to Pawtucket. As a result, North Providence became the smallest town in the state, with an area of 5.8 square miles; the population dropped from 20,495 to 1,303 citizens. A hundred years later, the population again peaked at 20,000.

With the advent of the nineteenth century, the areas of the town near the Woonasquatucket River, the West River, and the Wenscott Reservoir began to take on a more industrial flavor as mills were built. Except for the Fruit Hill area, all of the town's villages changed with the advent of the Industrial Revolution. In this essay, we will try to bring to you some of the little-known history of our town of North Providence.

In the early nineteenth century it became obvious that better roads were needed. Five turnpikes were constructed in North Providence with the cost of construction assumed by private companies. Turnpikes, as distinguished from ordinary roads, were those throughways with gates barring the progress of the traveler, at which payments were demanded for the privilege of using the road. The payments were called "tolls" and the gates were known as "tollgates." Beginning in 1805, the Louisquisset Turnpike was constructed when a company of the same name was formed to improve the old road. The tollgate of that road was at the northeast corner of Louisquisset and Mineral Spring. In 1806, a turnpike was built passing what is now Twin Rivers; it was called the Douglas Turnpike because it extended to Douglas, Massachusetts. Its tollgate was located just below the Wenscott Reservoir (Twin Rivers). Next was the Farnum Pike, started in 1808 and finished in 1828; this road was eventually named Waterman Avenue in North Providence as a tribute to Caleb Waterman, a wheelwright and undertaker in Centerdale during the nineteenth century. The Powder Mill Turnpike, named for the powder mill built during the Revolutionary War which operated only three years before exploding, is now known as Route 44 or Smith Street in North Providence. Finally, the Mineral Spring Turnpike, chartered in 1826 and named for a mineral spring in Pawtucket, gave residents easy access to Pawtucket when town meetings were held there.

Patriotism in North Providence was exemplified by two groups of public-spirited citizens: the North Providence Company of Militia and the Eastermost Company of Militia in Smithfield. These groups petitioned the legislature for a joint charter that was granted in 1774 in the name of The North Providence Rangers. This group was led by officers Captain Joseph Olney, Lieutenant John Angell, and Ensign Joseph Randall. The North Providence Rangers group was assimilated through the years by other similar military groups, and so its spirit lives on.

Usually towns and villages in New England had a town pound to hold stray cattle or sheep as opposed to the dogs and cats of today. A descendent of an old North Providence family, Hezekiah Olney, had the town pound on his land c. 1875 at the present site of Brooks Pharmacy in Woodville.

For humans, confinement was in jails called Bridewells. The dictionary definition of this word is "a house of correction for the confinement of disorderly persons." The name was derived from a palace built near Saint Bride's or Bridget's Well in London, which was turned into a workhouse. North Providence had Bridewells in Marieville, Woodville, Geneva, and Centerdale. The most bizarre location of such a confinement facility is recorded in 1888, when Lewis Woodward was directed to have two cells placed in the basement of the school at Marieville.

When we think of a theater in North Providence, most remember the Community Theater. Actually, the first place of entertainment was located in the Armory Hall, where numerous plays were held from the 1860s through 1892; the hall burned in 1892. Within the next fifteen years, Clarence Broley built another building on the same site which had stores on the ground level and a theater called Casino Motion Pictures on the second floor. By the 1930s, Napolean Trahan built a movie theater on Waterman Avenue called the Community Theater. At the time this theater was destroyed by fire in the 1970s, it was called the Hillside.

North Providence was not without its artistic side. Three well-known artists resided in Fruit Hill, two of them in the first decade of the twentieth century and one from the 1920s through 1940s. H. Cyrus Farnum lived in a house at 95 Olney Avenue which is still standing today. He painted brilliant outdoor scenes of Africa which were exhibited at the Butler Exchange in Providence. He died in 1925. George Whitaker, known as the "Dean of Rhode Island Artists," exhibited for many years at the Providence Art Club. He had studios at the Providence Art Club and also at his home at 1370 Smith Street where Janemor Apartments now stand. He painted abroad, chiefly with the Barbizon school. The third artist was Mabel Woodward, who in 1931 was living with her family at 36 Belvedere Boulevard. She died in 1944 and is noted for her oil paintings, especially coastal and beach scenes which today command as much as $20,000.

North Providence residents, like other early Americans, were concerned with establishing churches for their spiritual enrichment. The Baptist meeting house was built on upper Smithfield Road approaching the Wenscott Reservoir c. 1767. It had as its pastor Reverend Ezekiel Angell, who continued as pastor until his death in 1782 when he was succeeded by Rufus Tefft. In 1817, the church building was sold to John Hutchinson and the congregation moved to the site of the present Saint James Episcopal Church on Fruit Hill Avenue, where the second church in North Providence was established as a Baptist congregation in 1818. The third church was built in 1832 at Centerdale as the Free Will Baptist Church in the building that later became the town armory and the town entertainment center. The fourth pre-1890 church was called the Farmers' Chapel and was built in 1884 on Angell Road near the Lincoln town line. It served the farmers in the vicinity for more than half a century. In 1945, the Farmers' Chapel association sold the property, and by 1948 Mr. and Mrs. Norman Turner resided in the former church.

Many of us who belonged to scout troops probably remember a hike to the Peter Randall Reservation. Of course, we probably assumed that Peter Randall's home had been at that location. The true story is as follows. In 1929, a 30-acre tract on Smithfield Road was donated to the State of Rhode Island to be used as a park in memory of Peter Randall, an eighteenth-century resident of Providence. The donation was made by Mrs. Ellen Randall Appleby and her sister Mrs. Josephine Lee, both lineal descendants of Peter Randall, who never lived in this area himself. The land was originally owned by the Smith family and was sold to Edward Randall in 1824. It remained in the Randall family until the generous donation was made.

We have only scratched the surface of the history of our town. So much more can be said and perhaps it will be in future publications.

One

ALLENDALE

The village of Allendale was founded in 1822 by Zachariah Allen, who was the founder of the Allendale Mill in that same year. The architect of the mill complex was John Holden Greene, a collateral ancestor of this author. This mill was unique because of its pioneer use of fire retardant materials and innovative manufacturing machines. In addition, the first building seen as one enters the mill property is a mill store built in the Greek Revival style. The patriarch of Centerdale, Frank C. Angell, was born in this building in 1845. At that time, the first floor was used as a country store and the second was the residence of the Angell family. According to Angell's book, *Four Score Years*, this structure was called Scout's Hall by 1909.

Originally, just wool was manufactured at the Allendale Mill, but cotton was included later. Mr. Allen built gambrel-roof mill houses for his employees *c.* 1824, and during the 1840s several Gothic cottages were added; these buildings are shown in A.J. Downing's book, *The Architecture Of Country Houses*. The house at 515 Woonasquatucket Avenue is an example.

In 1847, Zachariah Allen built a stone Baptist Sunday school for the children of the mill workers. The architect was Thomas Tefft, who had collaborated with Henry Barnard to begin innovative school construction concepts. In 1850, the building at 545 Woonasquatucket Avenue was consecrated as a church. A brick addition on the southeast end of the complex was built in 1910, and the mill remained in operation until 1976 when part of the complex was converted to condominiums.

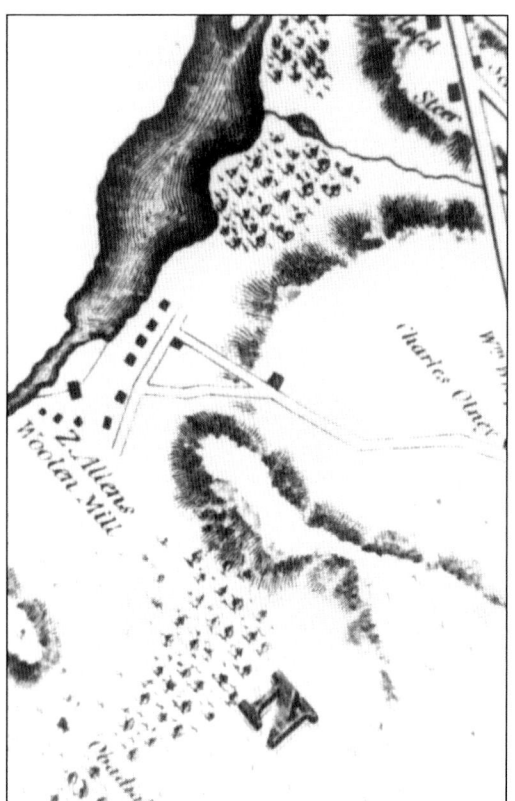

This is the village as it looked in 1835. Woonasquatucket Avenue did not exist at that time.

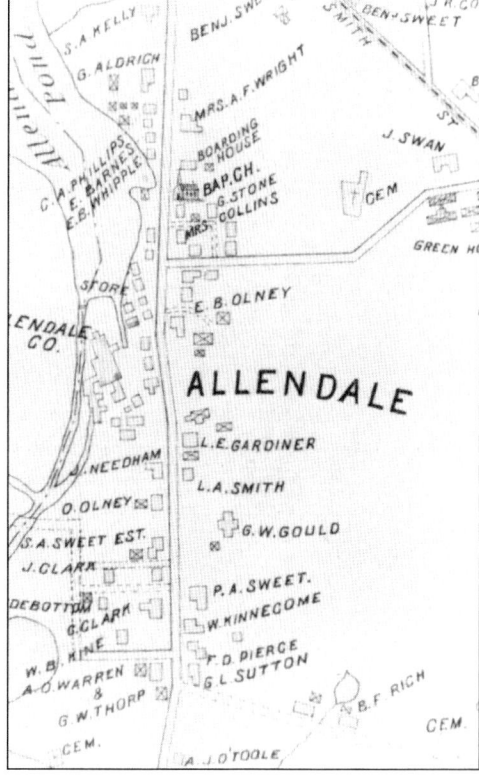

This 1895 map shows that with the mill as the center of employment, many new homes as well as mill houses were built in the area. Woonasquatucket Avenue was called River Avenue in 1895, and was renamed Woonasquatucket Avenue in 1907.

This engraving shows the Allendale Mill c. 1851. The company store is shown partially at the right This complex was built in 1822 by Zachariah Allen using innovations in fire retardant construction.

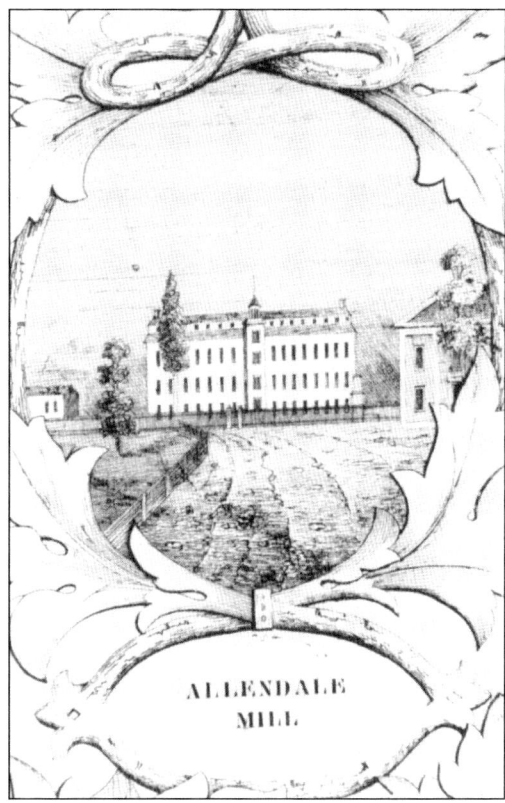

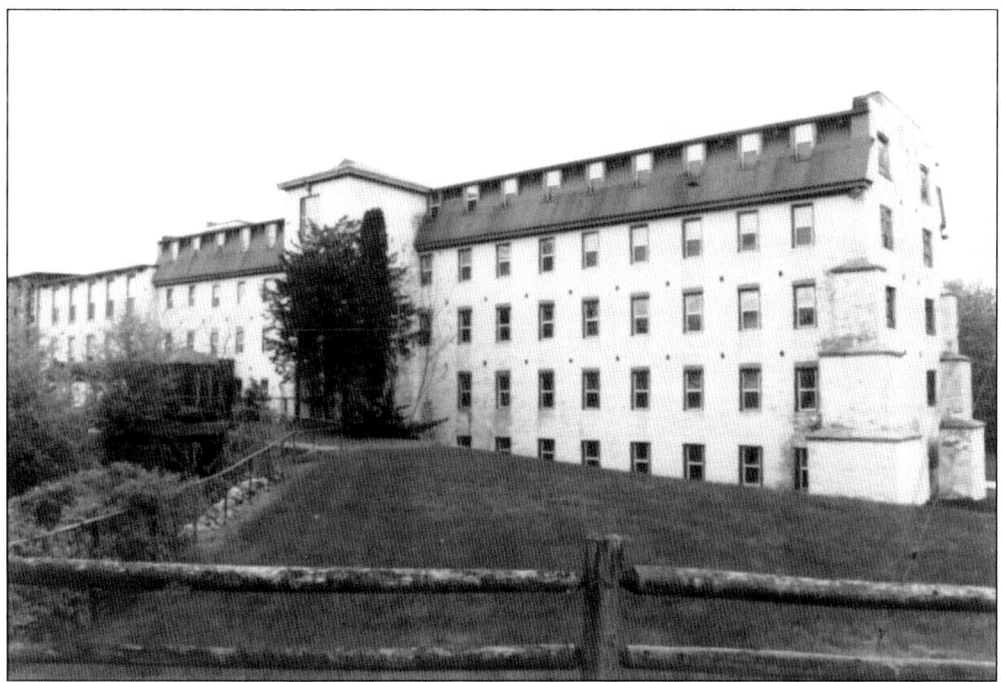

The mill is shown here as it appears today. It was open as a functioning mill until the 1960s. It now has been partially converted into a condominium complex.

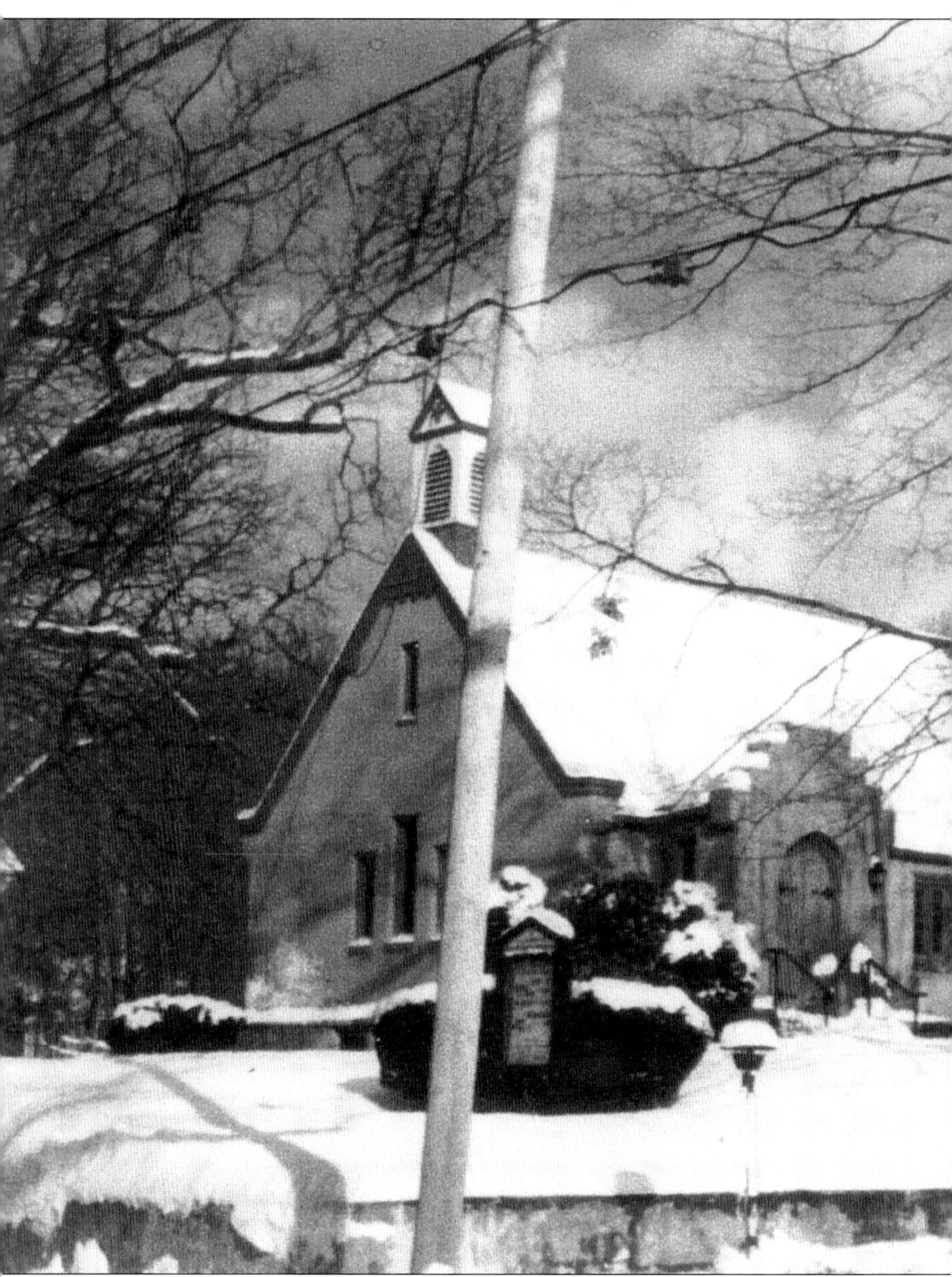
The Allendale Baptist Church appears here in a modern view. Additions, as seen here, were

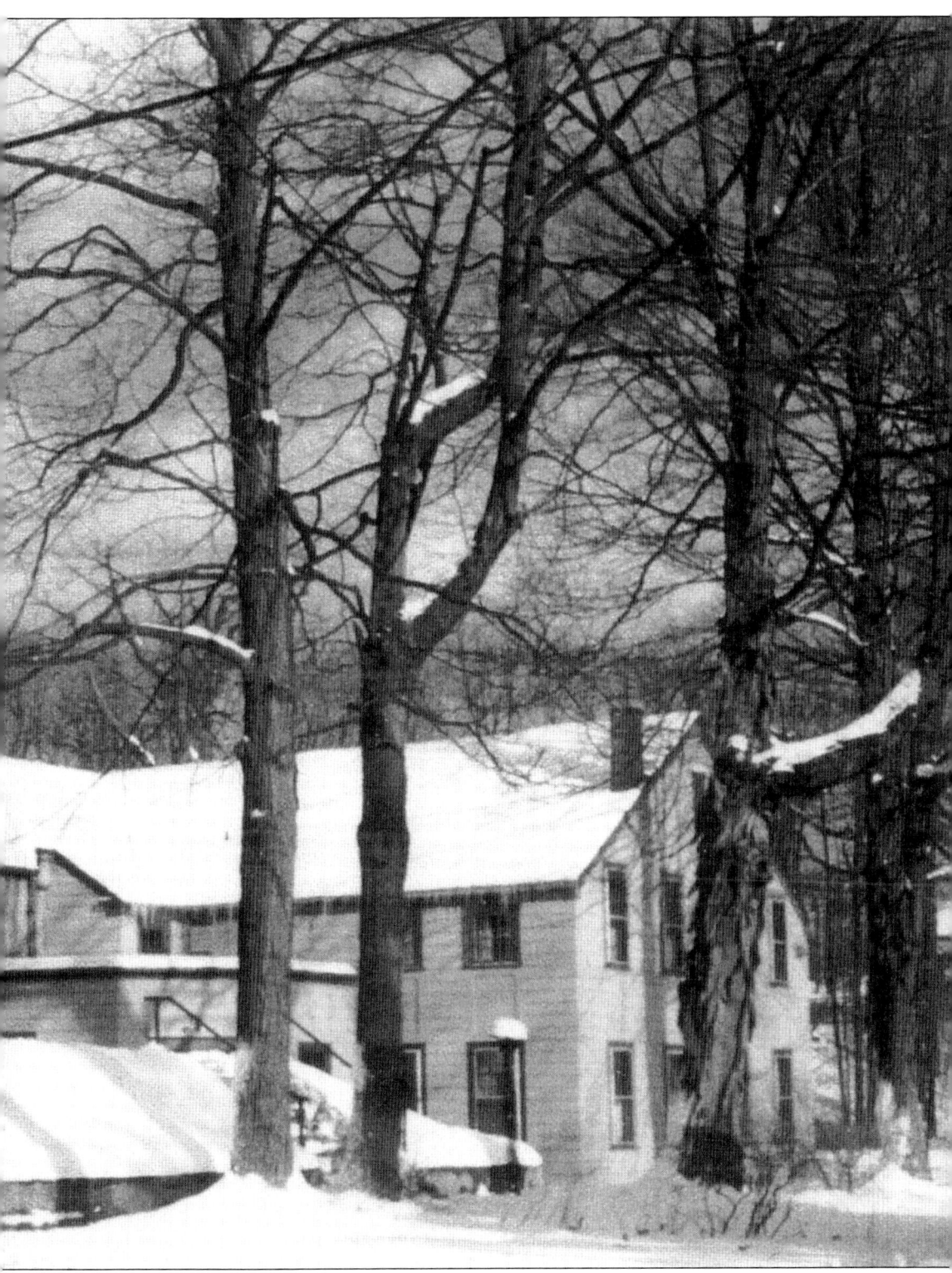
made in the 1930s and 1950s.

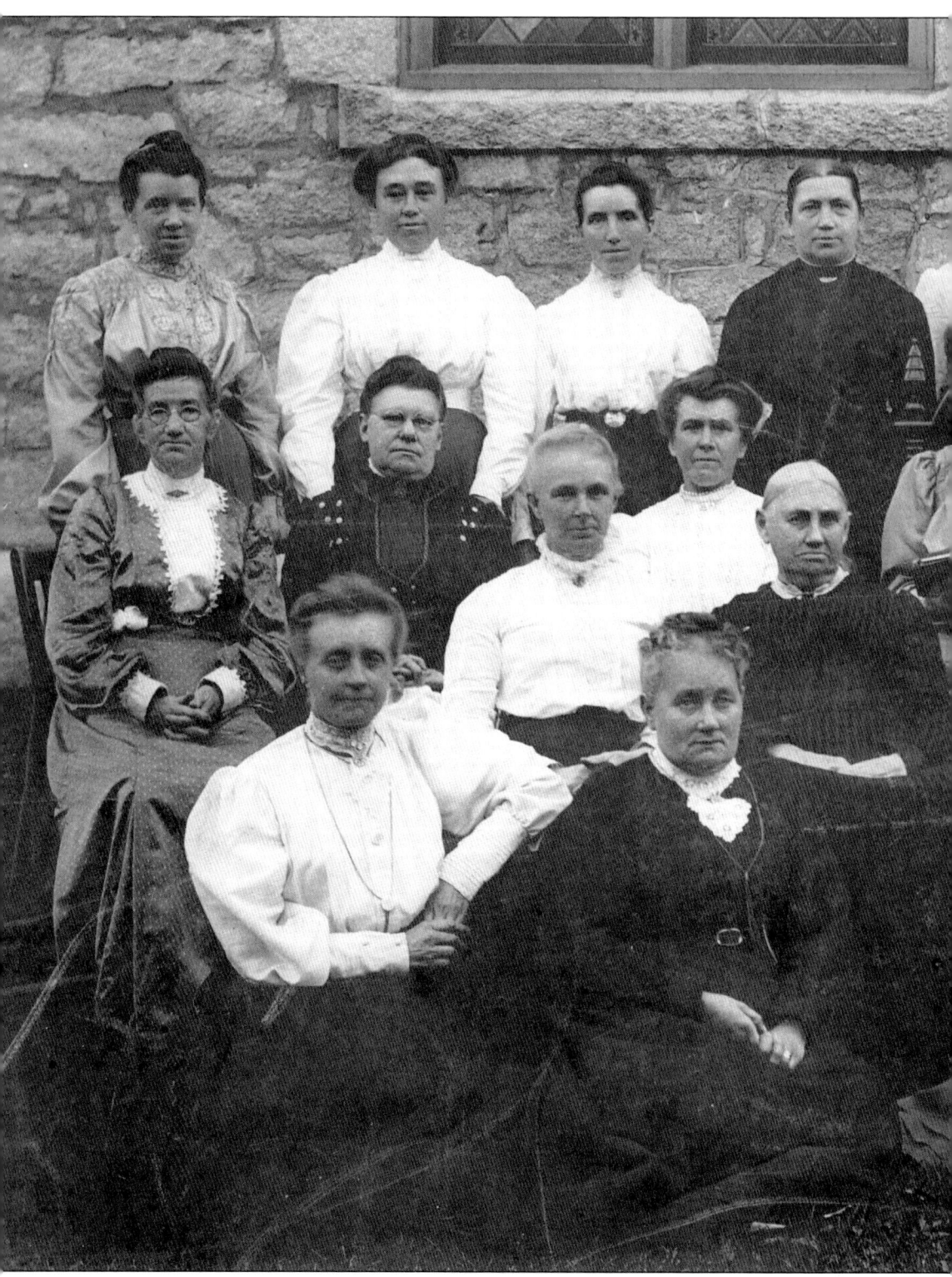
An Allendale Church group is pictured here in the late nineteenth or early twentieth century.

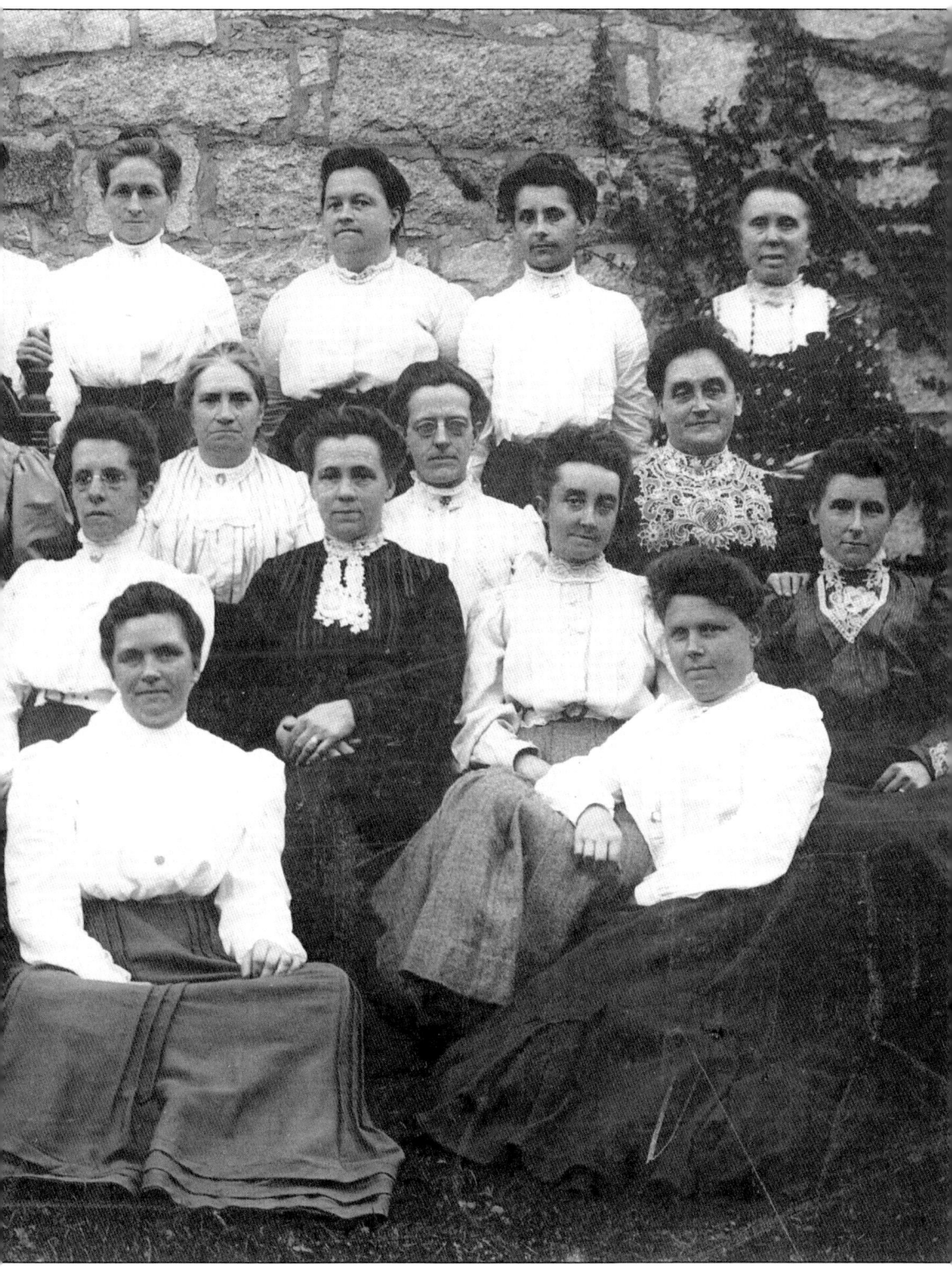

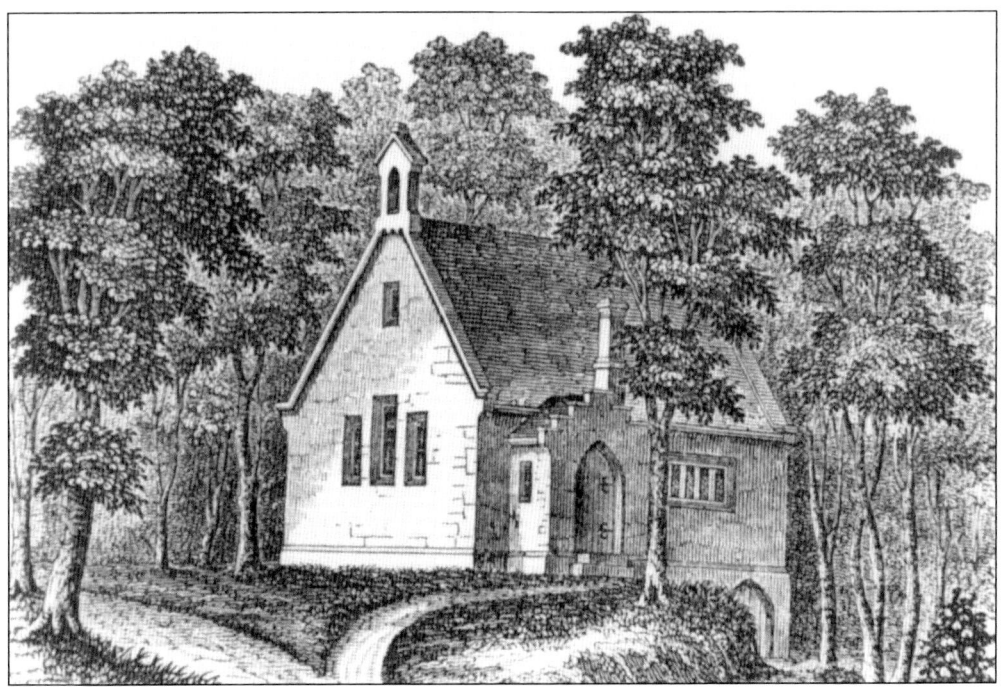

This schoolhouse, erected by Zachariah Allen, was shown in an 1848 publication of Henry Barnard. The basement room was intended to be a library, but was used as the primary school. The second floor was used as a lecture hall, and eventually the building became a church.

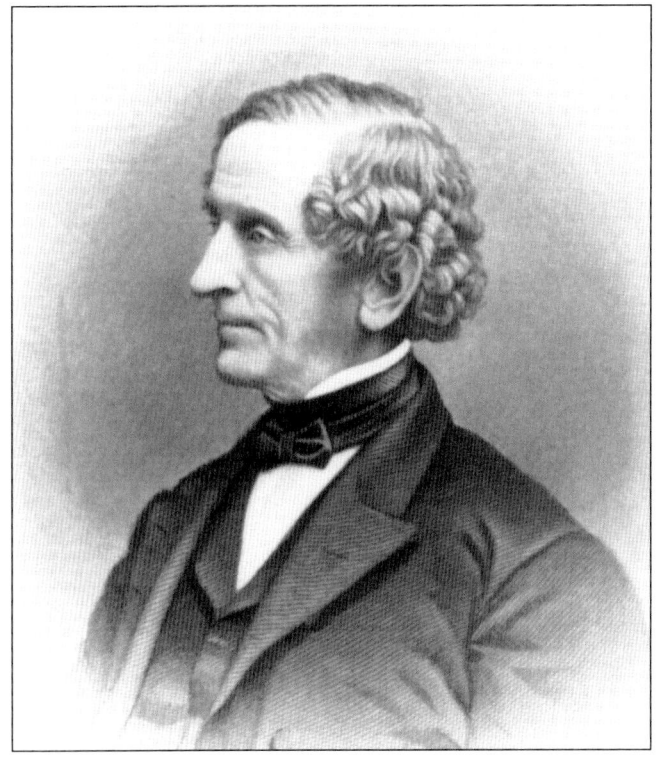

Zachariah Allen, an inventor, author, and reformer, was born in 1795 and died in 1882. He built the Allendale Mill and the mill houses, as well as the Allendale Baptist Church.

Two

CENTERDALE

In 1812, Israel Arnold purchased land on the west side of the Old Colonial Road (now Route 44), where he erected a mill and mill houses for his employees. Arnold called this mill village "Centre" because of its location at the geographical center of Scituate, Providence, Pawtucket, and Greenville. The village became known as Centremill c. 1830. In 1849, the village acquired its own post office and its name was designated as Centredale, although an 1851 map shows Centerdale. By 1893, the post office had officially changed its name to Centerdale.

Centerdale grew into a central shopping center for North Providence and surrounding areas until the second half of the twentieth century, when the advent of the mega-malls caused its decline as a shopping center. Few original eighteenth-century structures remain in Centerdale. An early house that is still standing at 2 Bourne Avenue, however, known as the Nathaniel Day house, was built c. 1737.

The first library in Centerdale was opened on July 4, 1870. This library was located between Ellery Motors and Robbins Funeral Home on Mineral Spring Avenue. Frank Angell along with Marcus Joslin and Alexander Harrington were the founders.

Early churches in Centerdale included the Centerdale Independent Methodist Church (founded in 1897), Saint Alban's Episcopal Church (1899), and the Free Will Baptist Church (c. 1832), which was located on the present-day site of Our Place. This Baptist church building was purchased by James Halsey Angell in 1863 and transformed into the Armory Hall that was used as a drill hall and entertainment center until it burned in 1892. Saint Lawrence Catholic Church was built in 1907 as more Catholic families moved to Centerdale.

The first school in Centerdale was built on Smith Street c. 1802/05. The second was constructed in 1848 and the third in 1886; both the second and third schools were located on Angell Avenue overlooking Smith Street. In 1959, the 1886 school burned in a spectacular fire and the present-day school was built later on the other end of Angell Avenue.

Centerdale today is the seat of the town's government and is slowly regaining some of its commercial flavor.

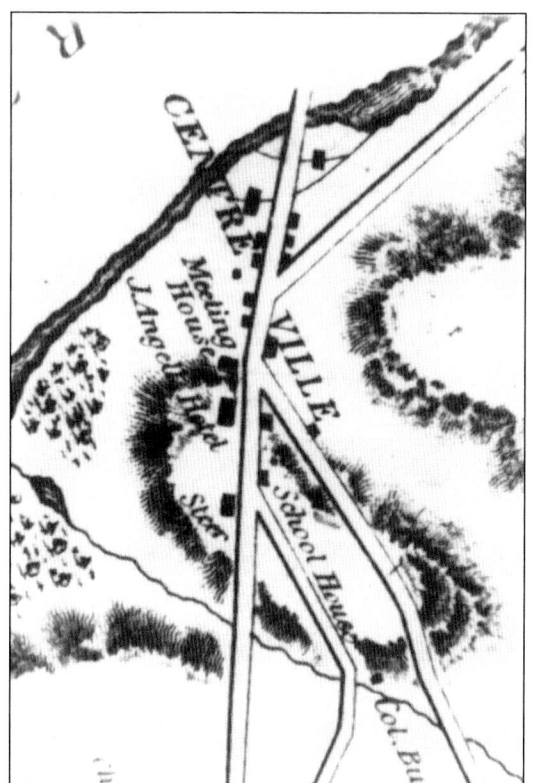

This map shows Centreville in 1835. The sites shown are the mill and mill houses, the 1832 Baptist meeting house (which became the Armory Hall), the James Angell Hotel, Asa Steere's slaughterhouse, the 1802 schoolhouse, and Colonel Burr's house (which was the 1730 James Olney house).

By 1895, Centerdale had grown considerably. In 1893, the post office had changed its official spelling of the village to Centerdale. The library was opened on July 4, 1870, and in 1879 a town hall and the third schoolhouse at the corner of Angell Avenue and Smith Street were built. The dotted line along Smith Street shows the route of the electric trolley system.

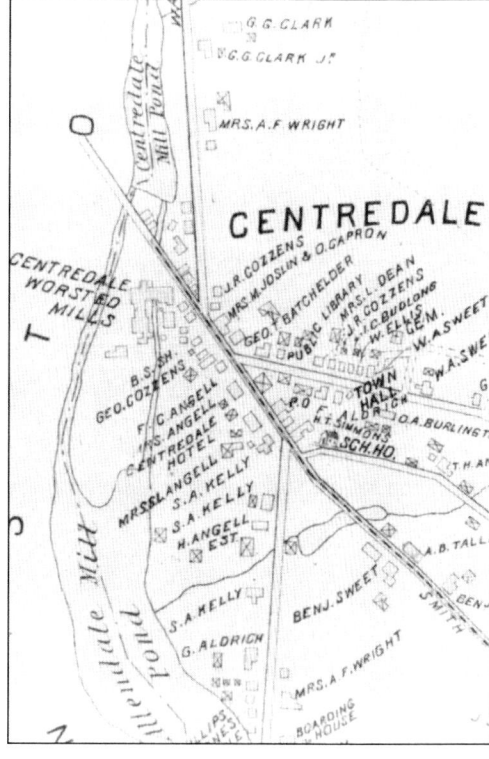

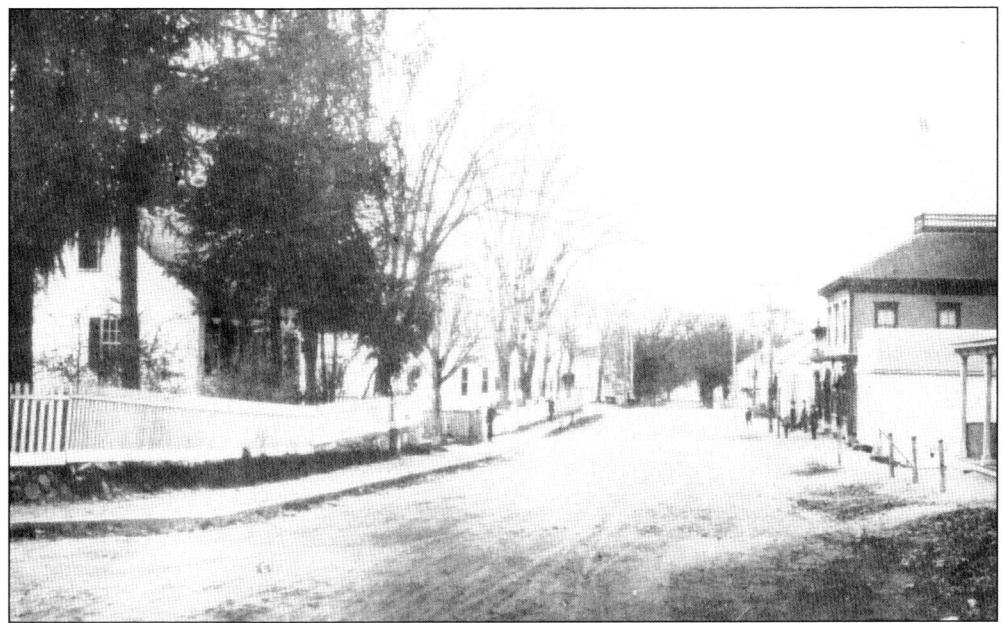

This pre-1893 photograph looks down Smith Street from the Woonasquatucket Avenue intersection. On the left, at Steere Avenue, is the Asa Steere house. Next is Frank Angell's house, and, following that, the tavern built by his grandfather. On the right after the porch is Lydia Wilcox's house, which became the first fire station. The final structure visible is Frank Angell's building.

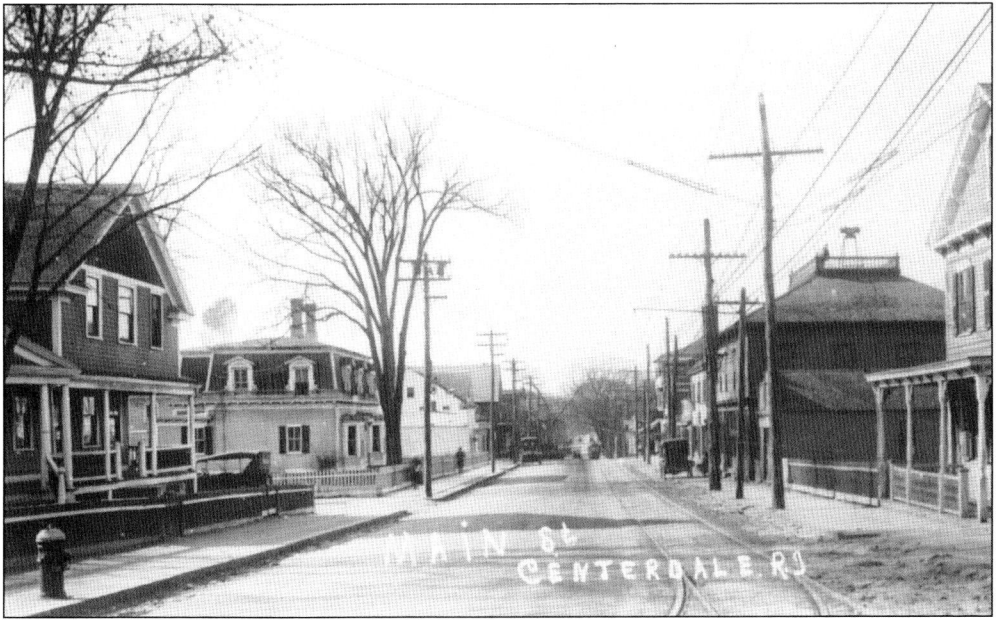

This c. 1910 photograph depicts the same scene. Notice the electric car tracks, which were installed in 1893.

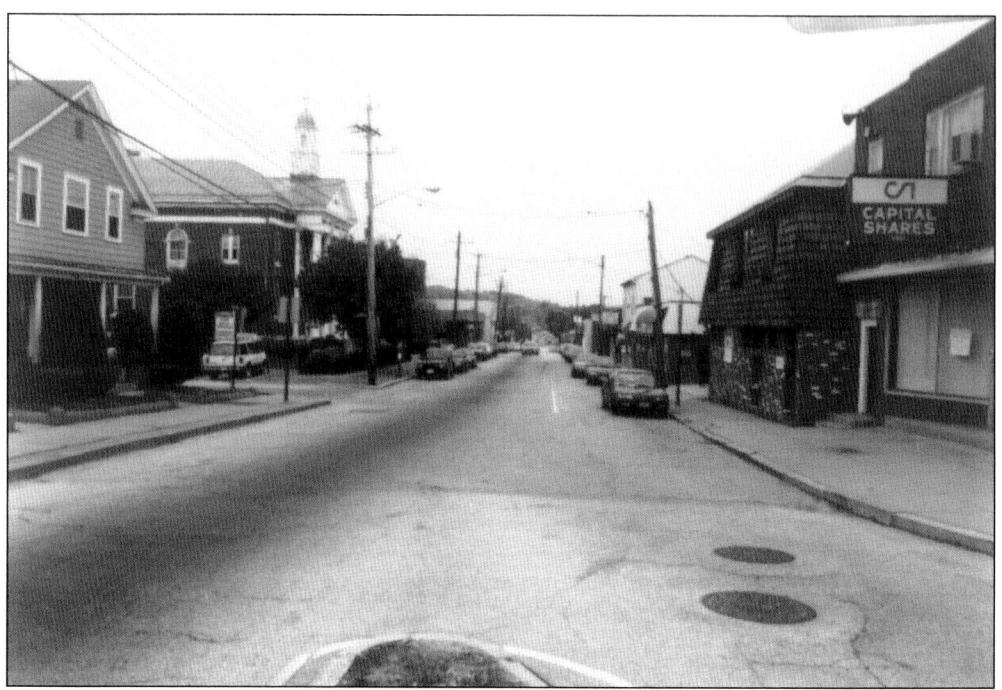
Centerdale is shown in 1996 from the Woonasquatucket/Smith Street intersection.

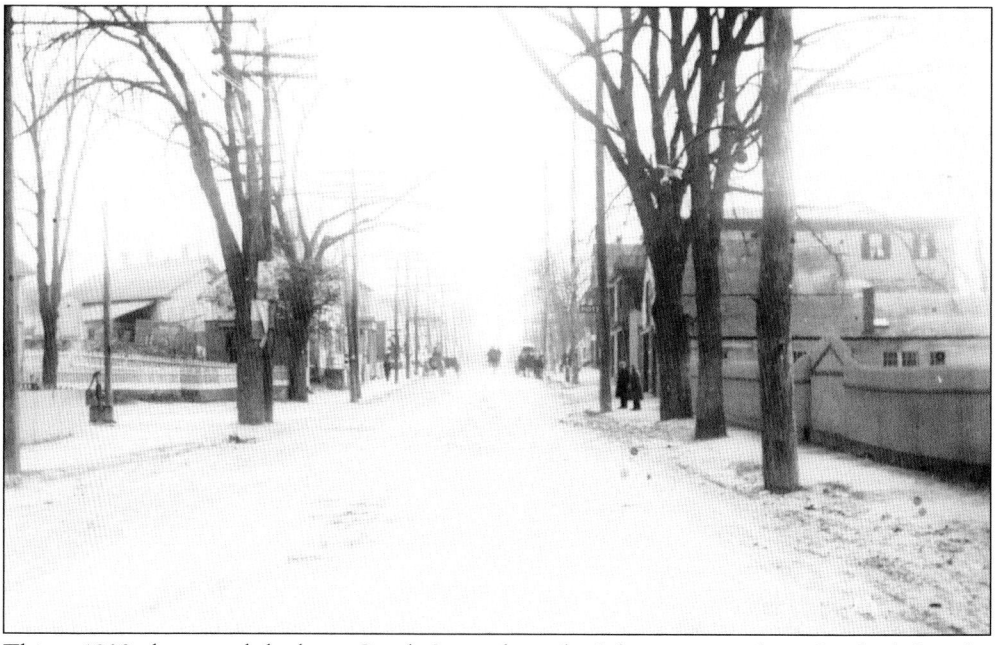
This c. 1900 photograph looks up Smith Street from the Johnston town line. On the left is the beginning of Waterman Avenue. In the distance is the Luther Carpenter house, and at the corner of Mineral Spring Avenue is the Winkleman and Finklestein Store. On the right are the mill fence, Sweet's Livery Stable, and the Broley Hotel. Electric car tracks are on the left.

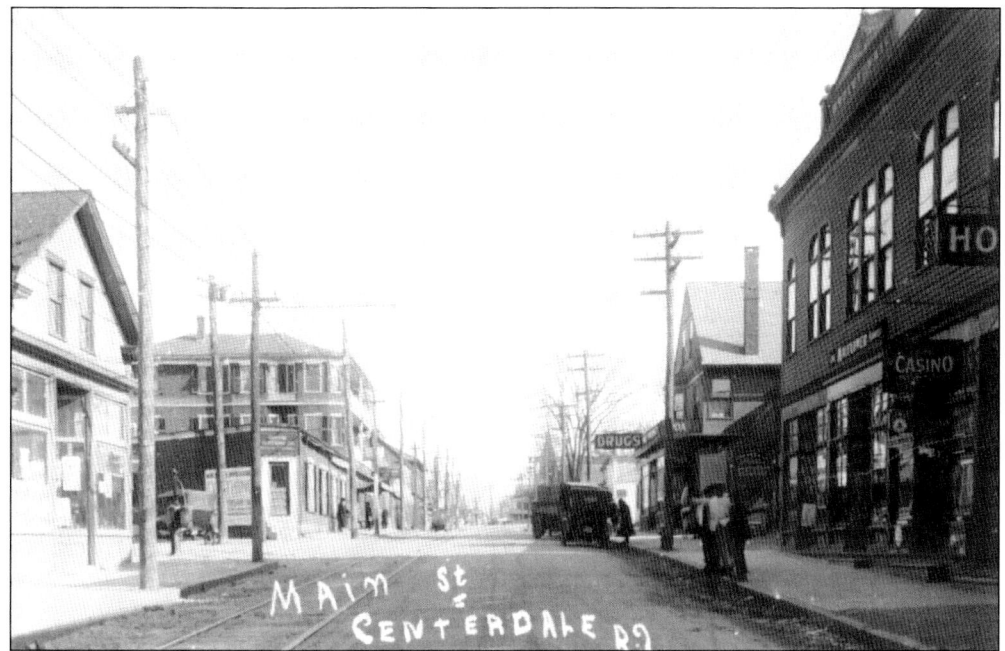

This c. 1910 view is from the Clarence Broley Hotel. On the right is Broley Hall, now called Our Place. That building housed Centerdale's first movie theater, "Casino Motion Pictures," on the second floor. Next is McKenna's Pharmacy at 2030 Smith Street. To the left are the Batchelder Bros. Store (which was the Luther Carpenter Store moved from Mineral Spring Avenue) and the Winkleman and Finklestein Store.

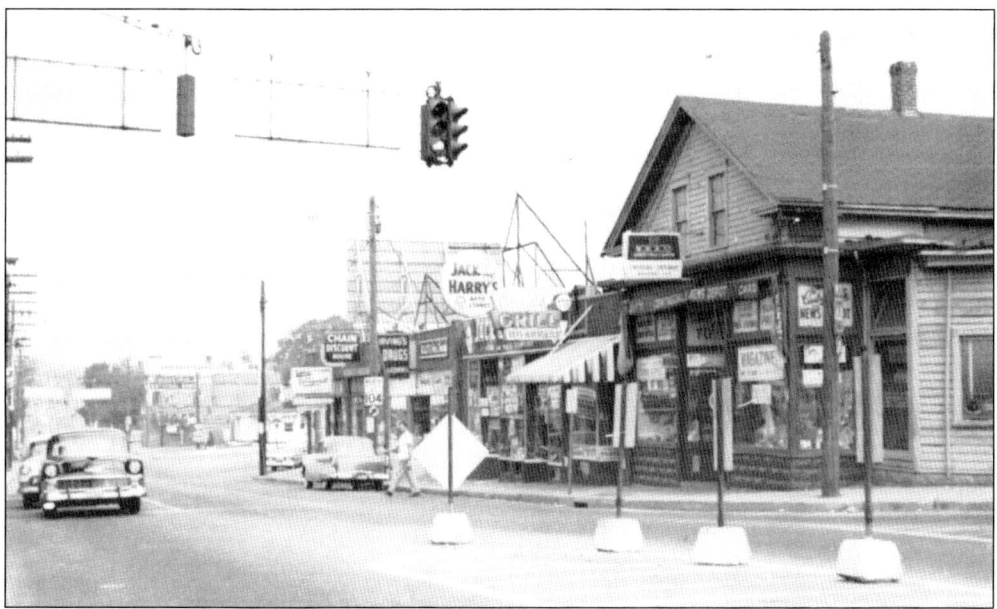

A 1950s Centerdale scene shows the village at its height as a business center. On the immediate right is Buonaccorsi's Centerdale News Depot, which was formerly the Batchelder Bros. Store. Other stores pictured are Charlie's Lunch, Jack and Harry's, Irving's Drug, and Chain discount. Darby's service station is in the distance. At that time, Smith Street was a two-way street.

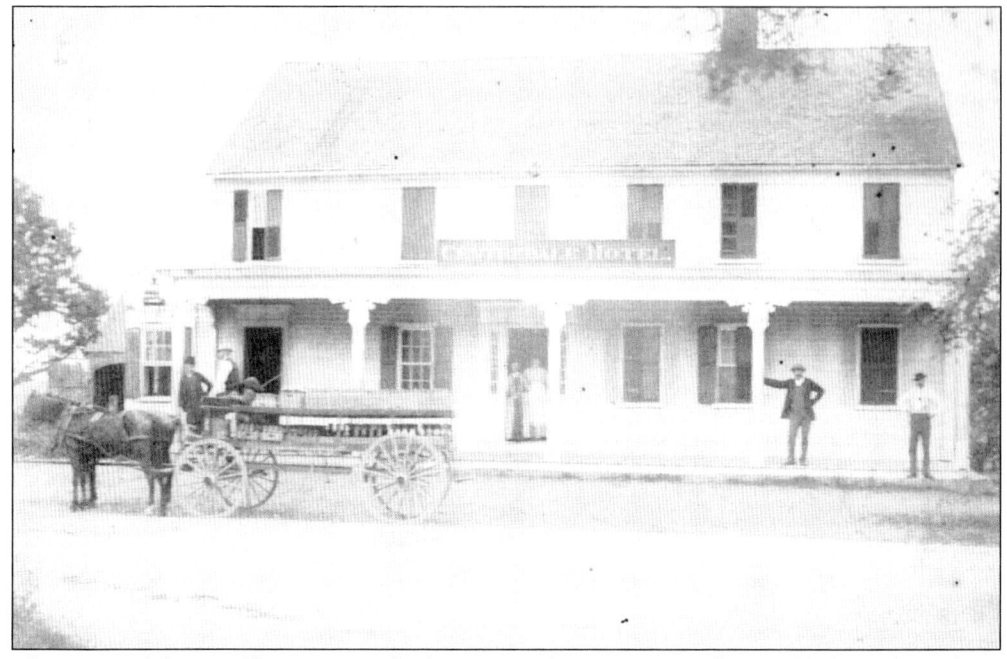

The Centredale Hotel/Tavern was built in 1824 by James Angell, grandfather of Frank C. Angell. From 1824 through the late nineteenth century, it was the center of the community. It served as a farmers' club room and also as the post office when James Halsey Angell was postmaster (c. 1854-1858). It had a total of ten fireplaces.

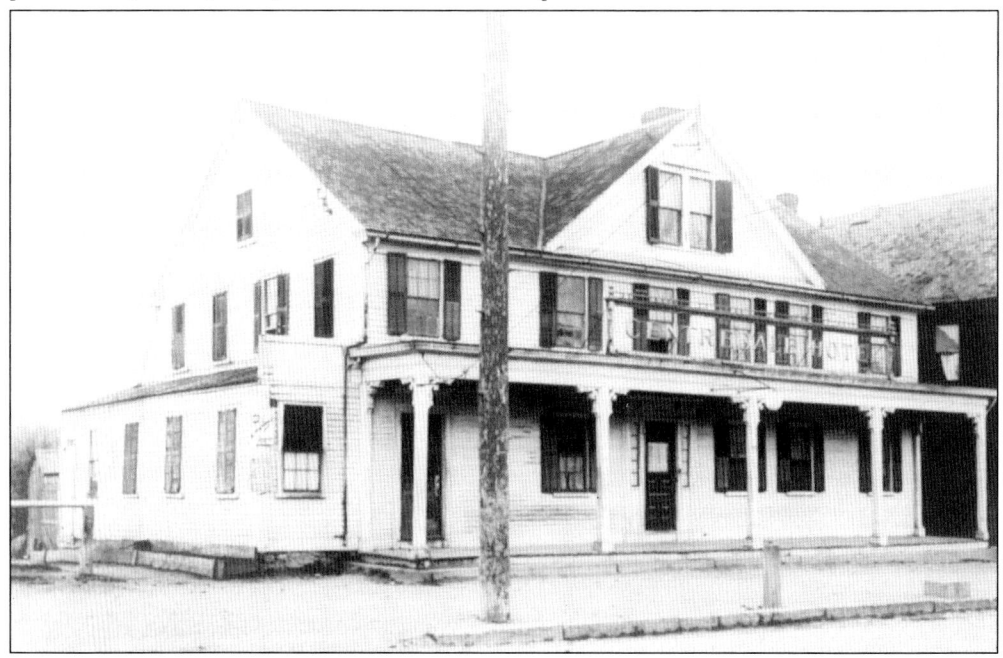

As the nineteenth century progressed, the tavern's exterior appearance changed. James Angell died in 1870 and the ownership went to his son, James Halsey Angell. From that time, the tavern was passed on through the Angell family until it was sold to Cassius Mathewson on August 25, 1897.

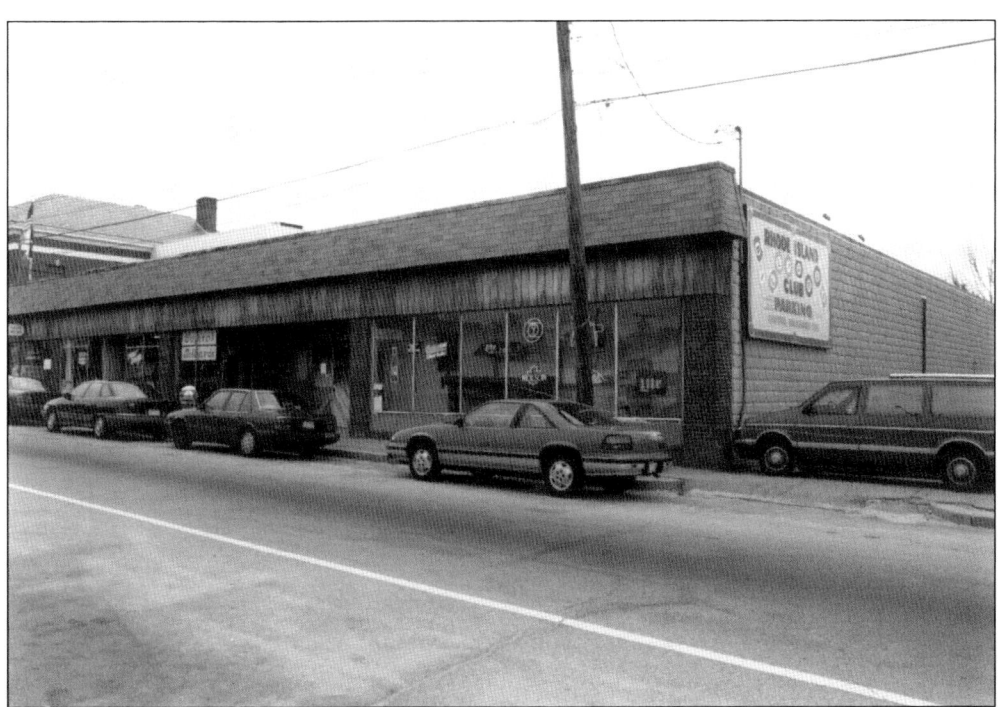

This is the site of the Centerdale Tavern as it looks today.

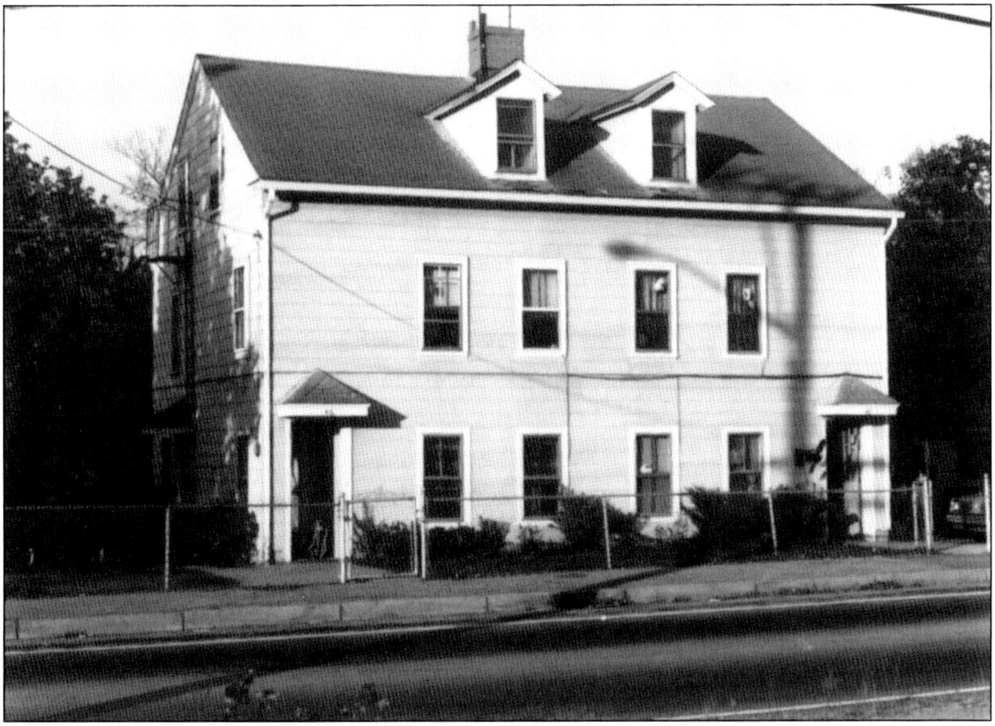

During the early nineteenth century, houses were built by the mill owners. This dwelling on Waterman Avenue is the only remaining mill house.

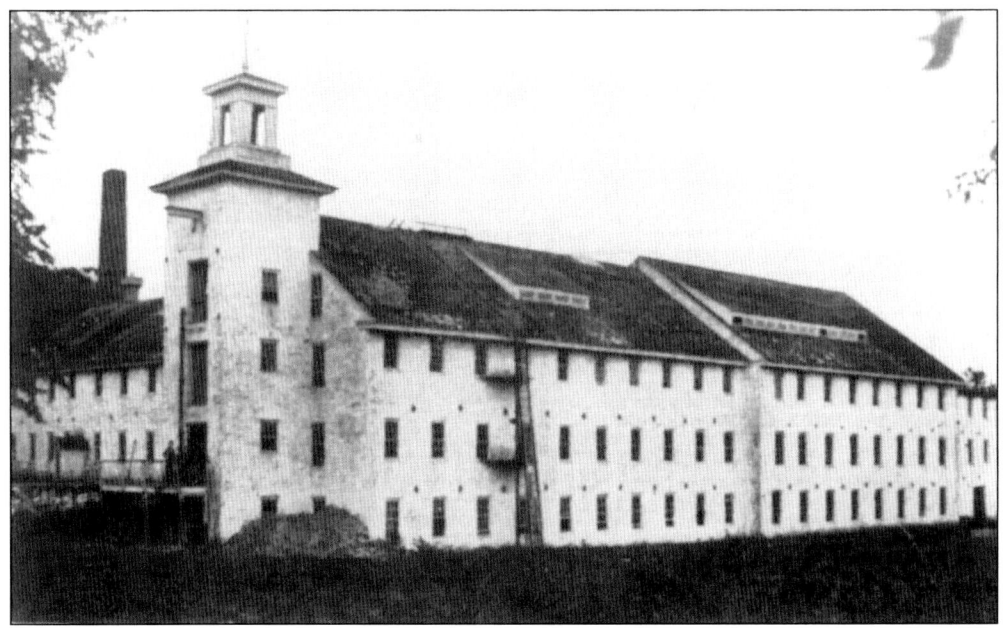

This is the Centerdale Mill in 1875. The first mill at this site burned in 1850 and a new mill was built in 1853 by James Cunliff. In 1859, Cunliff sold it to Amos Beckwith, owner of the Dyerville Mill. A new mill dam, an addition to the mill, and a Corliss steam engine enhanced the operation.

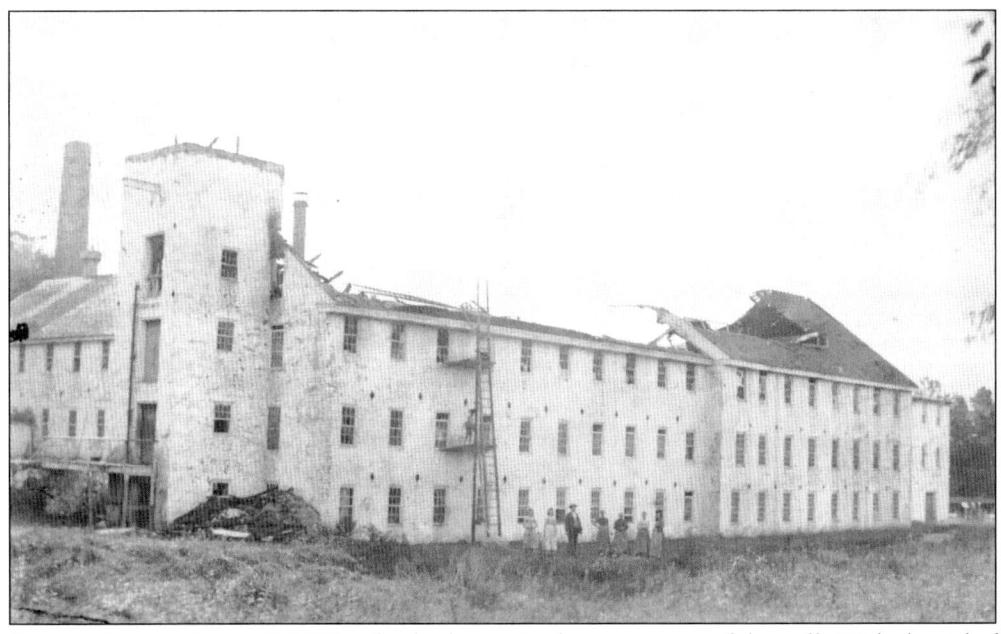

At noontime on August 7, 1889, a fire broke out in the upper story of the mill. With the aid of the Providence Fire Department, the mill was saved from destruction but suffered considerable damage. A few temporary repairs were made because of the poor business climate of the 1890s. In 1891, the property was sold to Henry H. Green and others.

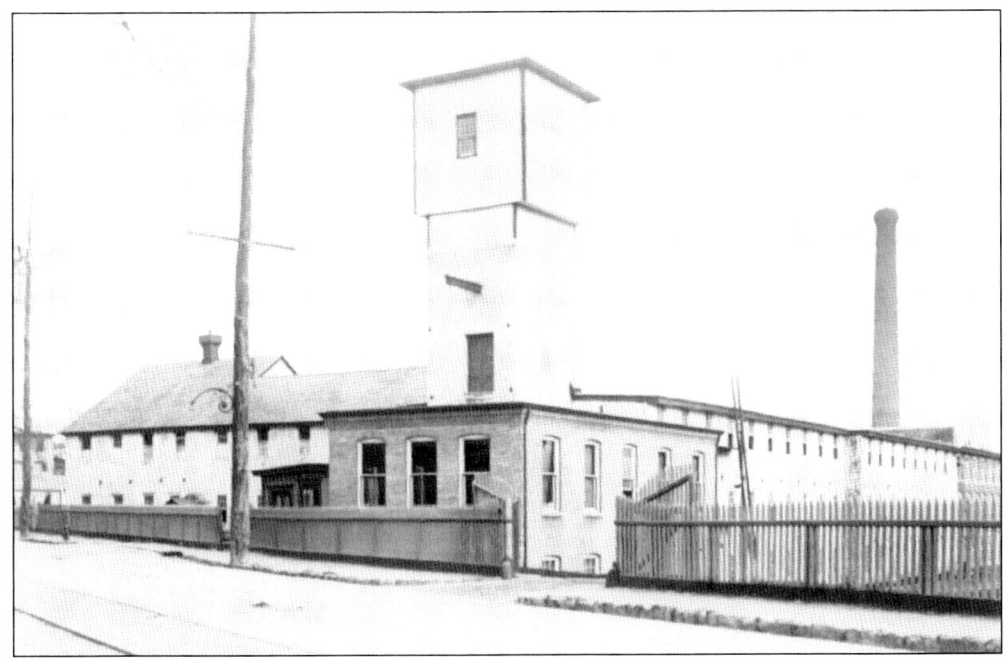

The Centerdale Mill appears here as it looked c. 1910. The mill had stopped manufacturing cotton and begun producing worsted yarn. The mill was owned by William Dracup, William Mackey, and James Lister Jr. at that time.

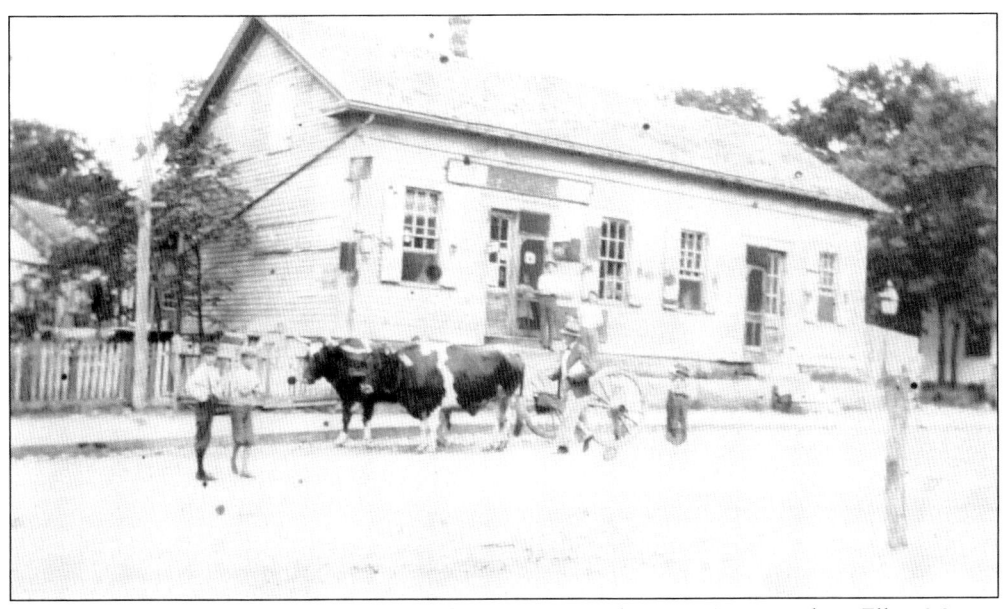

This is the Luther Carpenter Store c. 1900/1910 on Mineral Spring Avenue where Ellery Motors and Town Tavern are now located. The building was erected in 1847 and run by Mr. Carpenter until his death in 1886. George Batchelder purchased the store and it was moved to Smith Street. It eventually became Buonaccorsi's Centerdale News Depot at 2038 Smith Street.

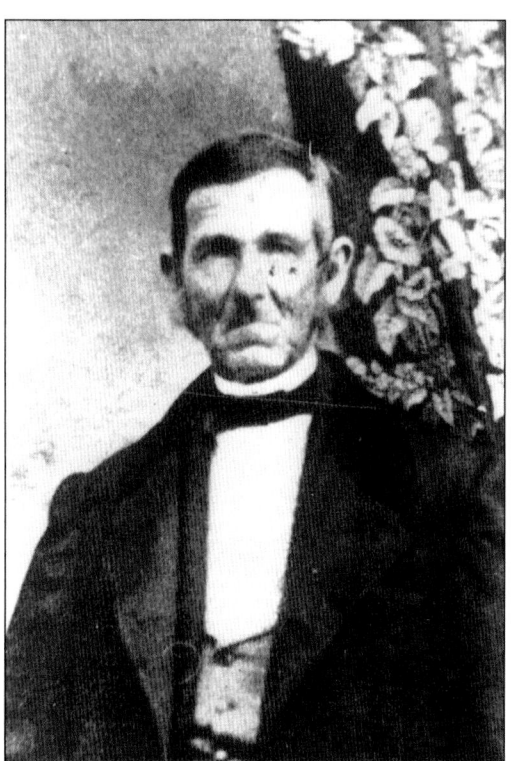

Luther Carpenter was the owner of the country store on Mineral Spring Avenue.

George T. Batchelder was the patriarch of the prosperous Centerdale Batchelders. Besides being owner of the Luther Carpenter store, he was a state senator and the Centerdale postmaster from November 1886 to October 1893.

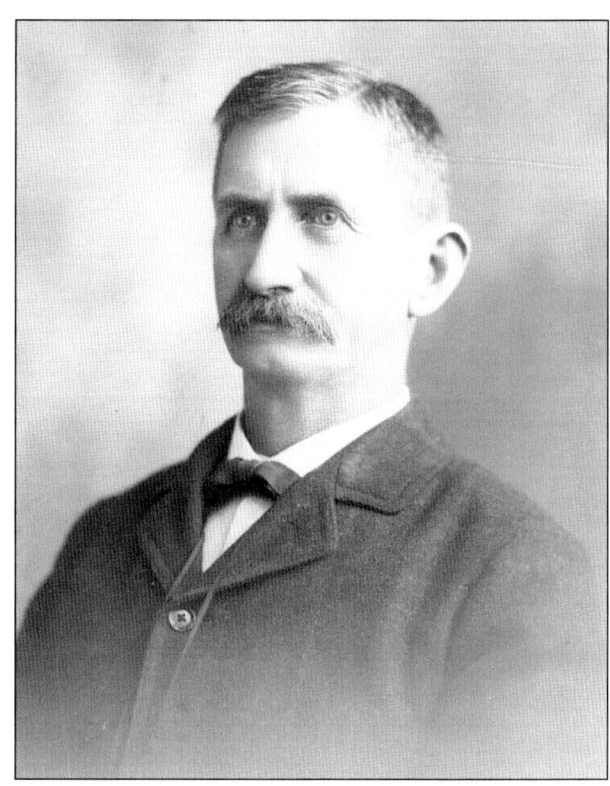

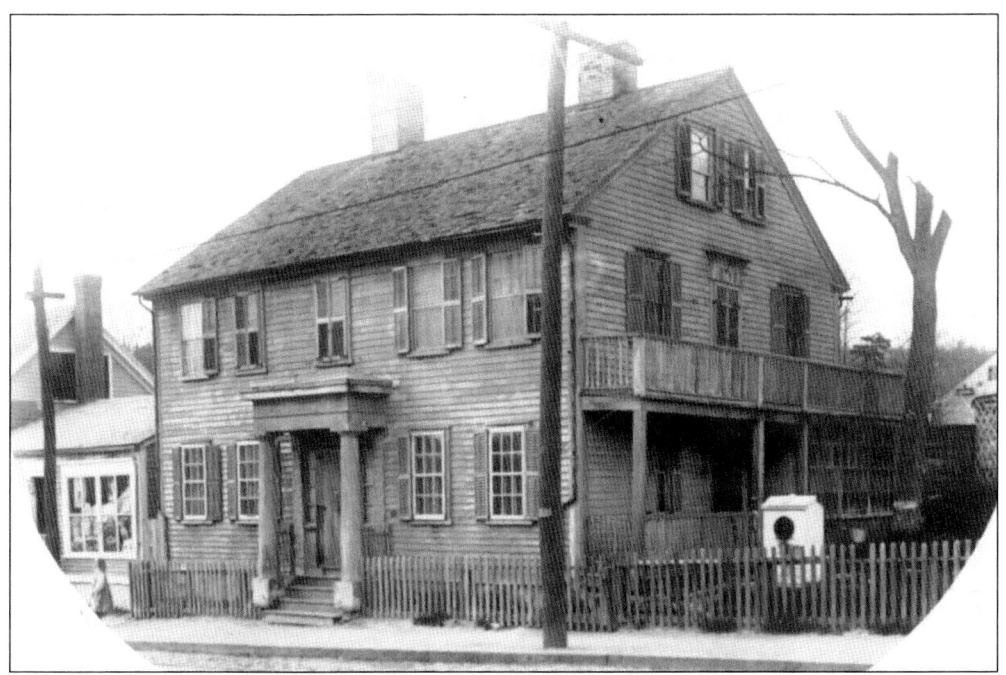

As the postcard caption states, this is Luther Carpenter's house, which faced Smith Street where Galligan's Antiques now stands. During the early twentieth century, the building was demolished to be replaced by the present brick building.

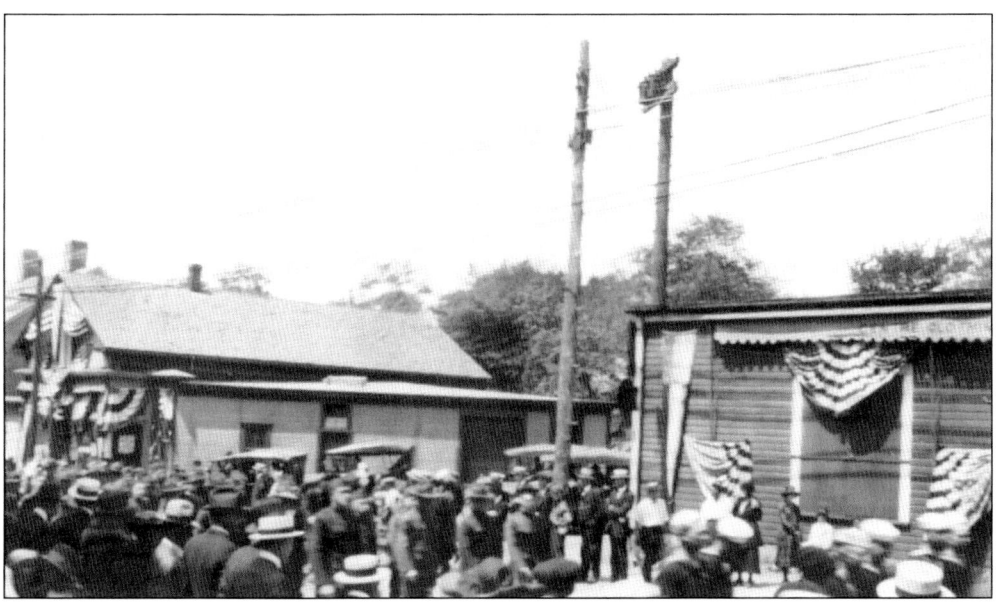

This is the intersection of Mineral Spring Avenue and Smith Street probably on July 4th in the 1920s. To the right we see the 1909 Winkleman and Finklestein Store. On the other corner of Mineral Spring and Smith Street is the old Luther Carpenter store (later moved to Smith Street with a one-story addition on the side).

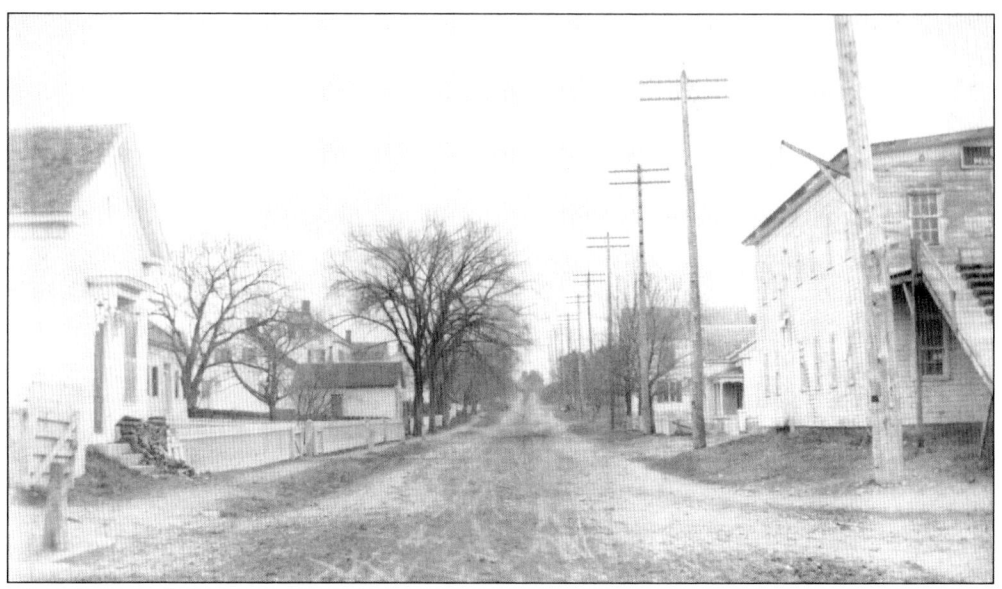

This photograph looks up Mineral Spring Avenue from just below the present site of Robbins Funeral Home. On the left is the 1870 North Providence Union Library. In the distance on the right is the 1879 first town hall. This photograph was taken by Frank C. Angell c. 1900.

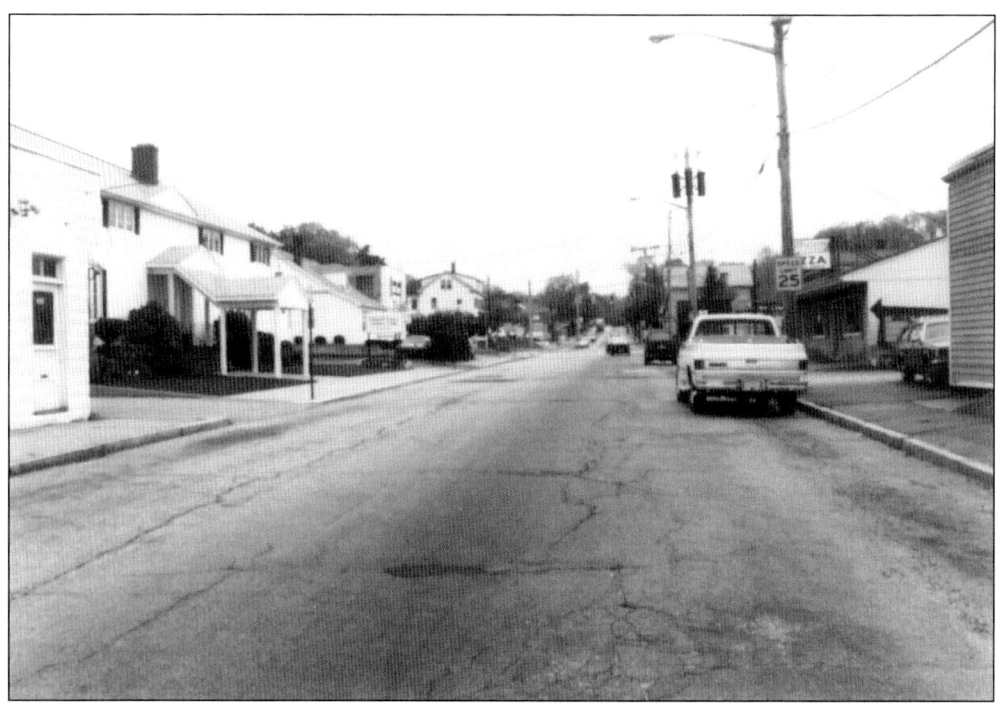

This photograph shows the same view today. Ellery Motors is on the left, followed by Robbins Funeral Home. The tall, double-shed, dormered house on the left in the distance is still standing today. On the right are the Winkleman and Finklestein building and the old town hall.

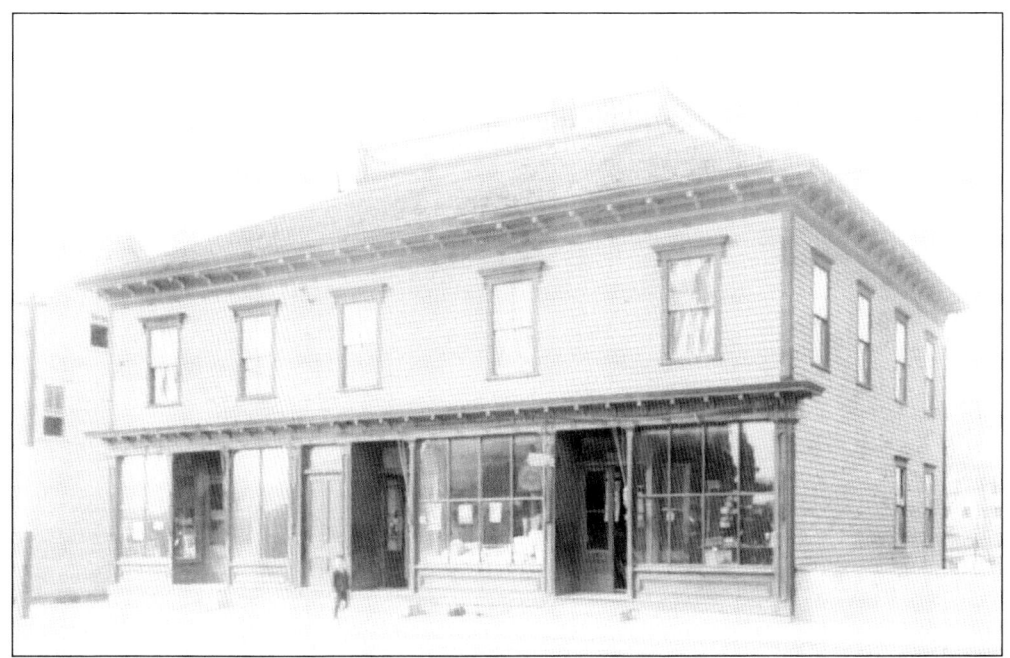

This is the Frank C. Angell building, which was built c. 1890s. It housed numerous businesses over the years including the U.S. Post Office and Fogarty's Clothing Store. This photograph dates from c. 1910. The second floor was used as the Masonic Hall until the present hall was built.

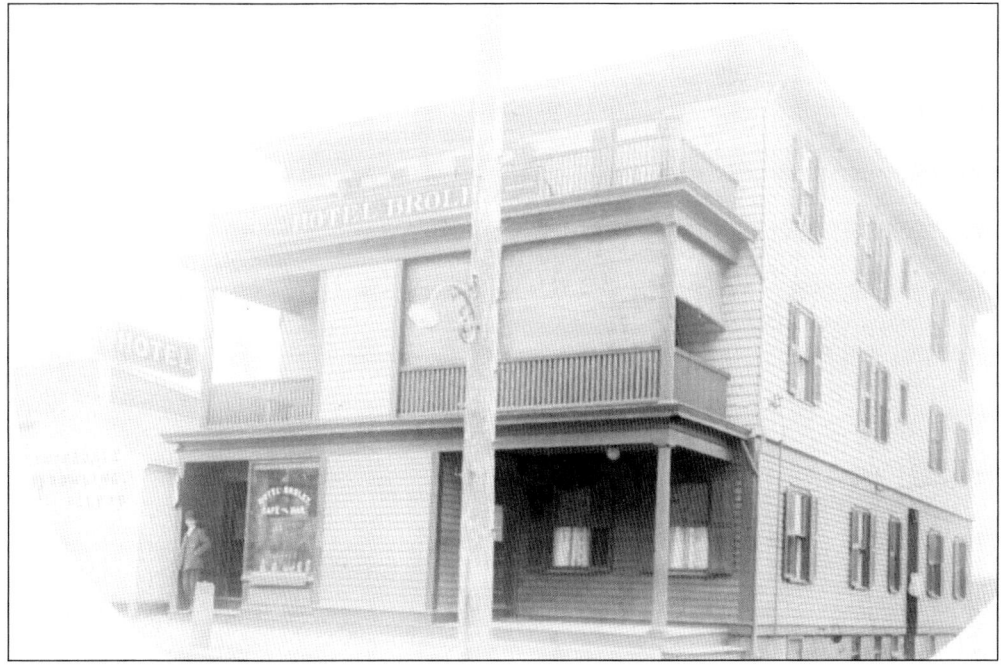

The Broley Hotel is shown here as it looked c. 1910. On the left in this photograph is a cafe and bar, and, to the left of that, the Centerdale Bowling Alleys. As the century progressed, the building became Adrian's Restaurant. The site is now an empty lot next to Our Place.

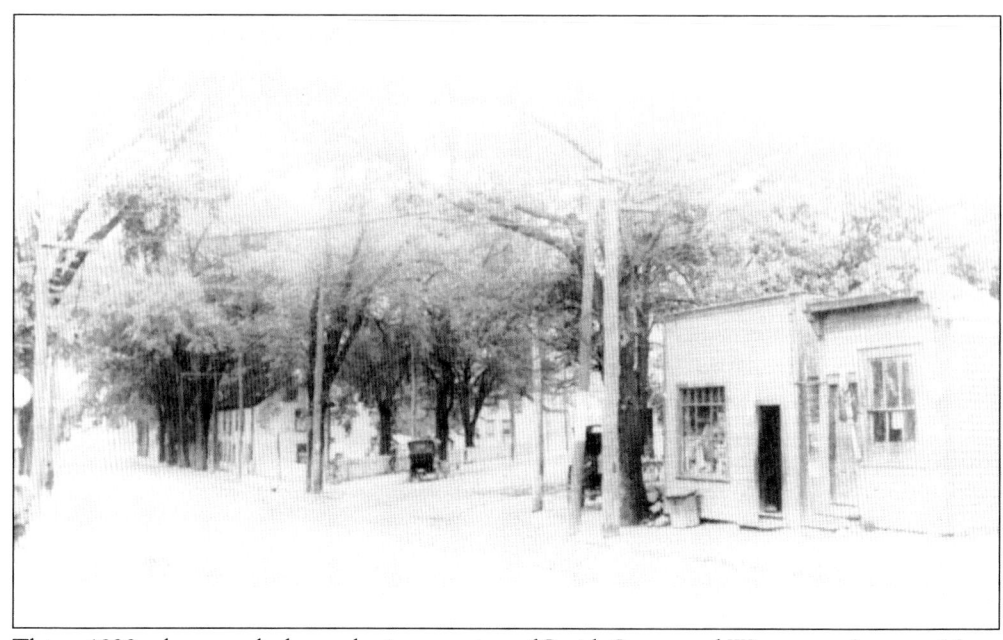

This c. 1920s photograph shows the intersection of Smith Street and Waterman Avenue. Many elm trees lined the road at that time. In the distance to the left of center, we see two mill houses. On the right is a small store which today is a parking lot.

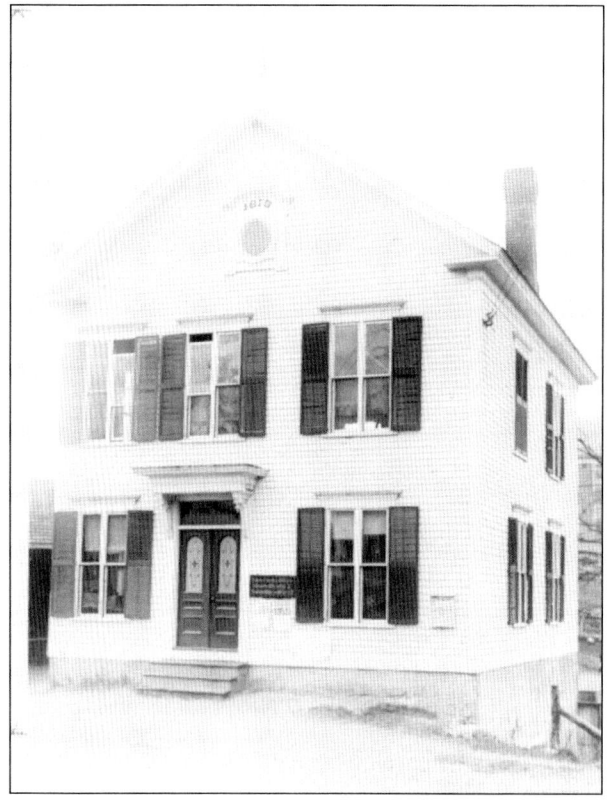

The old town hall was built in 1879 when North Providence gave up some of its land to Pawtucket and Providence and was left without a government business building. This photograph was taken c. 1910.

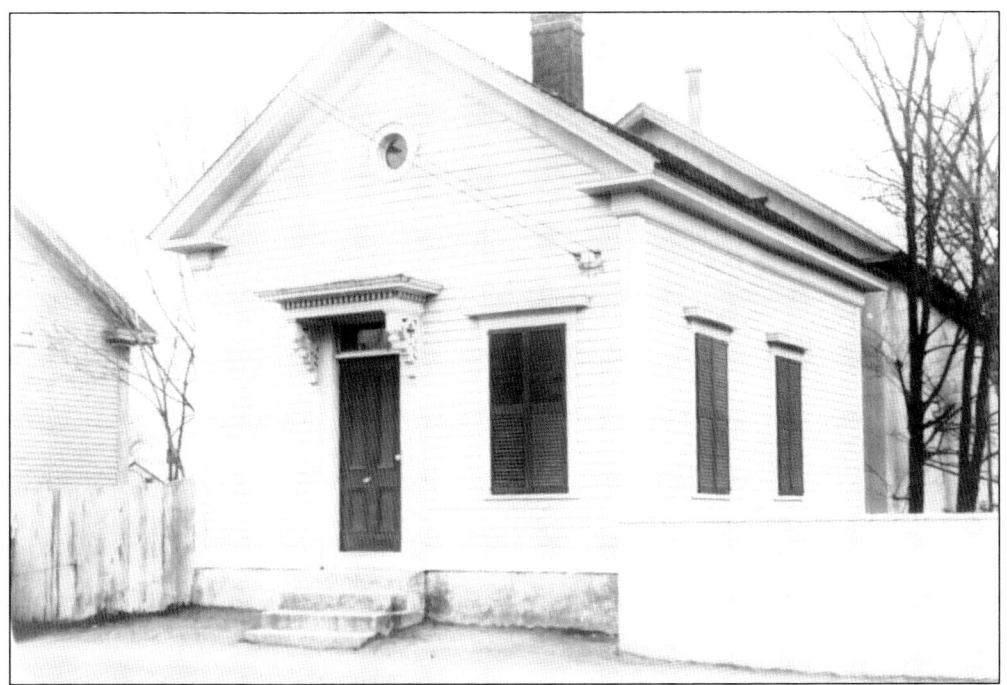

Seen here is the first library in North Providence, which was built and opened in 1870. It was called the Union Library until state funding allowed it to become the Union Free Library. Frank C. Angell was the leader in establishing this library and was the first librarian.

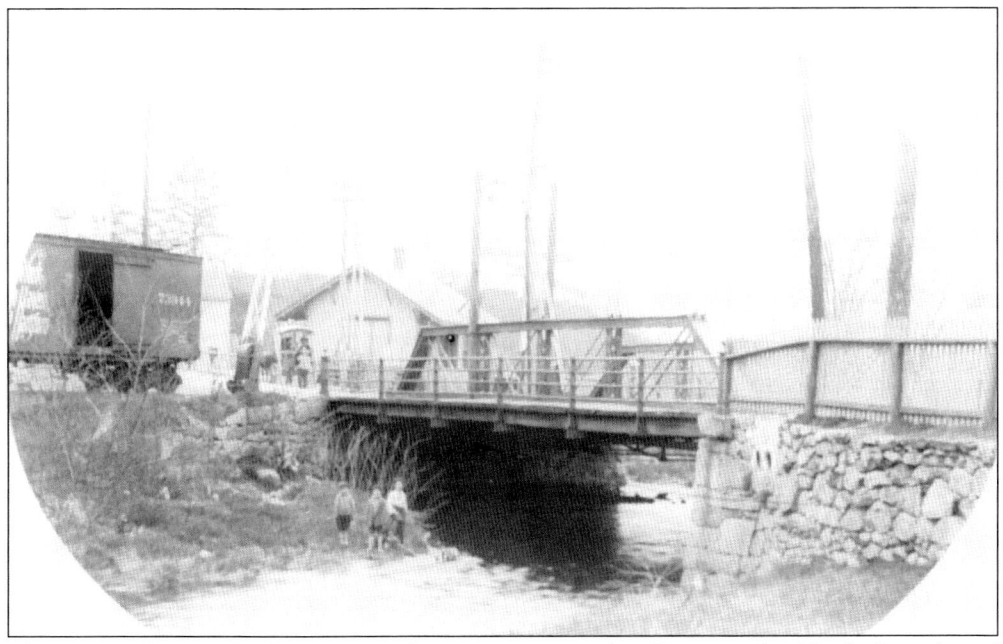

This scene depicts the bridge over the Woonasquatucket River at the North Providence/Johnston line. The Centerdale railroad station is on the left in this c. 1910 photograph.

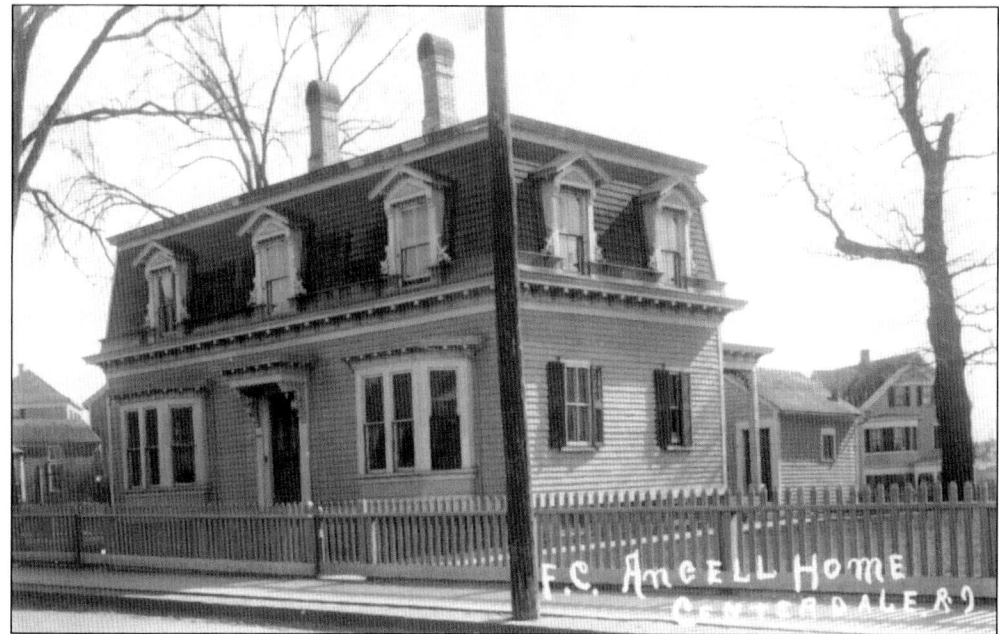

Seen here is the Frank C. Angell mansard-roof home, which is the present site of the second North Providence Town Hall. After Mr. Angell died in 1928, his house was moved to 20 Walter Avenue where it is located today. His barn became part of Robbins Funeral Home. The new town hall located on the site opened in 1931.

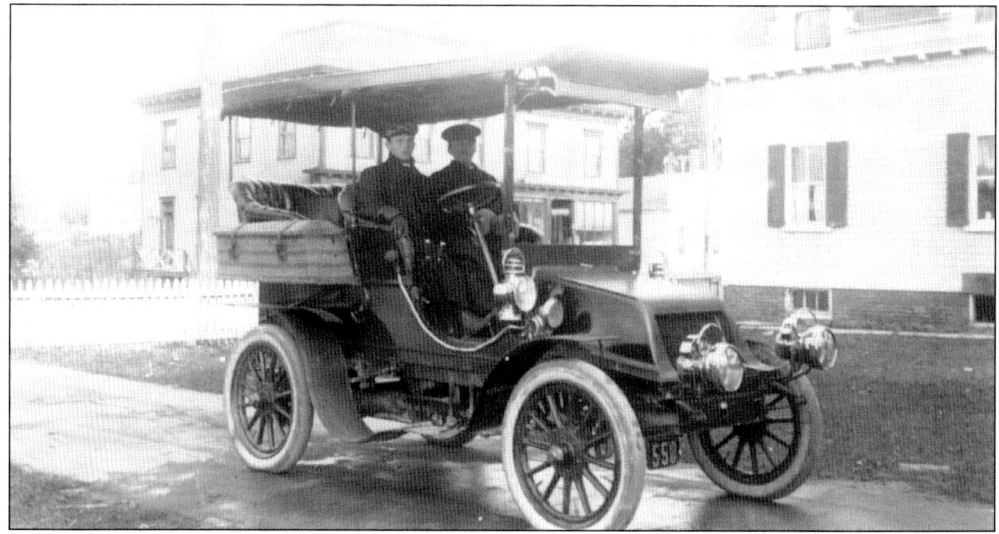

This image looks out from F.C. Angell's yard on Smith Street. In the background is the building where the post office and stores were located. To the right is his house. Seated in the automobile, a Winton 20-horsepower, are Frank C. Angell and, to the left, his driver. The photograph dates c. 1904.

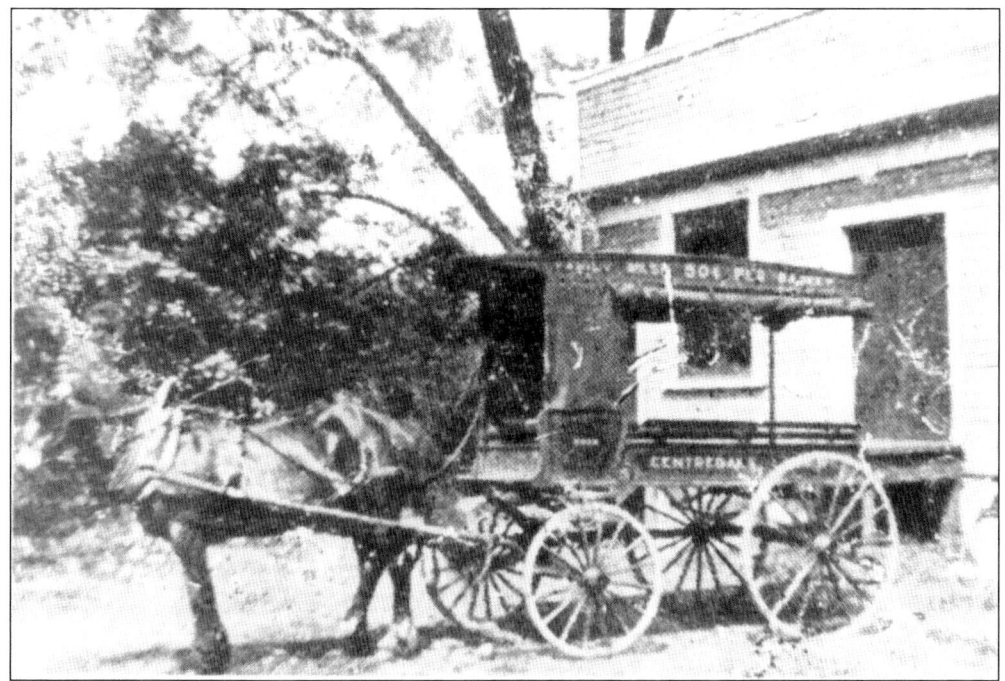

Unlike today, all businesses were independently owned in the village in the early days. This c. 1913 photograph shows the Centerdale Laundry, operated by Daniel P. McCarthy, at 41 Grover Street (located off Woonasquatucket Avenue).

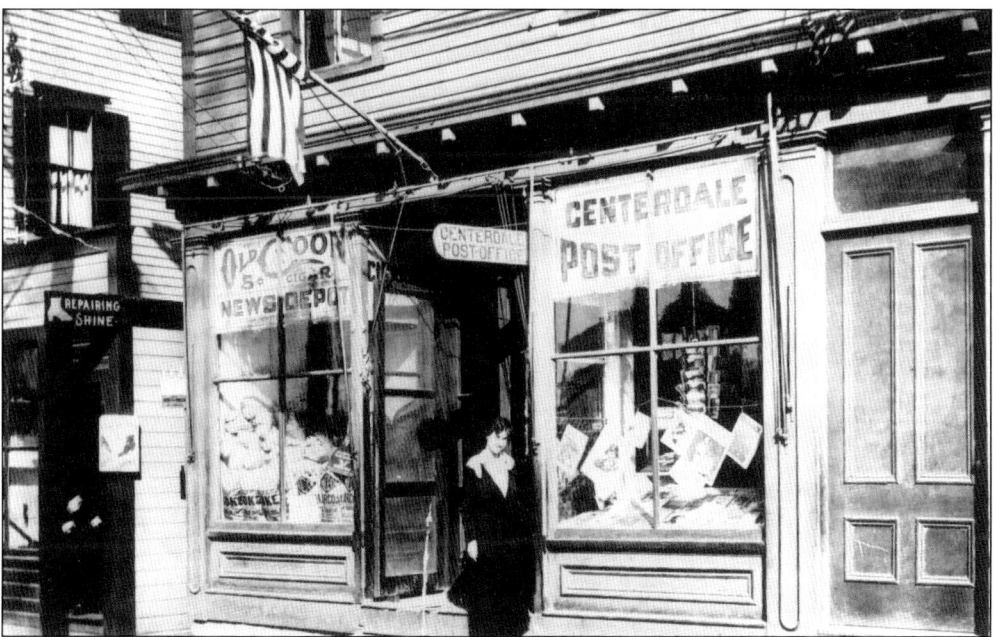

Shown here is Emma Baron in the doorway at 2007 Smith Street, which was at the left end of the F.C. Angell building. Baron was the postmistress from 1910 to 1915 when her brother Charles succeeded her. At that time, a person could not make a living running a post office, so the post office was usually part of another business.

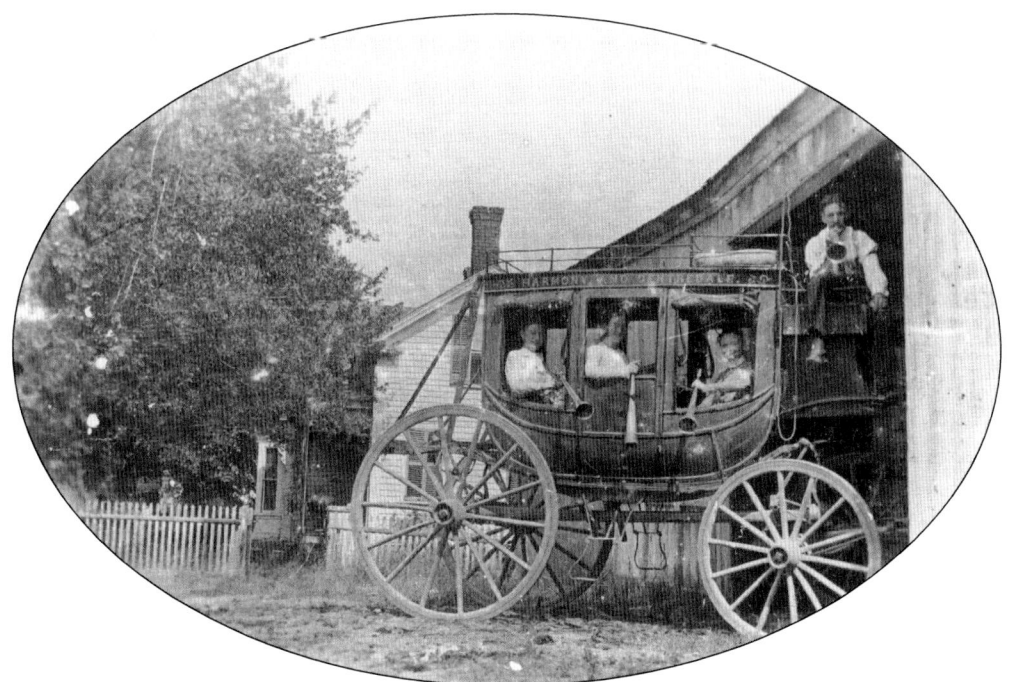

This holiday photograph was taken on July 4, 1901. Pictured from left to right are: Grace Merither, Maude Merither, Mary Ann Tilley (who was the daughter of the pastor of the Centerdale Independent Methodist Church), and Howard Leonard. The group was about to leave for the village of Harmony. A notation on the photograph states that they stayed up until 4:00 am.

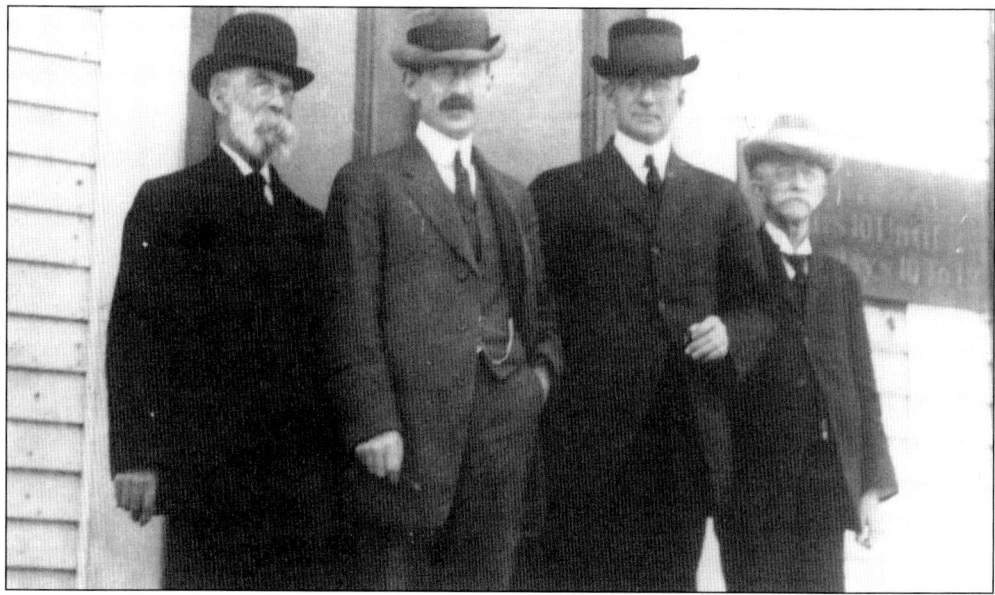

Four prominent citizens and leaders in the town are pictured in front of the 1879 town hall in this c. 1915 photograph. From left to right are: Thomas Holden Angell (the second town clerk), Herbert Fenner (the village undertaker), Louis Sweet (the third town clerk), and Frank C. Angell (the town treasurer for many years).

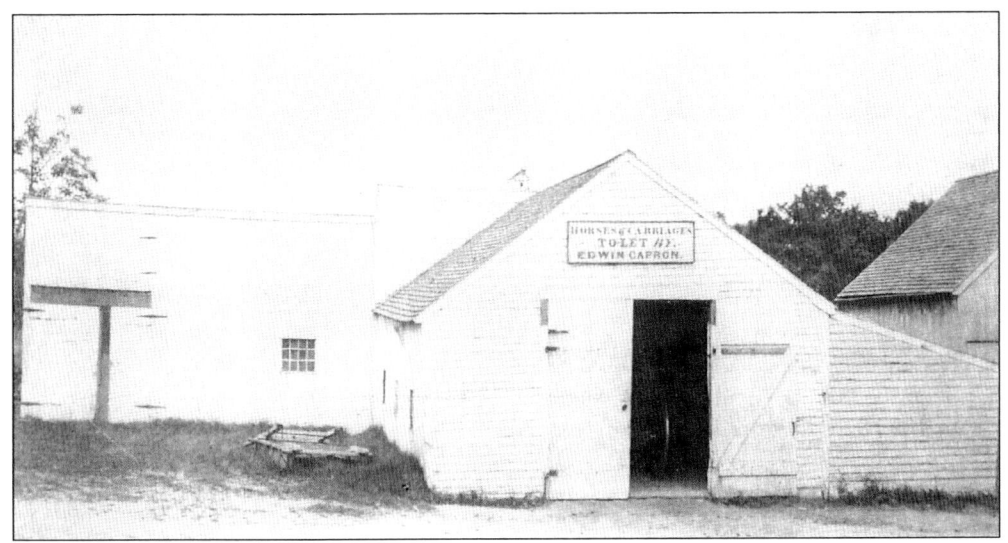

The first livery stable in Centerdale was established by Edwin Capron in 1831. Seen in this photograph is that building. Capron continued this business until his death in 1889. The stable was located on the same site as Sweet's Livery Stable.

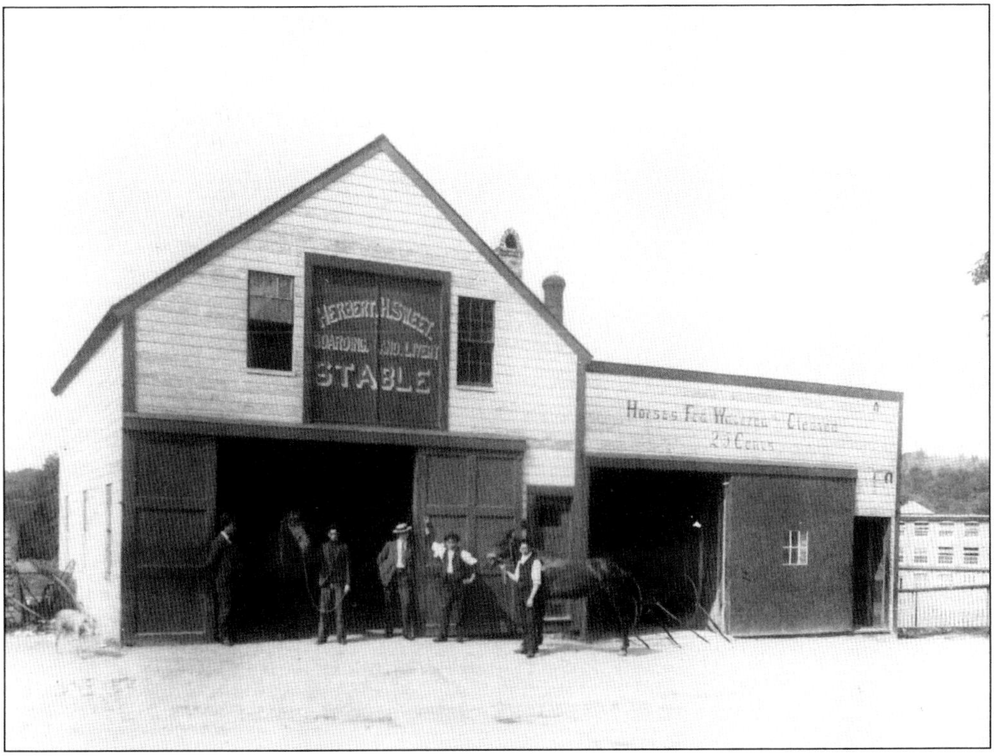

This is the Herbert H. Sweet Livery Stable near the Centerdale Mill. In recent years, a Christmas shop and Salvation Army were located at this site. Today, the site is a vacant lot. In this early twentieth-century photograph, from left to right are: Herbert H. Sweet, Barney McNally, Dennis Mackie, Pat McNally, and Billy Favreau. This land is still owned by a Sweet family grandson, Herbert Sweet.

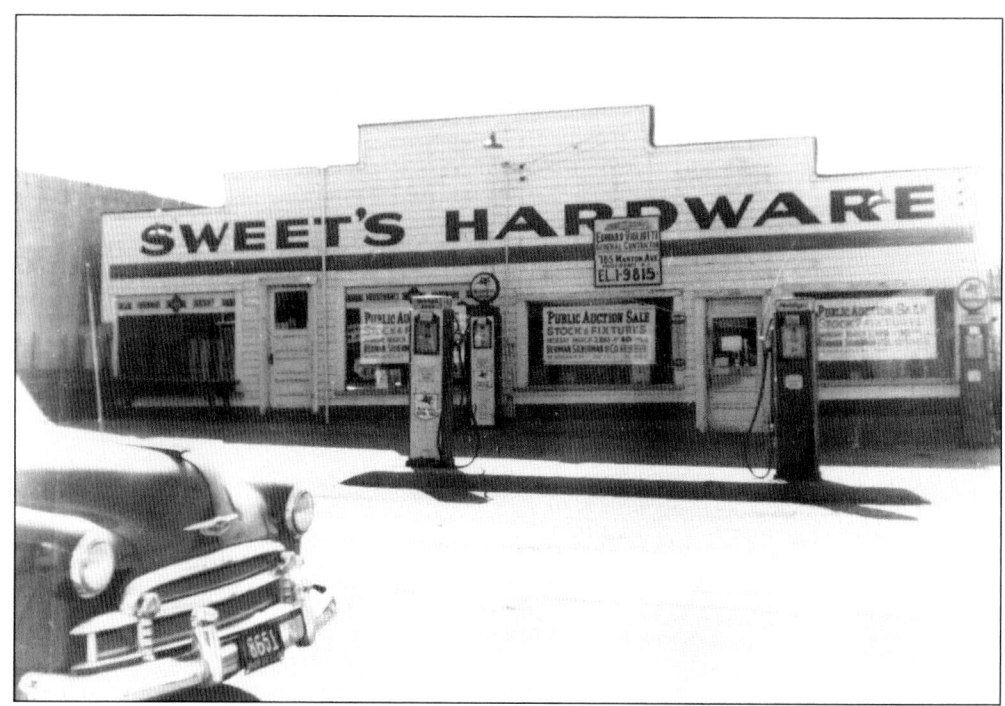

On the land where the livery stable was located, Henry Sweet built this hardware store and gas station. It was closed in 1953.

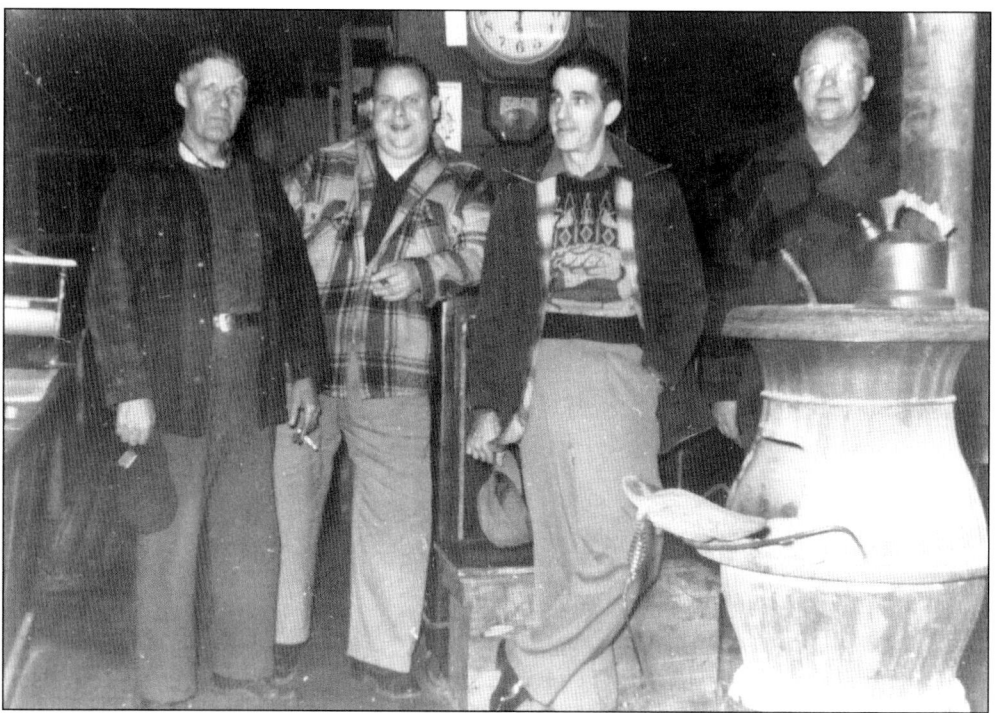

This scene shows the inside of Sweet's Hardware. From left to right are: Elmer Wallace, Ken Ingham, Russell Gregory, and Owner Henry E. Sweet.

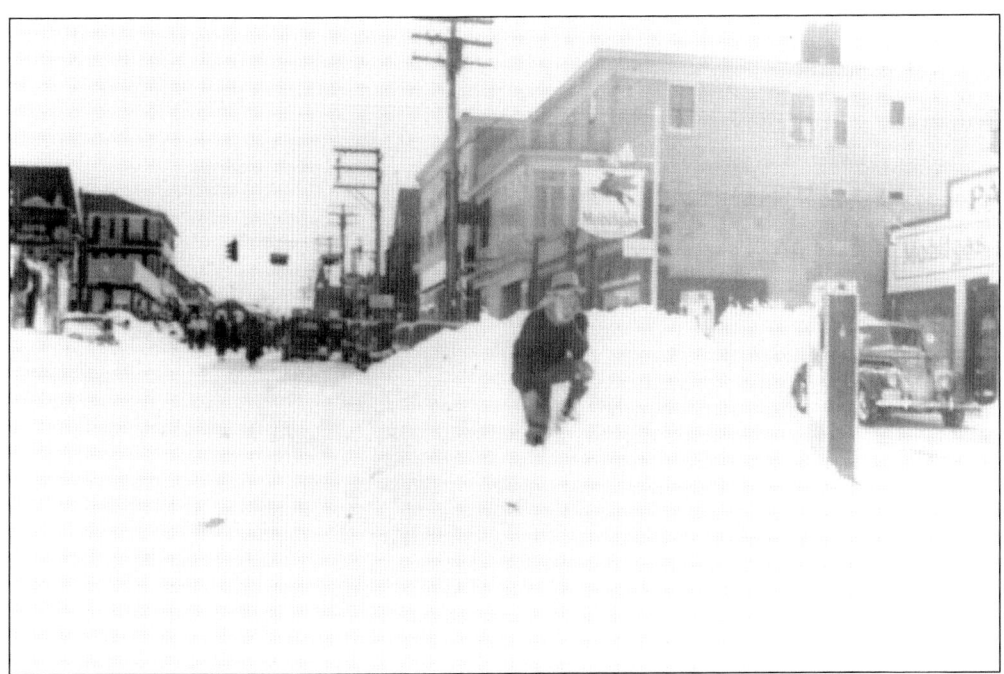

This winter scene in Centerdale looks toward Providence from Sweet's Hardware. This photograph was taken in 1940 showing Herbert Harvey Sweet.

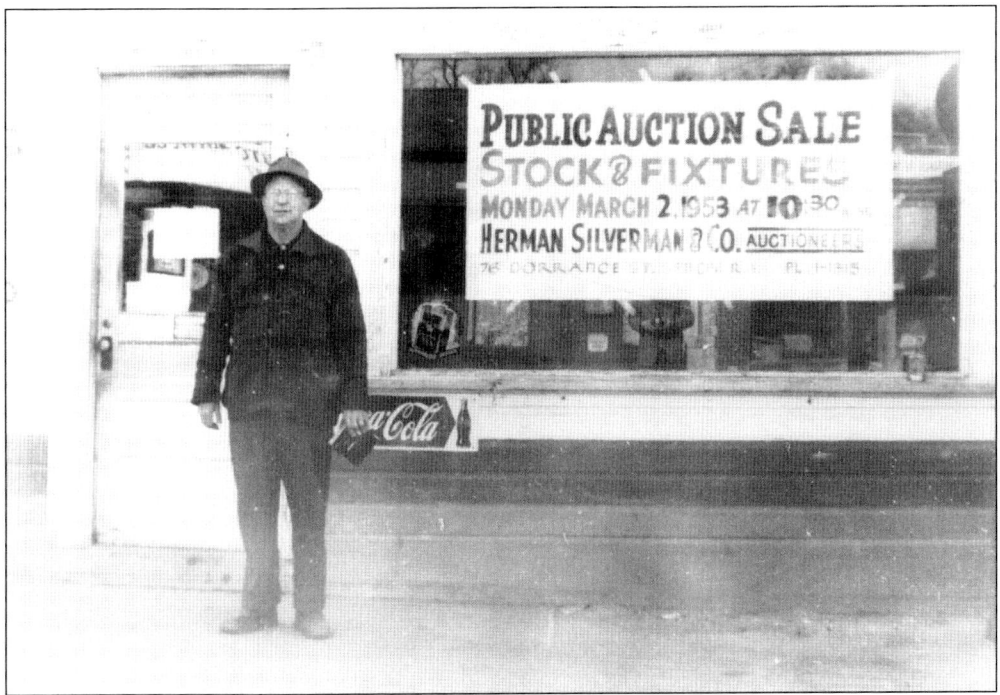

This photograph showing the final days of Sweet's Hardware reveals the notice of a public auction to be held on March 2, 1953. Standing beside the doorway is Henry Edwin Sweet, the owner.

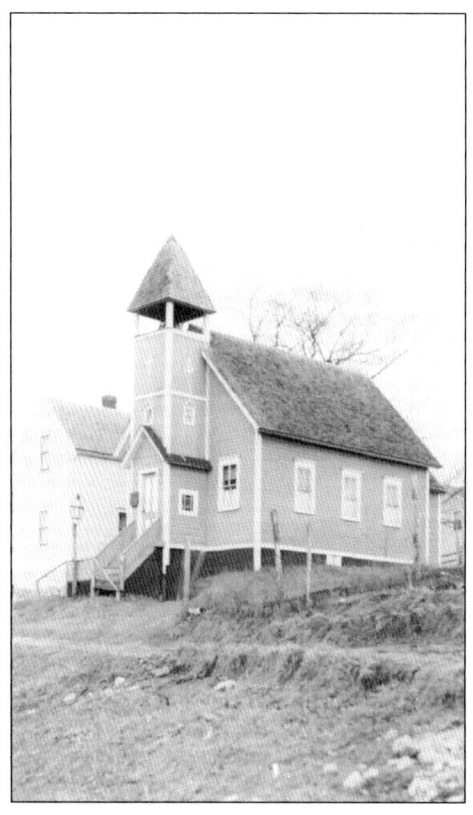

This is the Centerdale Independent Methodist Church on George Street. During the summer of 1896, William H. Tilley and others held open-air services which were so successful that a lot was purchased and a small church built. The church was dedicated on June 17, 1897. This photograph was taken c. 1900.

This is Reverend William H. Tilley, who was assistant pastor of the Independent Methodist Church. On June 27, 1901, he was formally ordained to the gospel ministry and was then elected pastor. He also worked for the Salvation Army. By the time of this photograph, he had lost his right arm and needed a strap to help carry items.

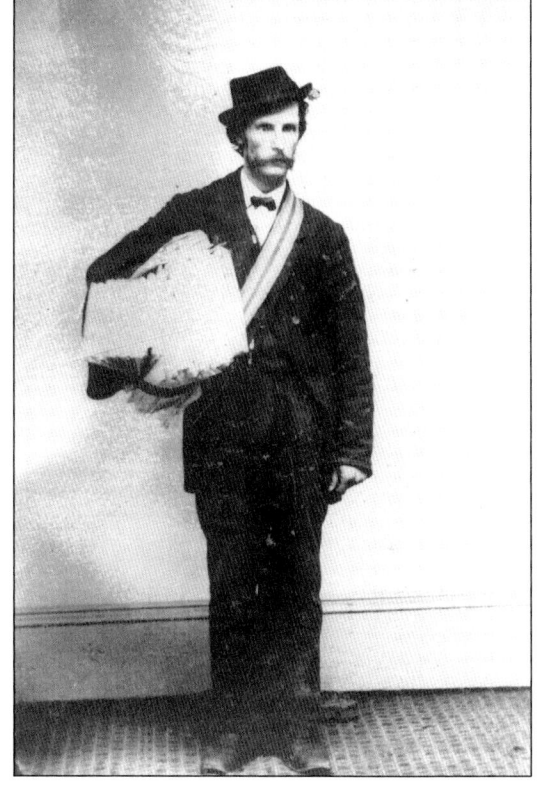

This is Saint Alban's Episcopal Church, which started as an Episcopal mission headed by Reverend James W. Colwell. In 1899, the congregation voted to build a church and appointed the building committee of F.C. Angell, William Dracup, and Reverend James W. Colwell. A formal dedication took place on January 1, 1906, and on June 16, 1906, the church was consecrated.

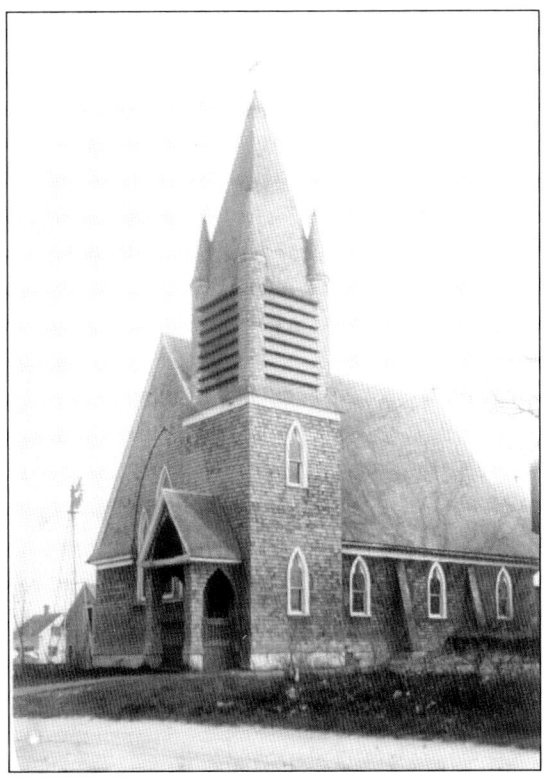

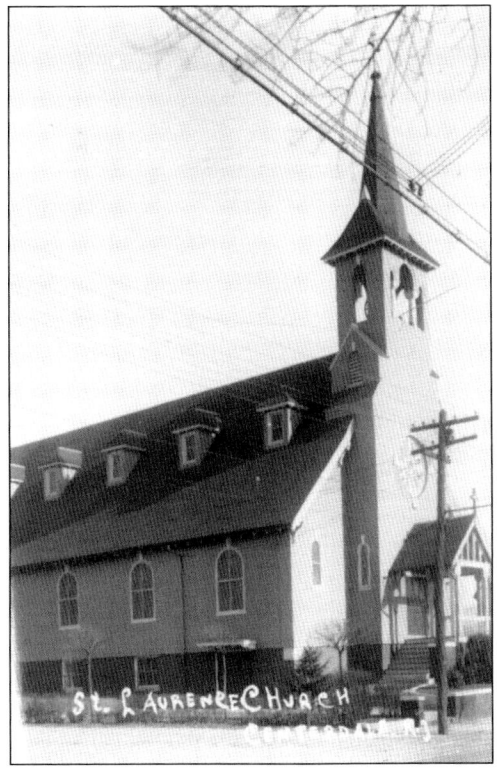

At the turn of the twentieth century, the number of Catholics in Centerdale had increased, so Bishop Harkins approved the formation of a new parish. The cornerstone for Saint Lawrence Church was laid on October 20, 1907. However, church services led by Reverend James Hardy began on October 13, 1907, in a room in Allendale.

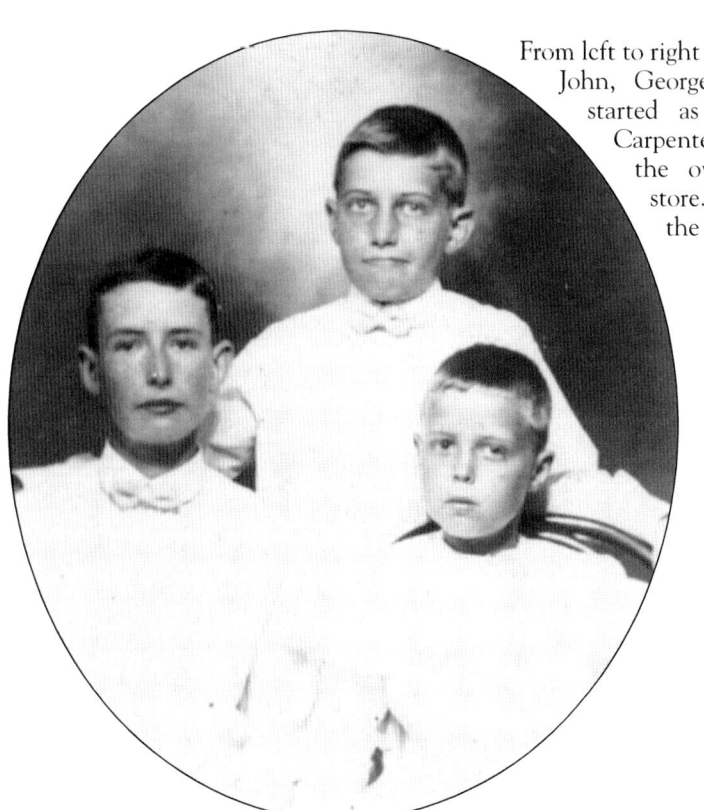

From left to right are the Batchelder brothers: John, George, and Earl. Their father started as an employee of Luther Carpenter and eventually became the owner of Luther's country store. His sons succeeded him in the business.

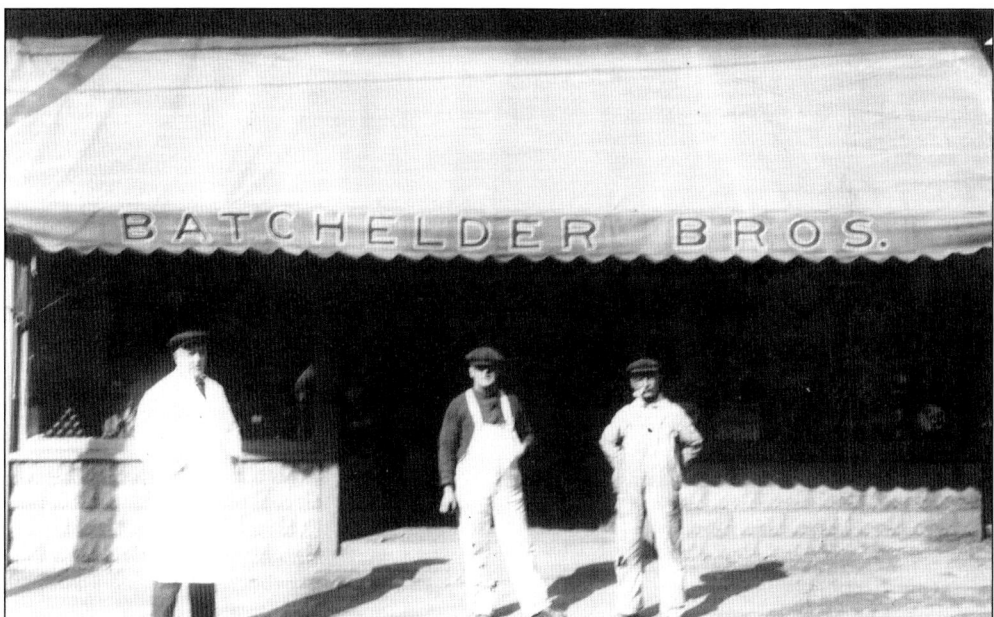

This photograph shows the Batchelder brothers as adults in front of their store at 2038 Smith Street at the corner of Smith Street and Mineral Spring Avenue. The building was moved to that site from Mineral Spring Avenue in the early 1900s. It eventually became Buonaccorsi's Centerdale News Depot.

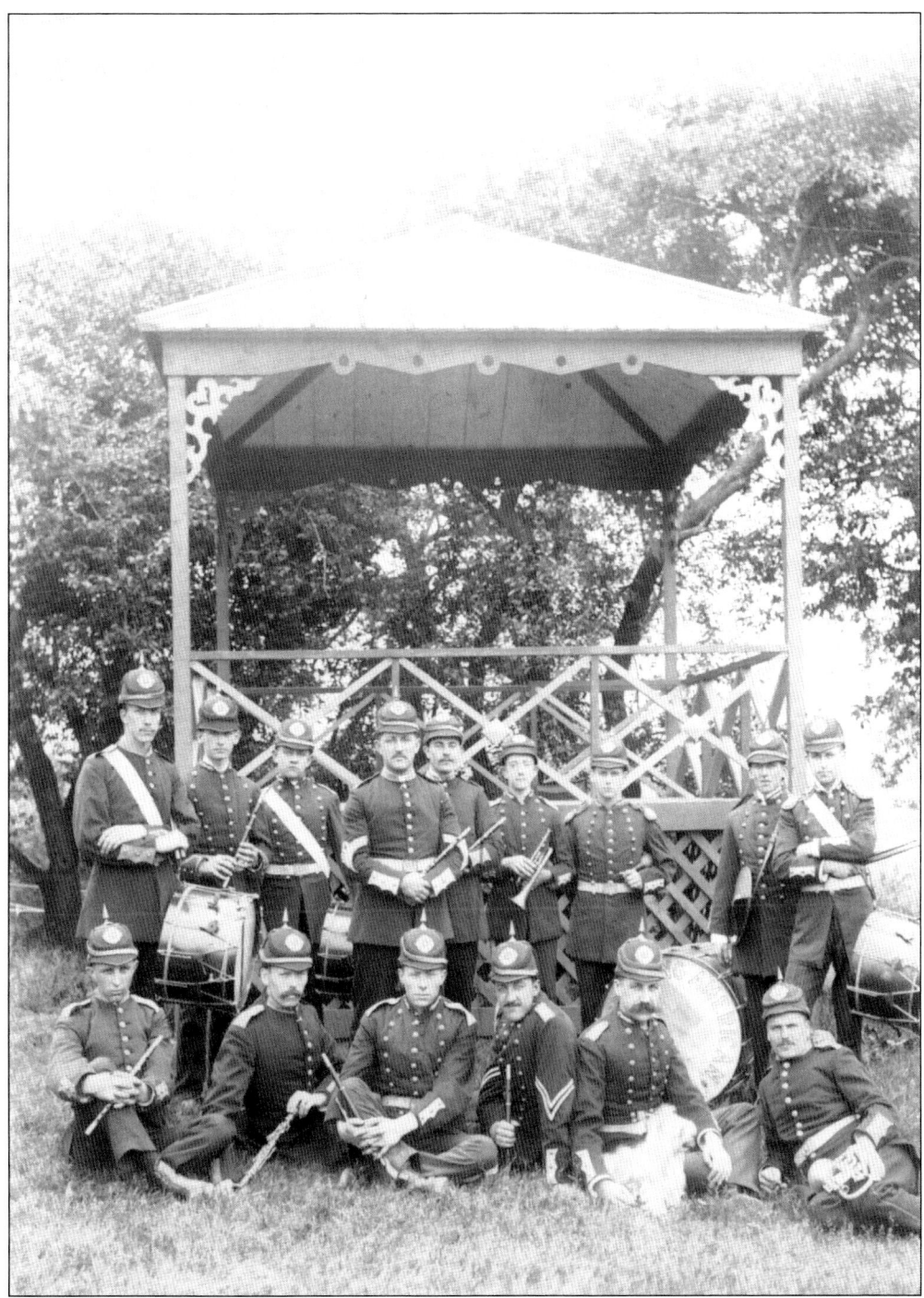

This is the Centerdale village band, named the Young American Band, c. 1885. It was formed in August 1884 through the efforts of Frank C. Angell and George Cozzens. Although it started with twelve members, it grew to twenty-five members and was known as a flute and drum ensemble. Rehearsals were held in the basement of the Armory Hall, but the fire in that building in 1892 started the decline of the band, which disbanded in 1894.

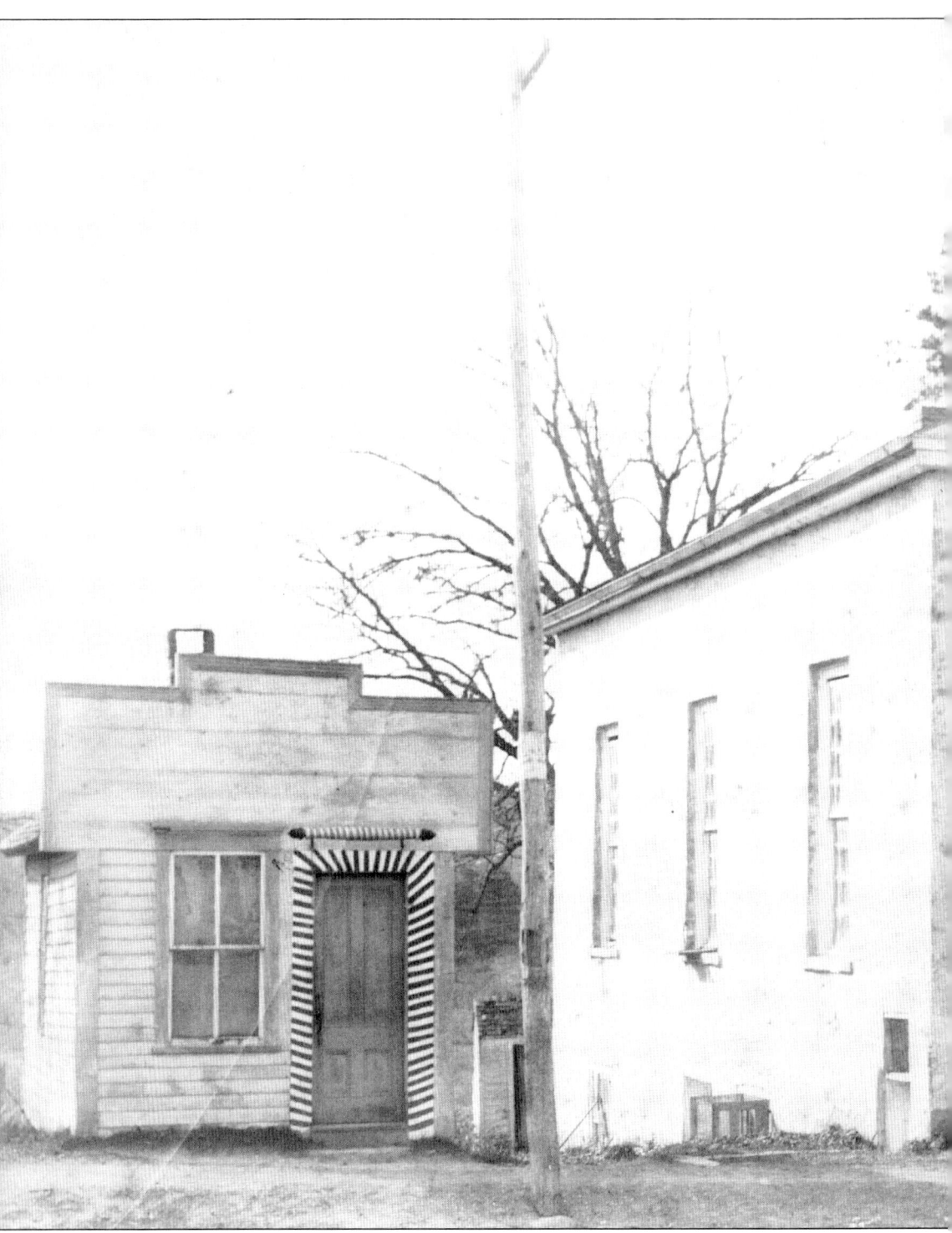

The Armory Hall, shown here c. 1885, was originally built as the Free Will Baptist Church in 1832. In 1847, it was sold to the Episcopal Society, who held services there until 1855. In 1863, James Halsey Angell bought the property and converted it into the Armory Hall military

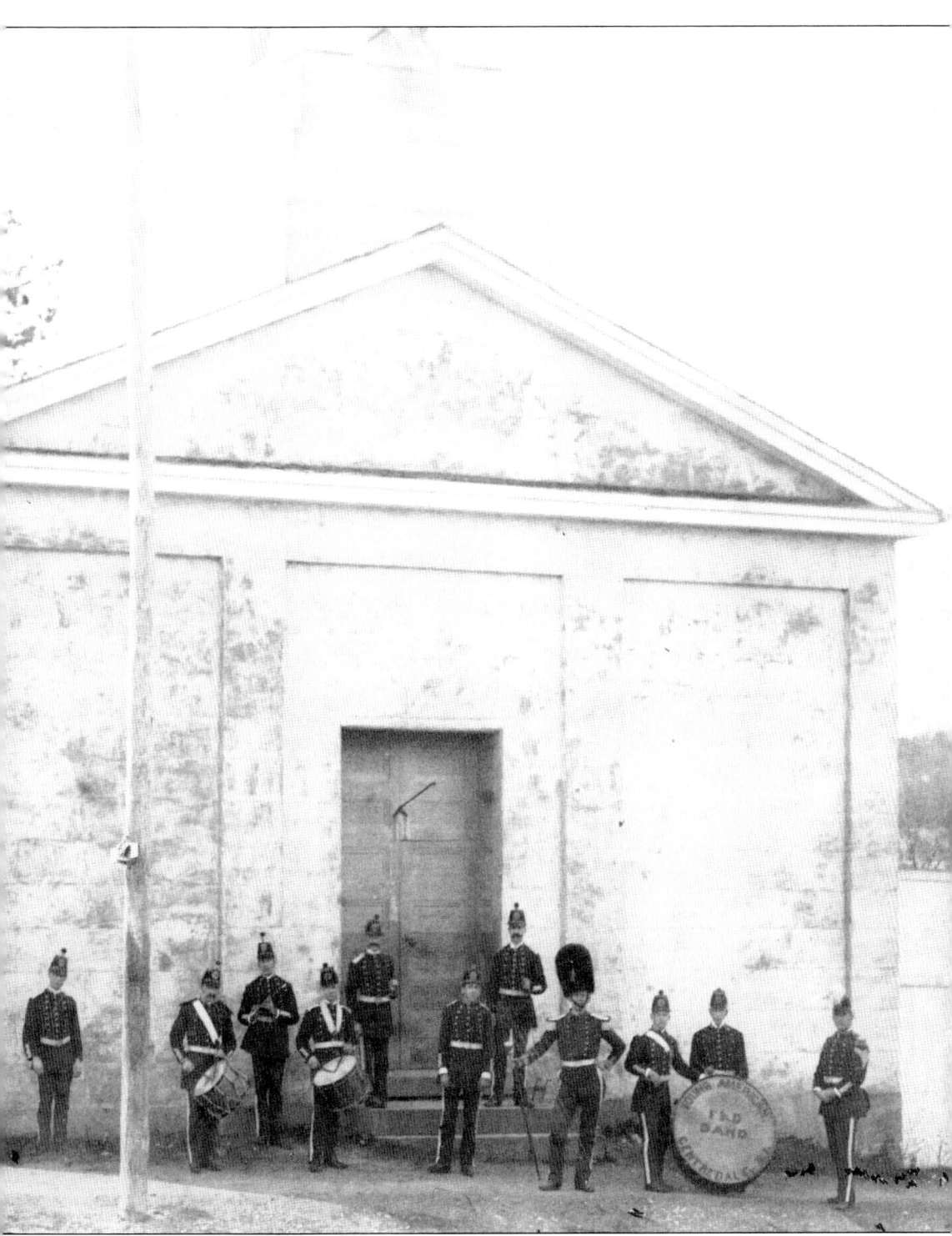
complex during the Civil War. After the war, the building was remodeled into a public hall. A barber shop is next to the hall in this photograph. In 1892, both buildings were destroyed by fire. This is now the site of Our Place.

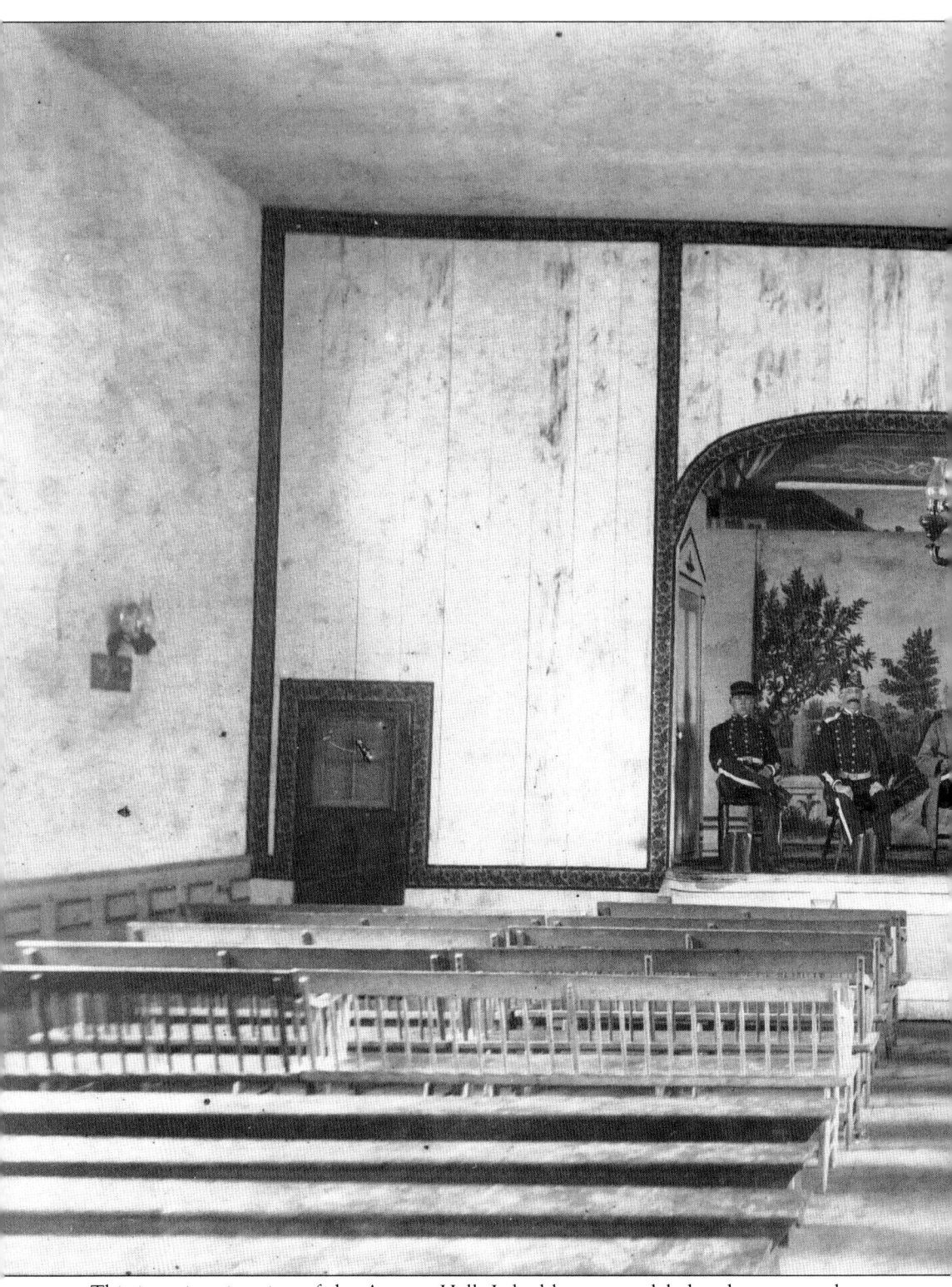
This is an interior view of the Armory Hall. It had been remodeled and a stage and scenery

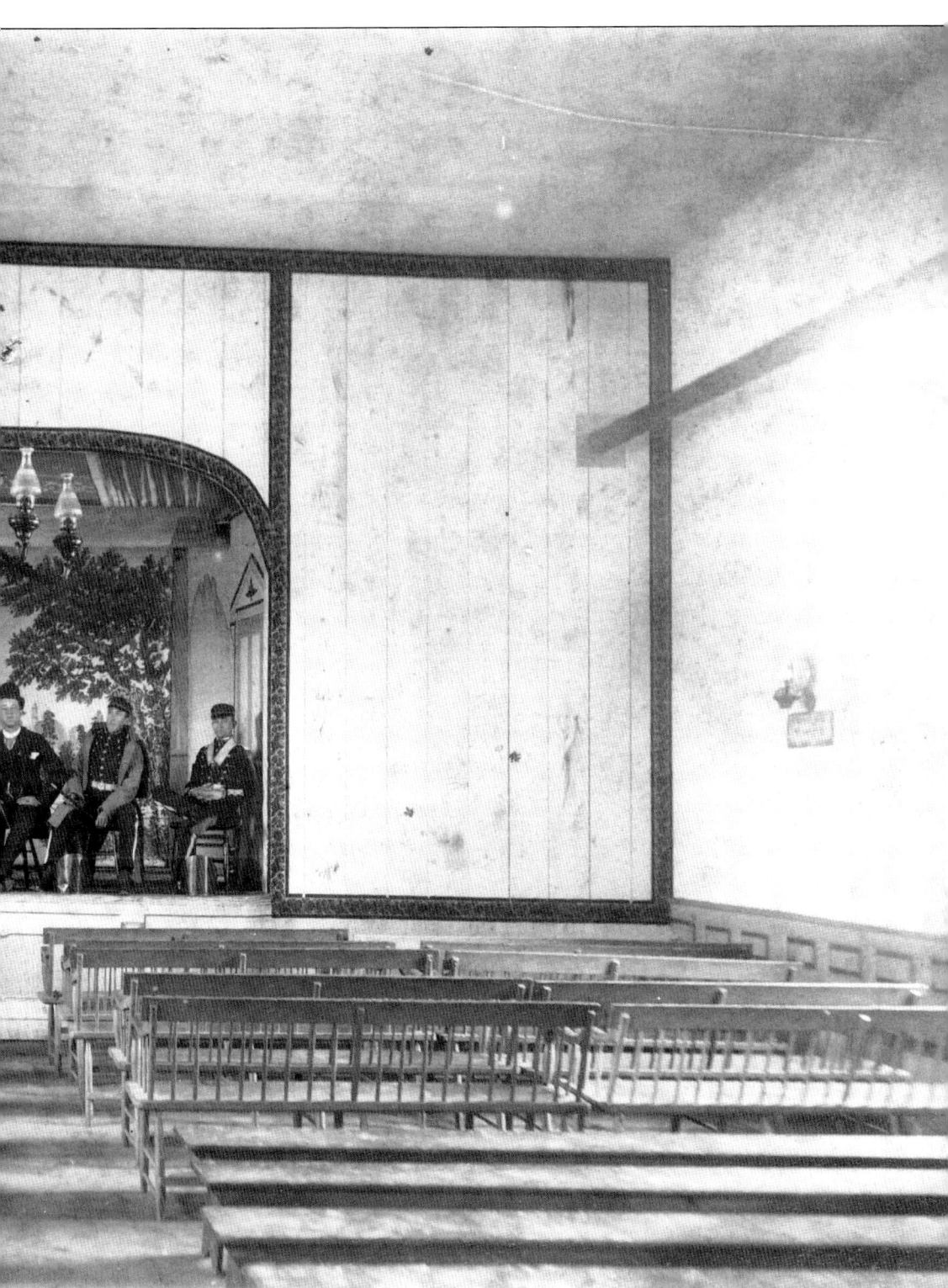
were added.

Grand Exhibition

— AT —

Armory Hall, Centredale,

— ON —

Saturday Eve'g, Oct. 31.

The public are respectfully invited to attend an Exhibition as above, where will be performed the comic Drama, entitled

All is not Gold That Glitters!

Jasper Plum,	Mr. J. Marsh
Stephen Plum,	A. W. Harrington
Frederic Plum,	F. C. Angell
Toby Twinkle,	M. M. Joslin
Sir Arthur Lovelle,	H. J. Turner
Harris,	Mr. J. Nichols
Lady Valeria,	Miss A. F. Westcott
Lady Leatherbridge,	Miss. S. Lapham
Martha Gibbs,	Miss J. M. Burlingame

SONGS, by . . C. E. TUTLOW.

To be followed by the side splitting farce, entitled

Betsey Baker!

Mr. Marmaduke Mouser,	Mr. J. Marsh
Mr. Crumny,	M. M. Joslin
Mrs. Crumny,	Miss J. M. Burlingame
Betsey Baker,	Miss A. F. Westcott

The whole to conclude, with Celebrated

CLOG DANCE

By C. E. Tutlow.

Tickets. - - - - 25 Cents.
Children, - - - - 15 "

Doors open at a quarter to 7 o'clock.
Performance to commence at 7.30 o'clock

An Orchestra will enliven the occasion under the leadership of Mr. James Olney.

The proceeds to be devoted to the raising of a Public Library for the village of Centredale.

A. Crawford Greene, Printer, Railroad Hall, Providence, R. I.

This broadside was hung as an advertisement for entertainment held at the Armory Hall on October 31, 1868, as a fund-raiser for the building of the 1870 Union Library.

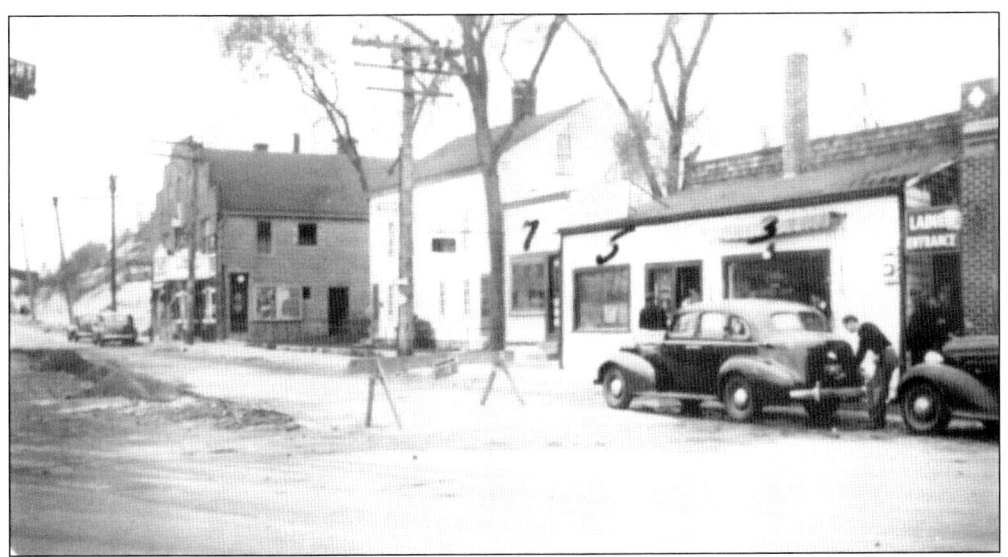

This image looks along Waterman Avenue in the 1930s. At the far right is the brick column of the present Diamond Home Specialties company. All of the following buildings are now gone: #3, #5 (a business that was originally the John Cozzen's house), #7 (Skinny's Restaurant, owned by Ed Scunzio), an old mill dwelling, and the then-new Community Theater.

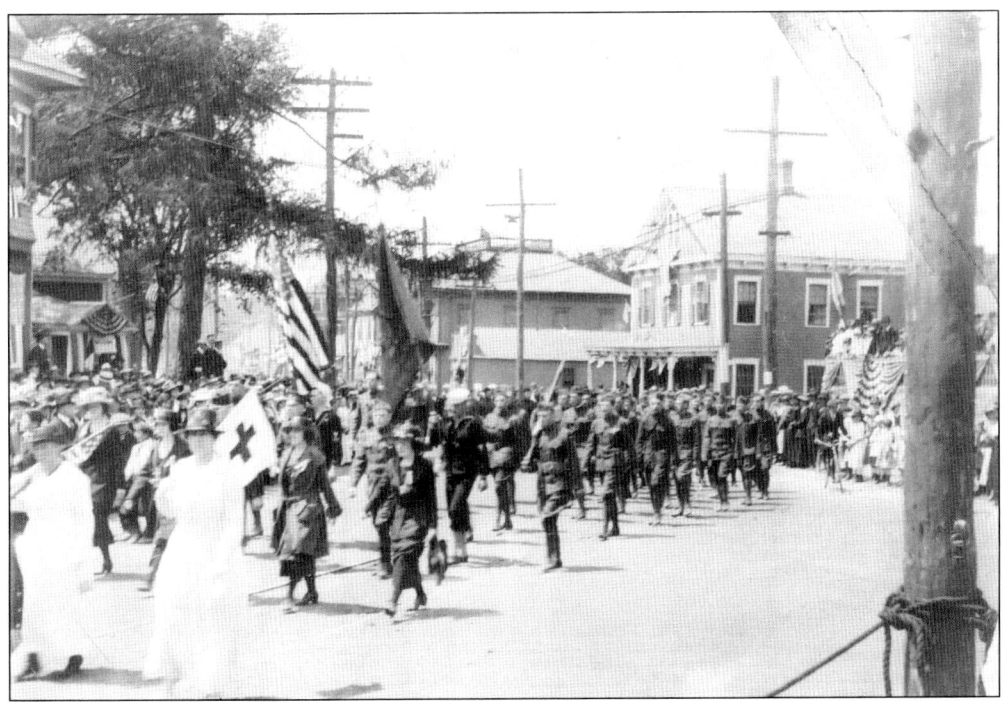

This town parade probably occurred after WW I. The group is entering Woonasquatucket Avenue. All buildings seen are those previously described.

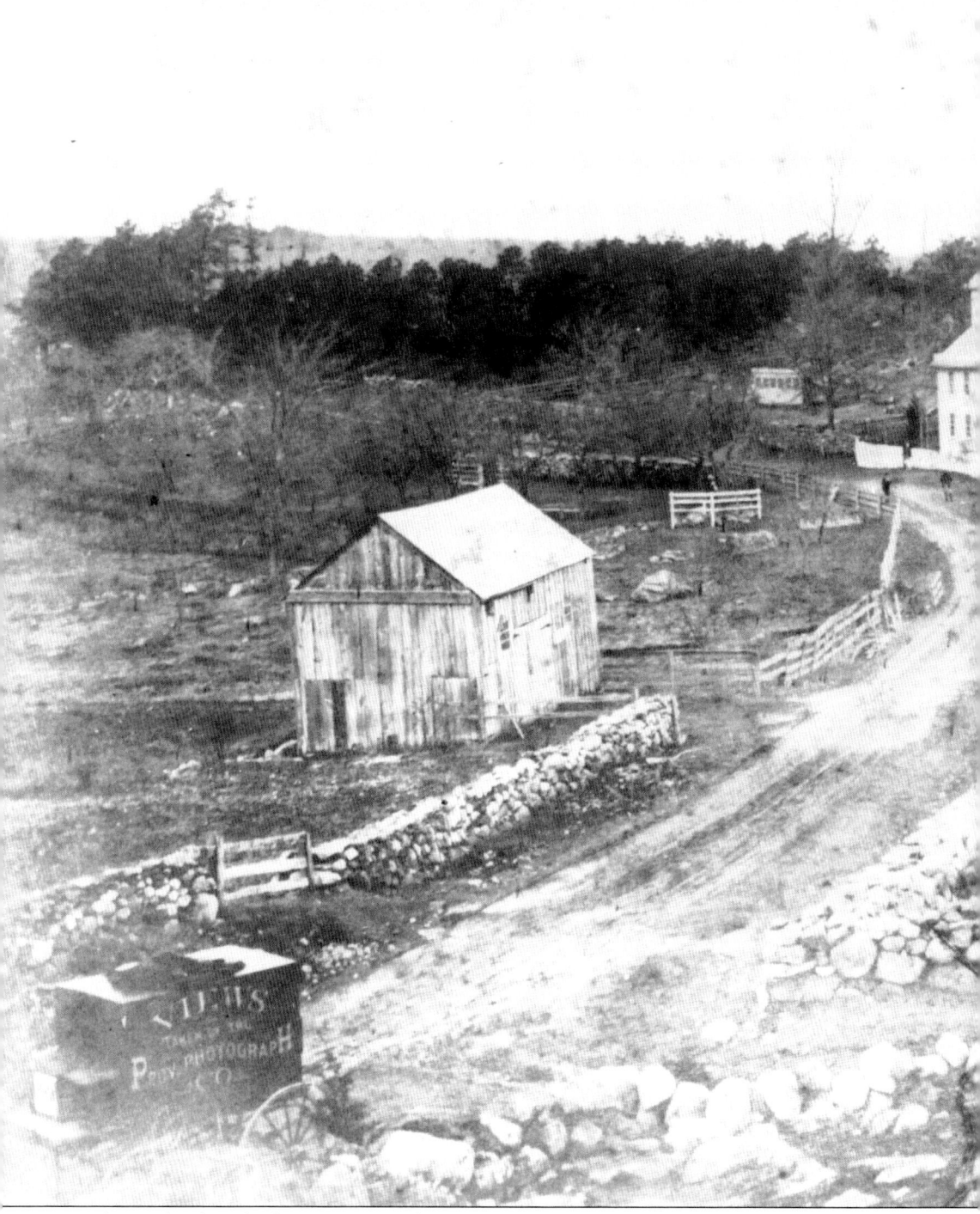

This is the farm built c. 1730 on what is now Angell Avenue by James Olney. James was a direct descendent of Thomas Olney of Providence, an original settler with Roger Williams. This photograph was taken c. 1892. James Olney died in 1770 and his will offers the following bequests: " to my wife, the benefit of my negro woman and to my sons, Emor and Samuel, my

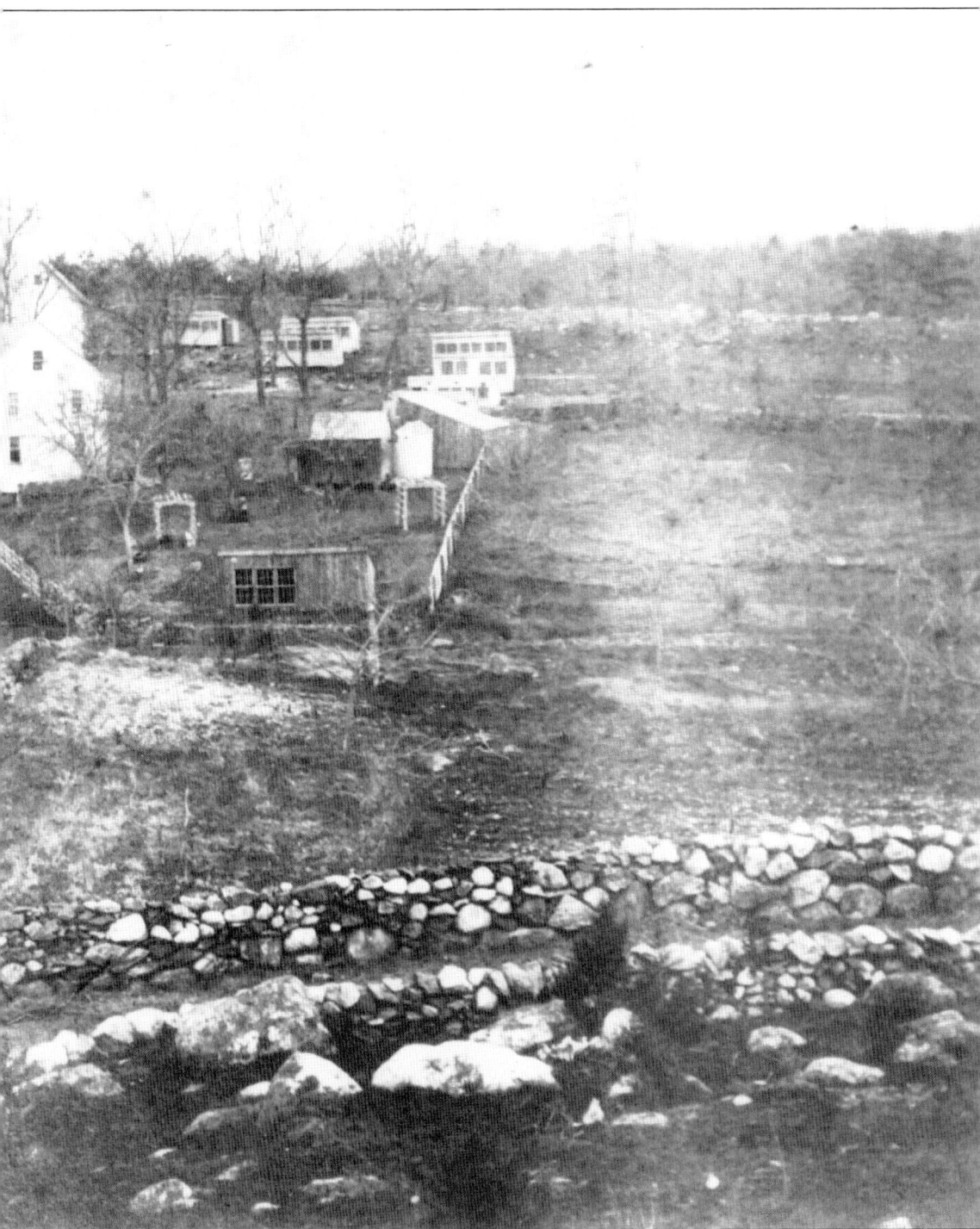

negro man to be shared so long as he behaves himself well they may not sell him, but if he misbehaves, then he may be sold." In the nineteenth century, the farm became the property of the Thomas H. Angell family for whom the street was named.

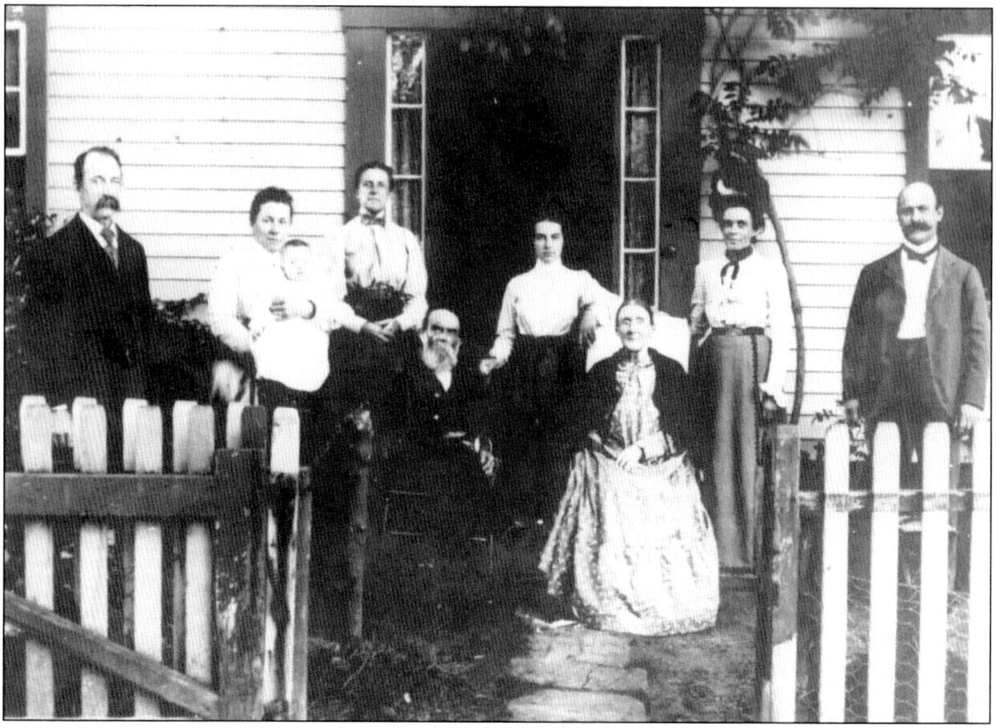

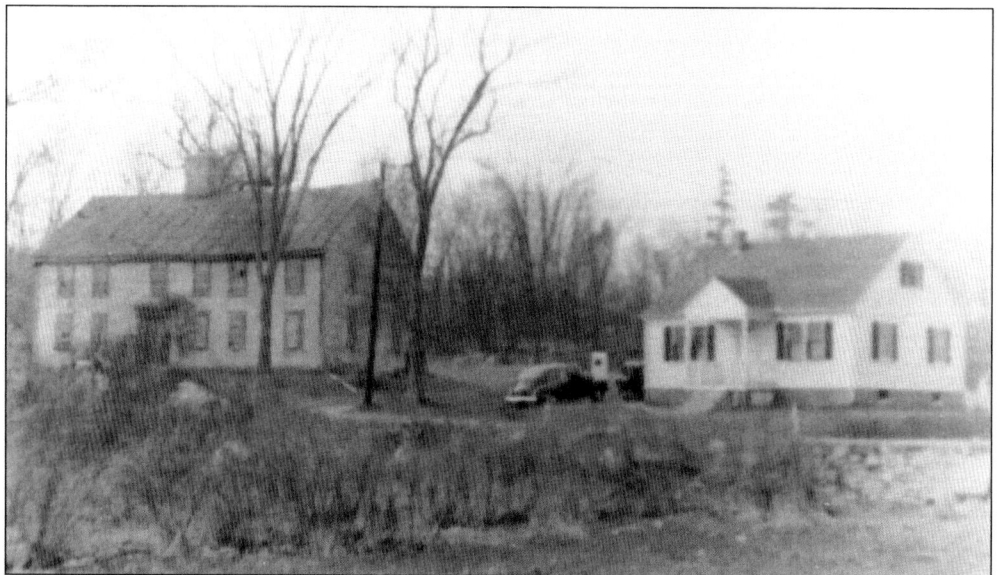

This 1900 photograph shows the front yard of the old house on Angell Avenue. Pictured are, from left to right: Walter Angell, wife Gertrude (holding their daughter Edith), Aunt Nell, Thomas H. Angell (the second town clerk), Gertrude Angell, Patience (Appleby) Angell (the wife of T.H. Angell), and Lillian and Easton Inman.

This 1930s photograph depicts the old James Olney house and the new Sidney Angell house on the right. Sidney Angell, the son of Walter and Gertrude Angell and grandson of T.H. Angell, was born in 1905. He is still living in the new Cape style house on Angell Avenue today. The old house is long gone.

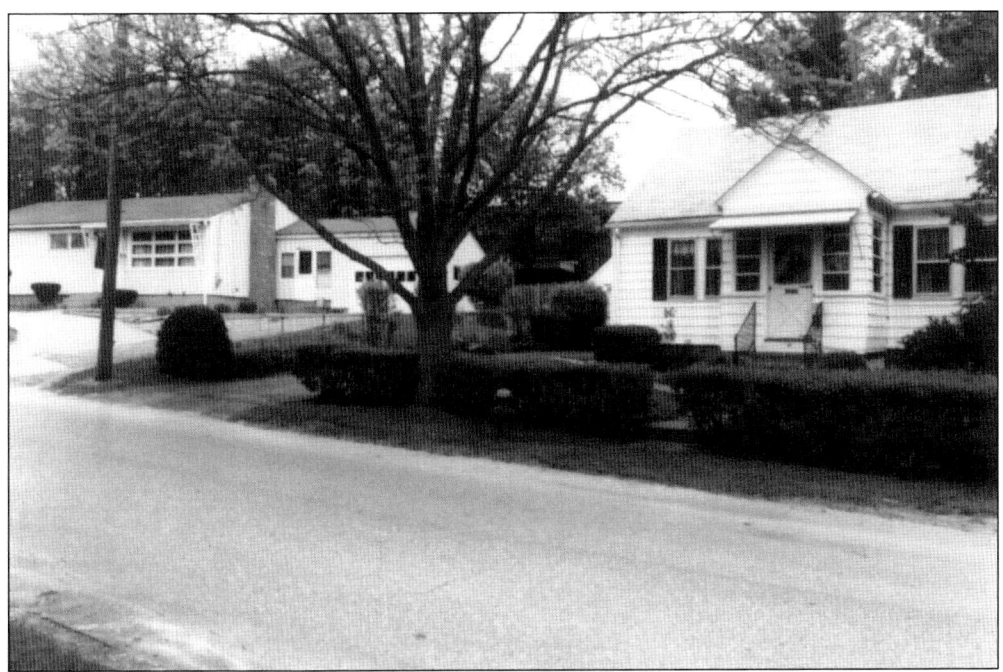

This shows the site of the James Olney house as it appears today on Angell Avenue

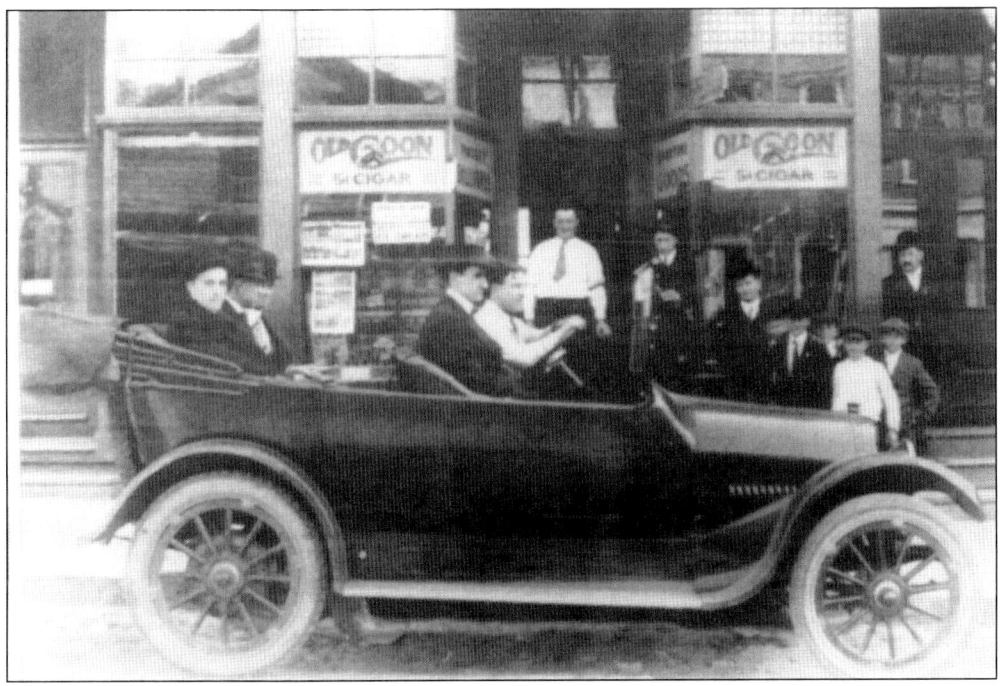

Here is James O'Reilly at the wheel of his car in front of his business. Jim and his brother William (standing in the doorway) were once proprietors of a small variety store and poolroom at 2046 Smith Street in the Clarence Broley building now known as Our Place. (*Observer* photograph.)

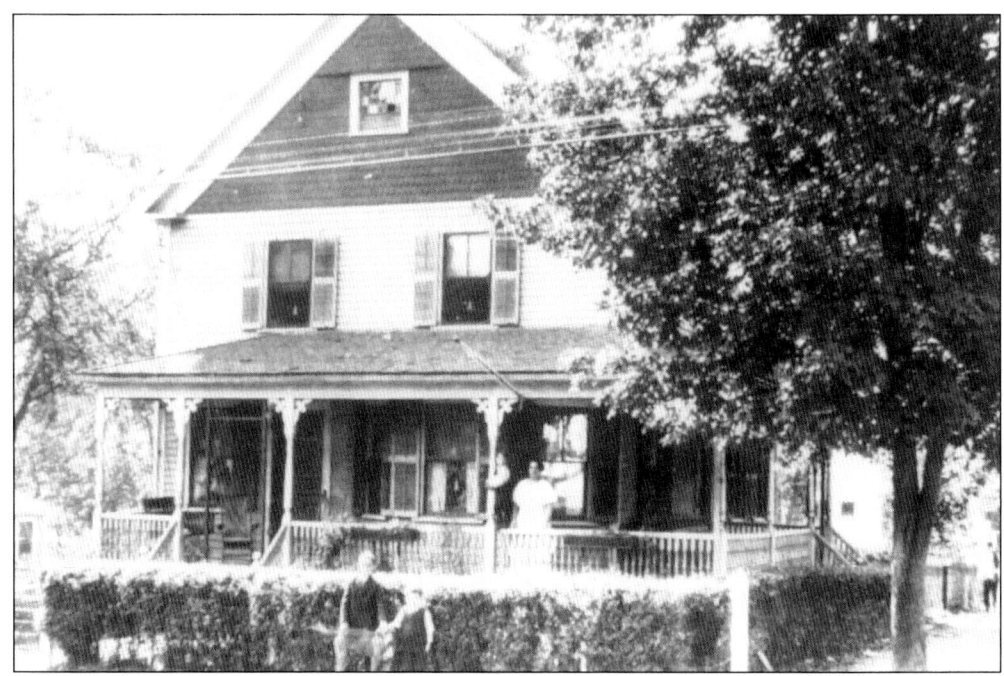

This is the James O'Reilly home at 640 Woonasquatucket Avenue as it looked in 1915. Family members are on the porch and on the sidewalk.

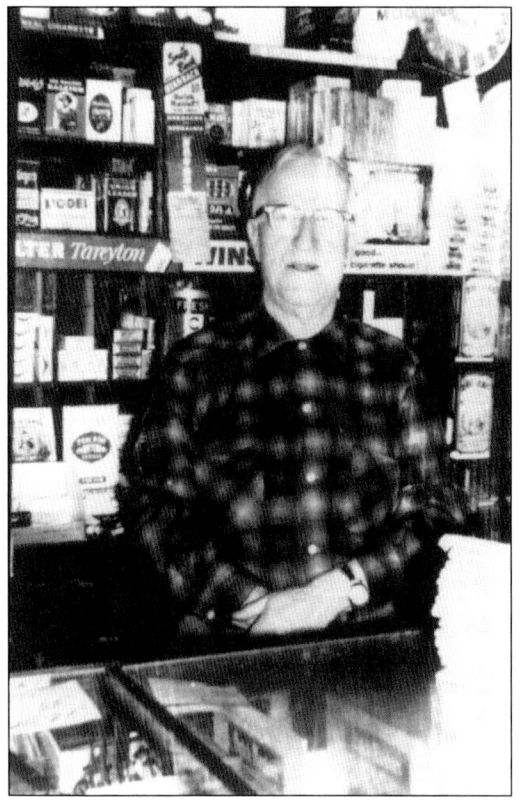

In later years, Jim O'Reilly operated another variety and sporting goods store across from the present town hall at 2009 Smith Street This photograph shows him behind the counter in his later years.

A late 1930s parade passed in front of the new Napolean Trahan Community Theater. On the left end of the theater building was a small candy store called Leona's Sweet Shoppe. That business was operated at one time by Jim O'Reilly's wife.

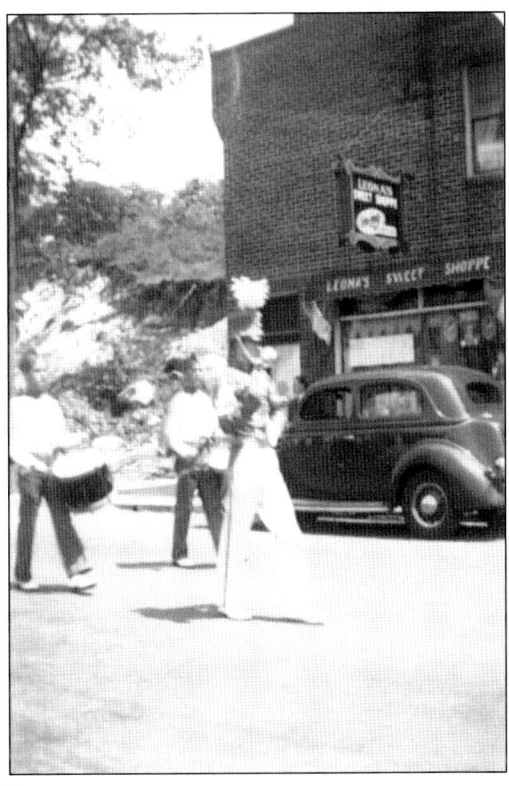

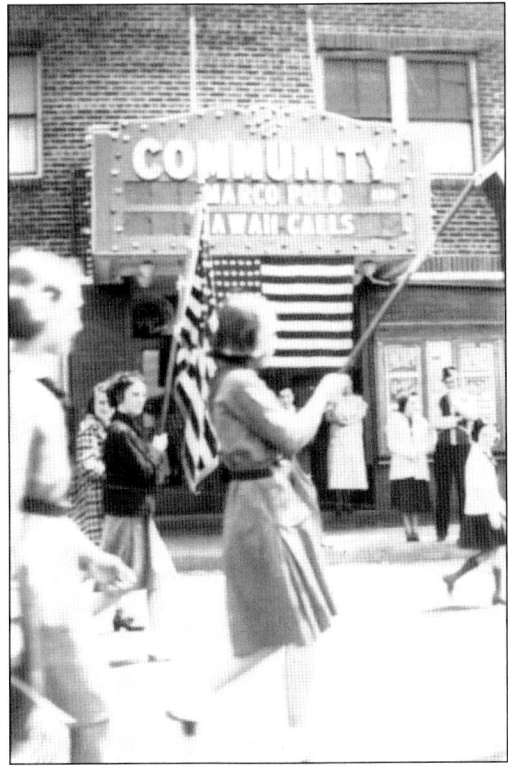

At this point, the parade passes the Community Theater sign. Daphne Reynolds is seen holding the flag.

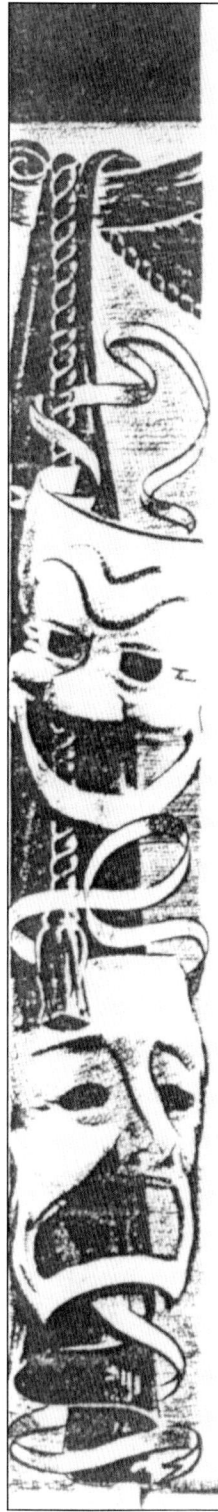

COMMUNITY

THEATRE—Centerdale, R. I. Phone: Centerdale 0842
"North Providence Theatre of Distinction"

Continuous Performances Every Evening from
6:30 to 10:30 P. M.—Doors Open 6:15 P. M.
Sunday and Holidays Continuous from 2:15 P. M.
Sat. Matinee at 1:15 P. M.

Use Our Free Parking Space

SUN., MON. and TUES., JUNE 12, 13 and 14

Sunday Continuous from 2:15 P. M.

2 — GREAT FEATURES — 2

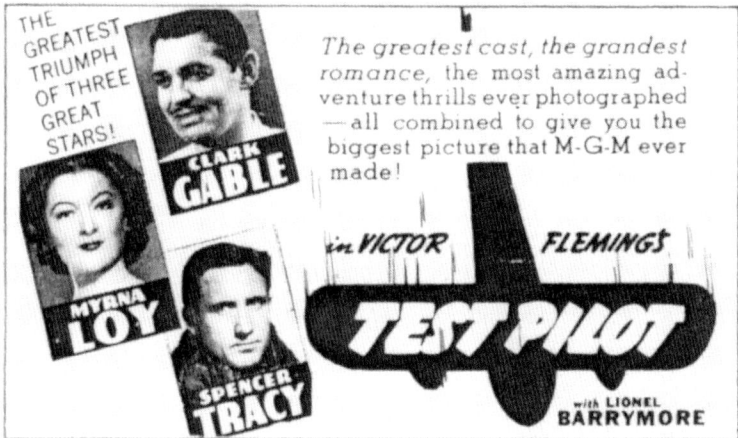

THE GREATEST TRIUMPH OF THREE GREAT STARS!

CLARK GABLE
MYRNA LOY
SPENCER TRACY

The greatest cast, the grandest romance, the most amazing adventure thrills ever photographed — all combined to give you the biggest picture that M-G-M ever made!

in VICTOR FLEMING'S
Test Pilot
with LIONEL BARRYMORE

— also —

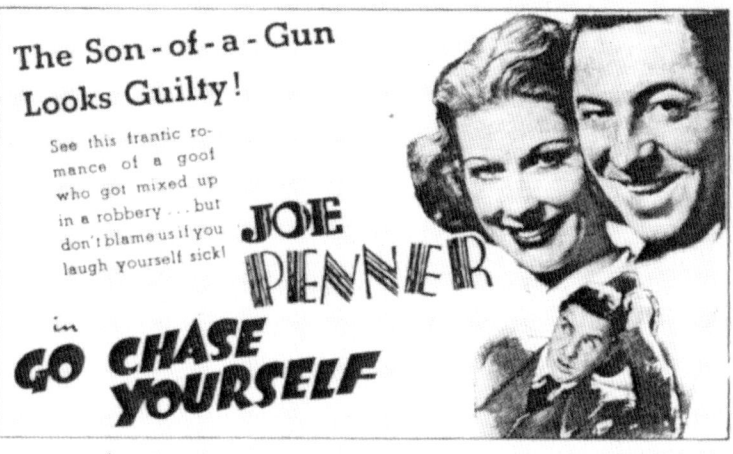

The Son-of-a-Gun Looks Guilty!

See this frantic romance of a goof who got mixed up in a robbery ... but don't blame us if you laugh yourself sick!

JOE PENNER in
GO CHASE YOURSELF

NOTE—"Test Pilot" Will Be Shown Monday and Tuesday at 8:00 P. M.

A 1938 flyer advertises upcoming events at the Community Theater.

Three

FRUIT HILL

In the early 1800s, Williams Thayer was either given a cherry tree or planted one from seed, depending on which source one consults. According to all sources, however, this cherry tree was the influence for the name Fruit Hill. By the turn of the twentieth century, Fruit Hill had become a very desirable residential area and remains so today.

The Olney family members were the first settlers in this area c. 1757. Ezra Olney built a house at what is now Capitol View Avenue. When he died in 1801, his estate was divided among his four children (Samuel, Cyrus, Rosilla, and Phebe) and wife.

In 1760, a distant cousin of Ezra's, Epenetus Olney, built a house at the site of the present Fruit Hill Apartments. This landmark has over the years been a tavern (c. 1800), the first post office in western North Providence (1825), and a private school founded by the Drowne family (1835). Stanton Belden bought the school in 1840 and continued to operate it until the Civil War. Mr. Belden demolished the old building and built the present Victorian house.

The earliest known public school in Fruit Hill was located at the intersection of Fruit Hill Avenue and Smith Street as early as 1765. By 1795, that school was gone. In 1828, when public education became mandatory, the Fruit Hill district school was built at the corner of Mount Pleasant and Elmcrest Avenues. This was also the site of the first Saint Augustine's Church. That school building was replaced on the same site in 1865. Nine years later when that land became part of Providence, Fruit Hill was without a school. Fortunately, that building was leased to North Providence until 1879 when a new Fruit Hill School was built on Fruit Hill Avenue at what is now the site of the VFW Hall. After 1879, the 1865 schoolhouse was moved to 28 Olney Avenue

The earliest surviving home in Fruit Hill is at 157 Olney Avenue; it was built c. 1767 by Stephen Whipple, a shoemaker. Fruit Hill was also home to an enclave of artists around the turn of the century. Fortunately, many of the early homes in the area remain intact to this day.

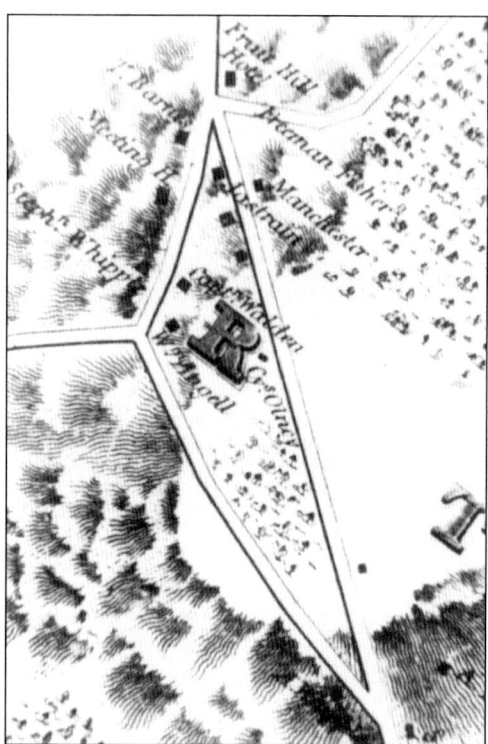

This 1835 map shows how sparsely populated Fruit Hill was in the early nineteenth century. In spite of this, it was the center of western North Providence in the eighteenth and early nineteenth centuries. It had a blacksmith, a wheelwright, a Baptist meeting house, and a school as early as 1765.

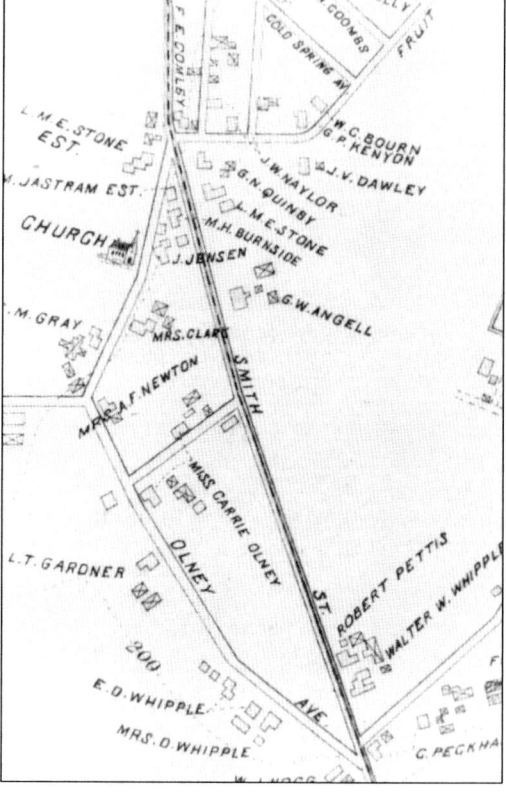

This 1895 map shows how much growth had taken place since 1835. New streets off upper Fruit Hill Avenue had been platted as well as others off High Service Avenue. High Service Avenue at the lower right was built as a road to the High Service Water Reservoir, presently the site of Fatima Hospital. Miss Carrie Olney owned the bulk of the land within the triangle.

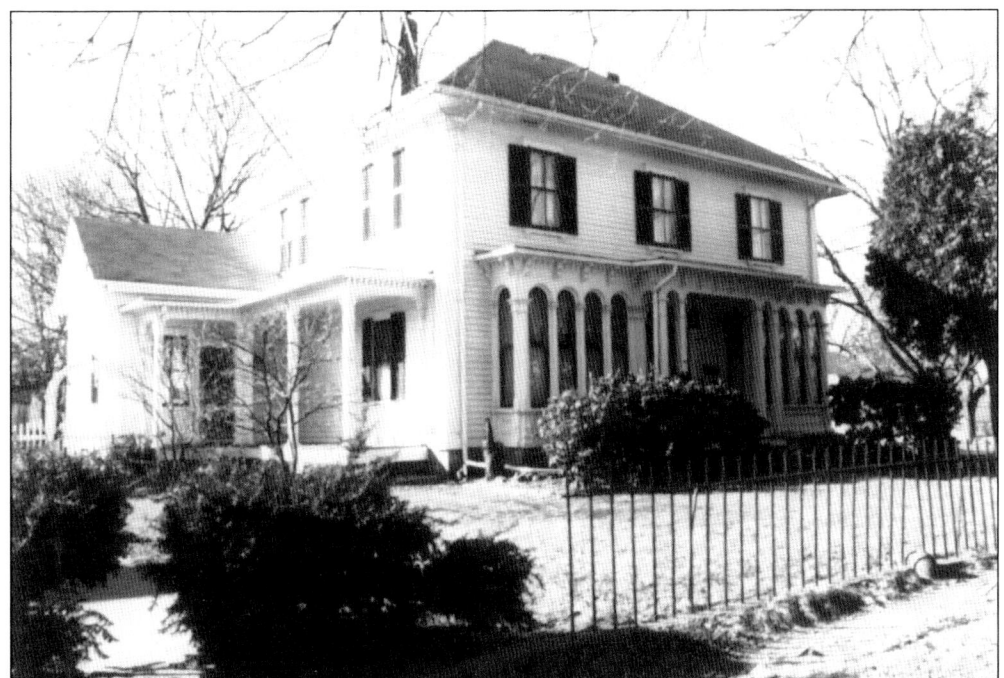

Ira Olney built this house at 59 Homewood Avenue in 1861 on the site of another smaller house built by his father Cyrus Olney. All of the land within Fruit Hill was part of a large tract owned by Ira's grandfather, Ezra Olney.

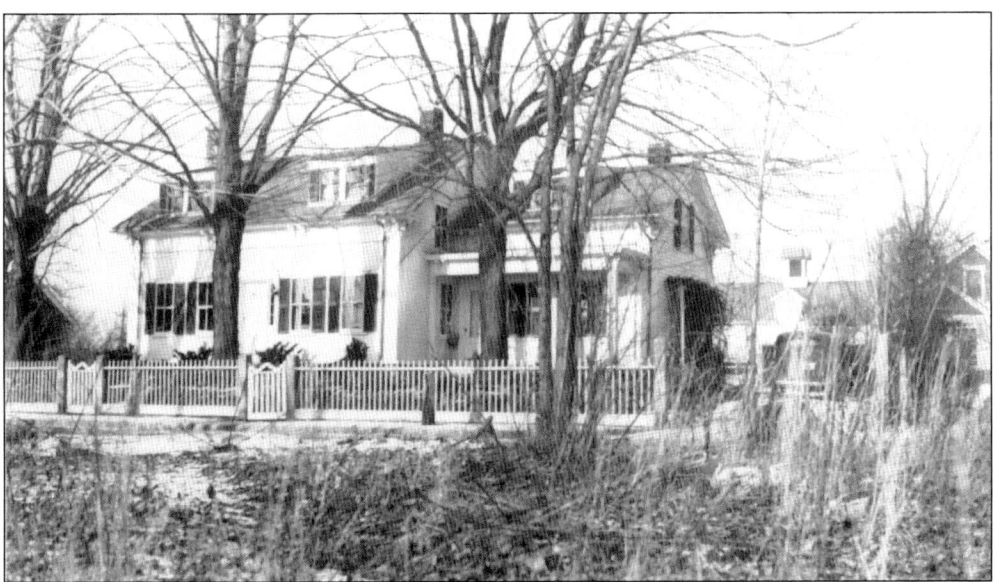

In 1861, Ira Olney sold his mother a 59.5-rod tract of land at the present 119 Olney Avenue. By the end of 1862, the same tract was sold to Ira's brother, Edward Wales Olney, by their mother together with a house. This c. 1938 photograph shows the house and barn. The house has been the residence of Barbara A. and Thomas E. Greene since 1972.

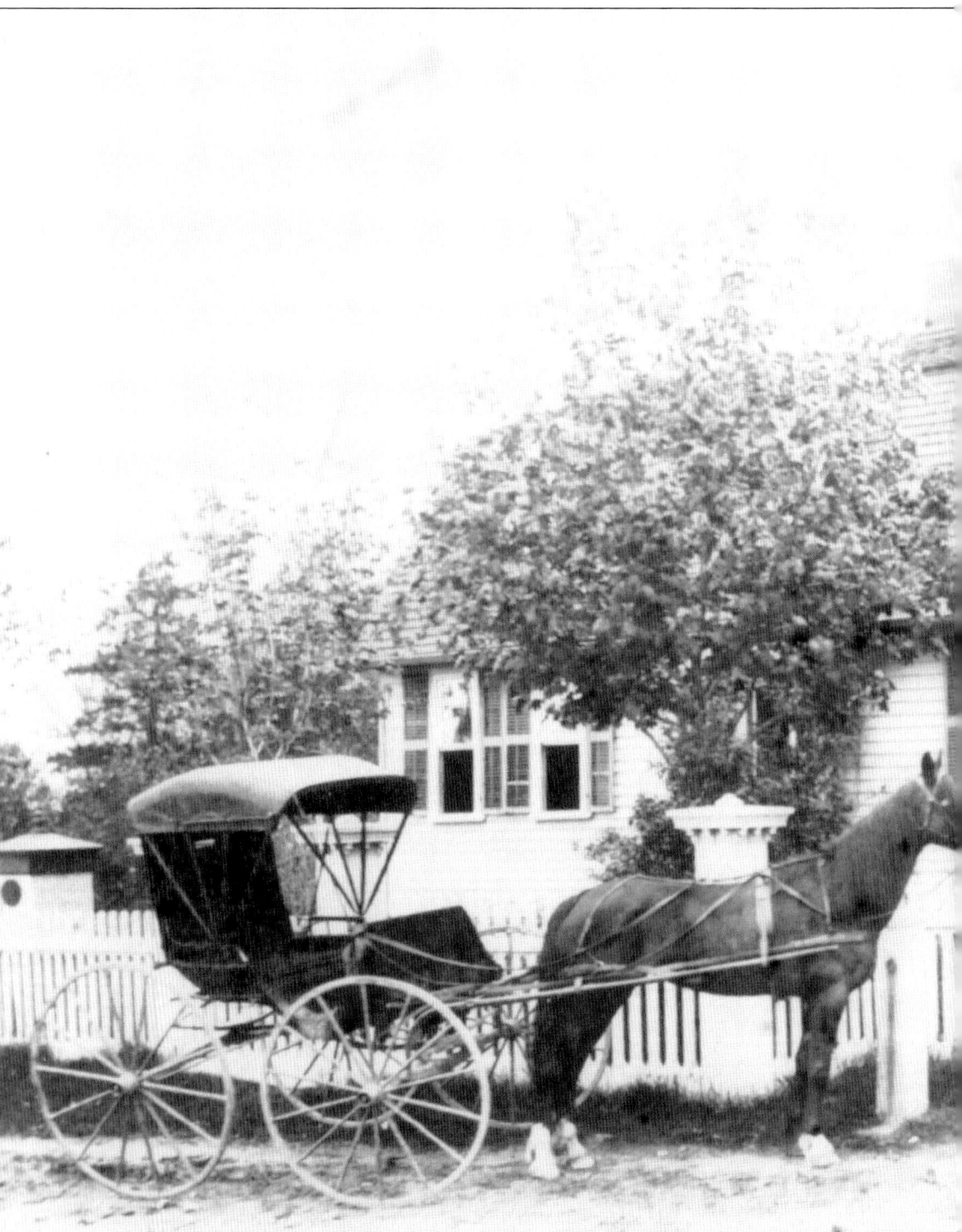

The Stephen Whipple House was built in 1767. Stephen, born in 1735 and a cousin of the nearby Whipple family, was a shoemaker. He bought the land and built the house at the present 157 Olney Avenue. The house went through several owners and was finally sold to William

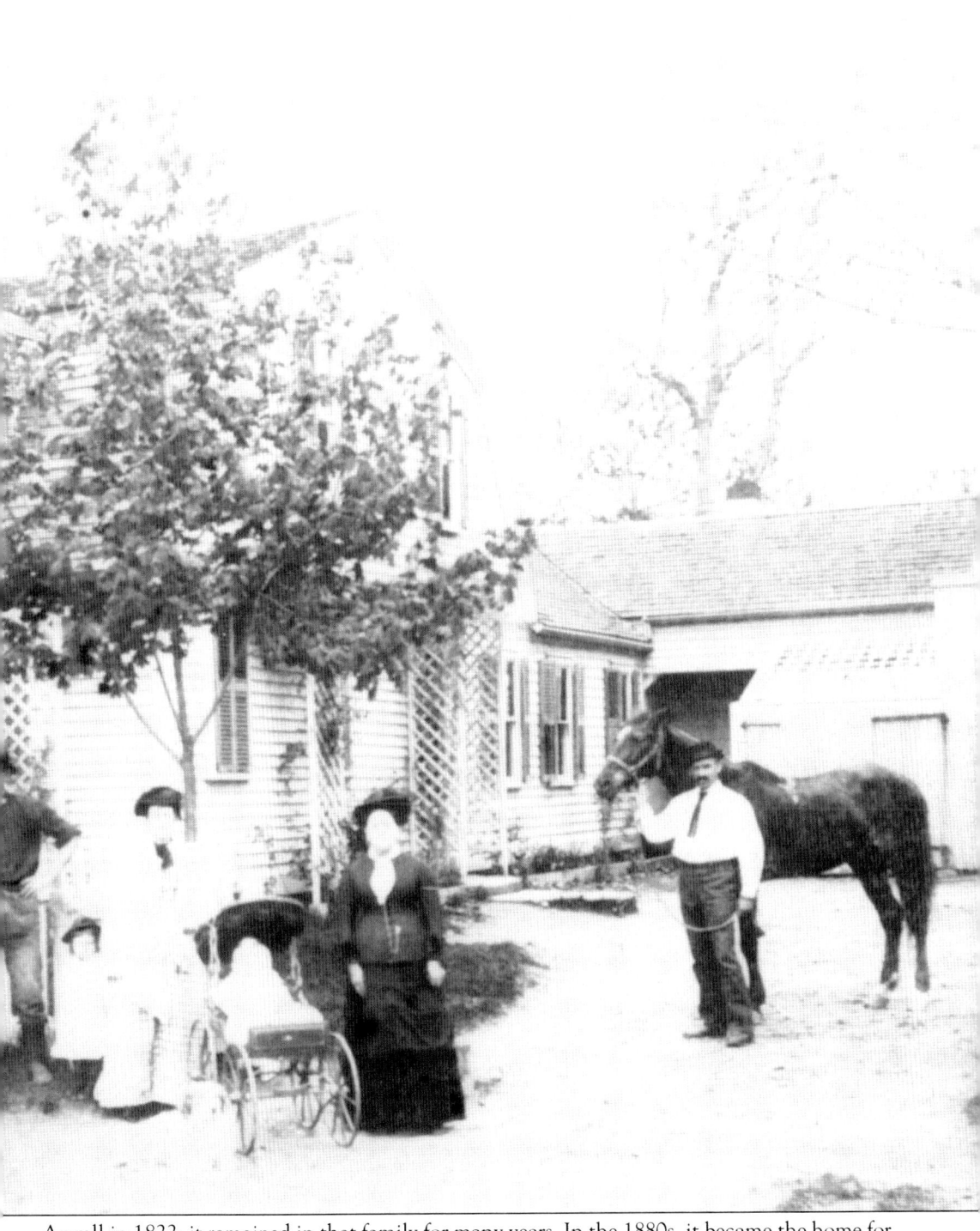

Angell in 1822; it remained in that family for many years. In the 1880s, it became the home for the Newton family who are pictured below. This photograph was taken c. 1890.

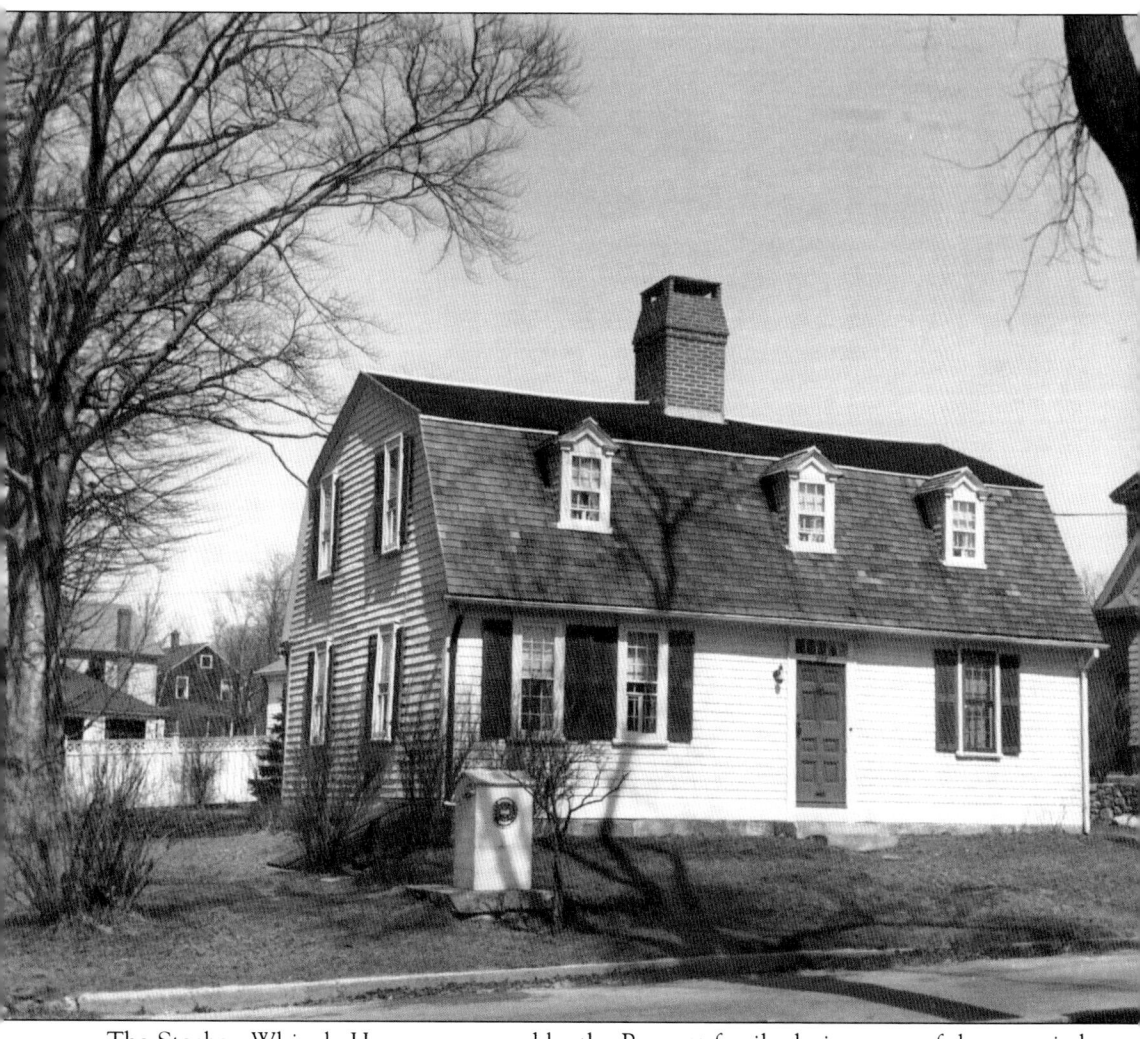

The Stephen Whipple House was owned by the Bennett family during most of the twentieth century. In 1995 it became the property of William M. Woodward and Joseph Hanley. This photograph dates to the mid-twentieth century. The well house is no longer on the site.

This is the original building that was located at the corner of Smith Street and Fruit Hill Avenue. It was a private school from 1835 to 1861. Before 1835, it was a private home, a tavern, and the North Providence Post Office from 1825 until 1849.

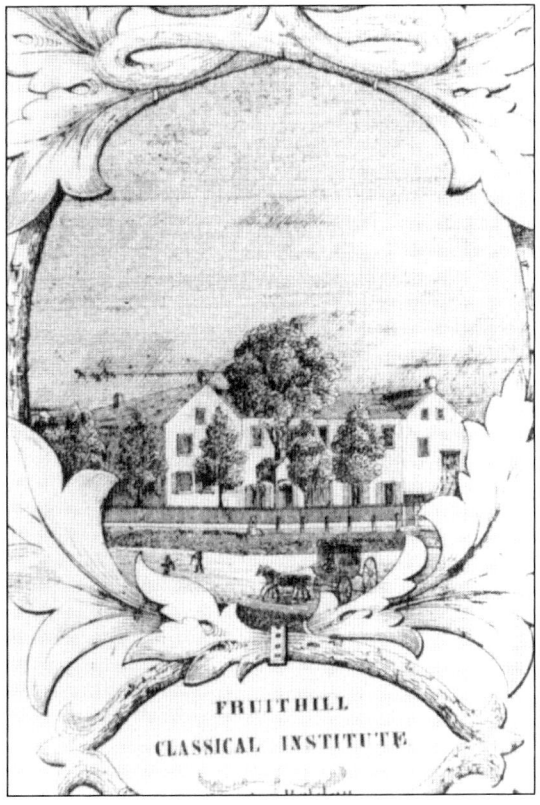

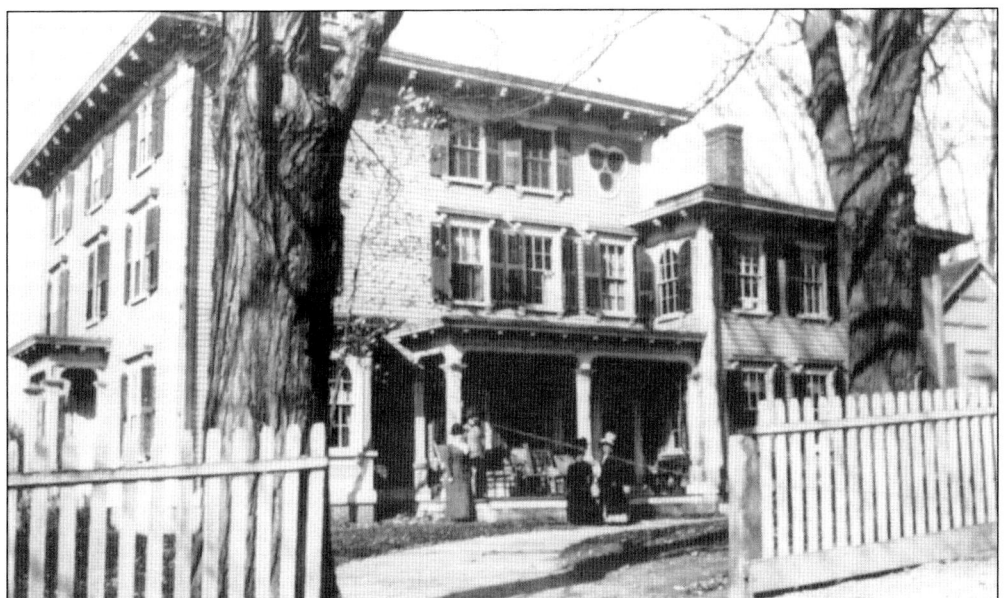

Stanton Belden built this Victorian structure c. 1861 to replace the old Fruit Hill Classical Institute. Rooms were rented out because Fruit Hill was sparsely populated and considered a resort area for people from Providence and the nearby area. The air on the hill was considered very healthy. Since the 1940s, this building has been known as the Fruit Hill Apartments.

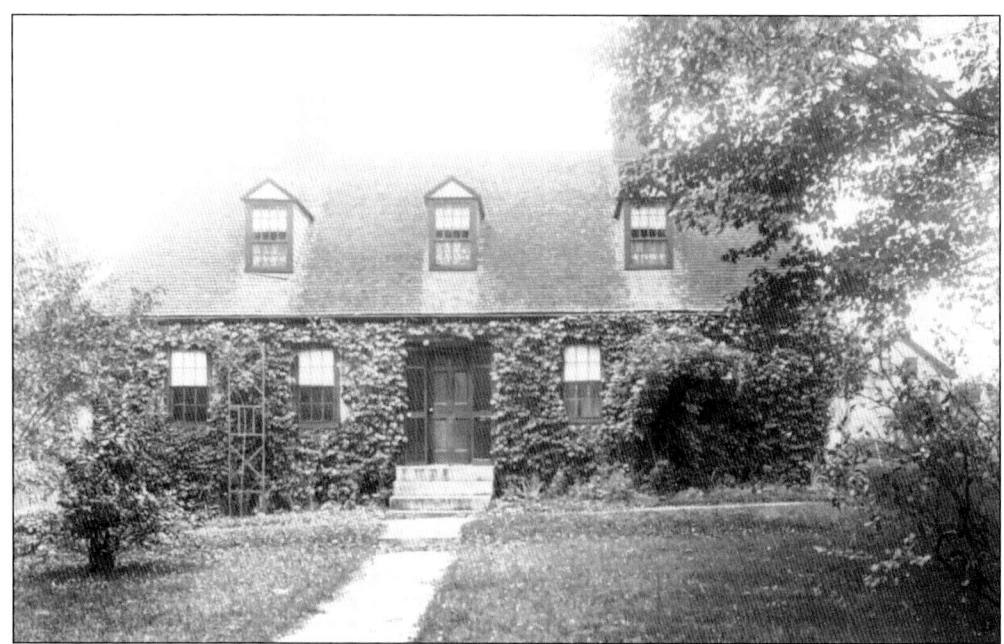

This house at 516 Fruit Hill Avenue is known as the Joseph Naylor house. Naylor bought it in 1875 from John Barker, who had purchased the land in 1867. This is a stone house which remained in the Naylor family late into the twentieth century.

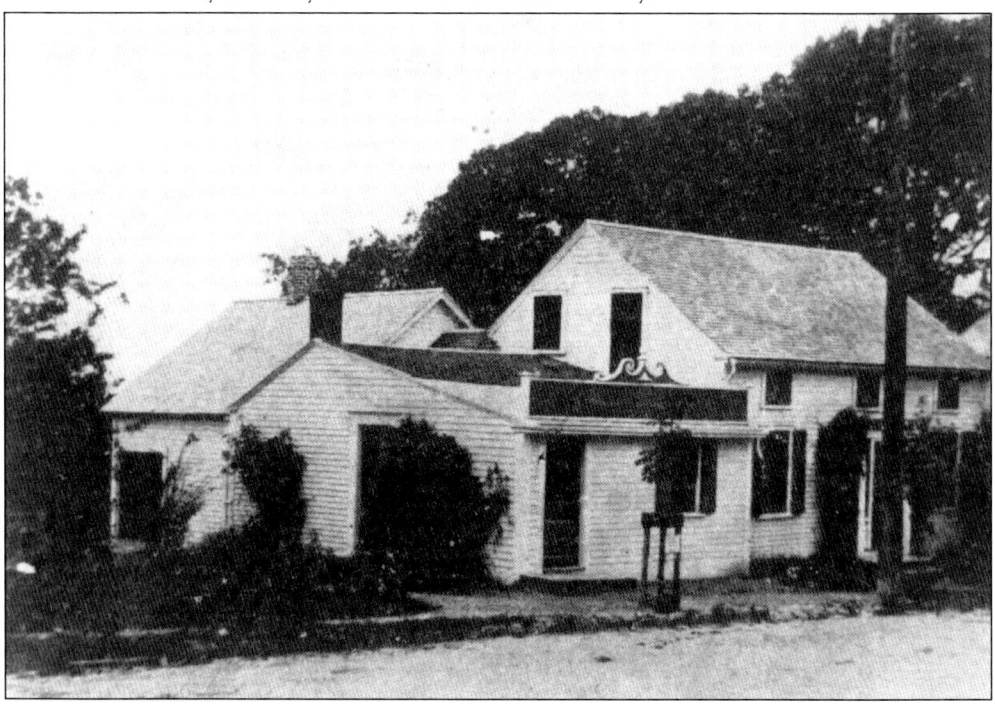

This 1914 photograph is of the building formerly at 1596 Smith Street called the Belvidere Club. Built c. 1795, the building was purchased in 1904 by the North Providence Improvement Association. It became a private club and the first Fruit Hill fire equipment was housed in the rear of the building around 1909.

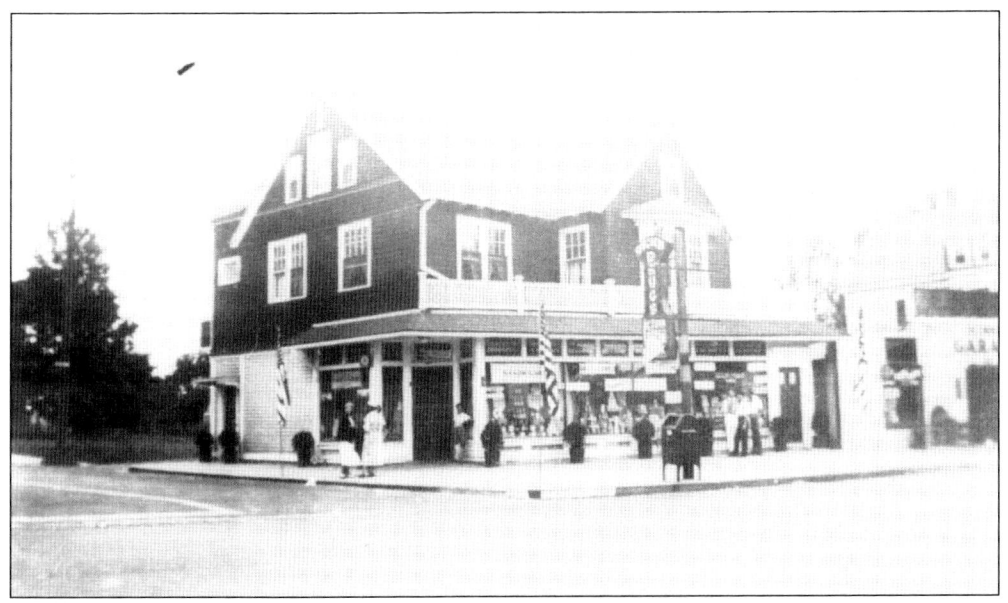

This March 1937 photograph depicts Dick's Drug Store. David L. Dick opened this business in Fruit Hill c. 1914. He worked as the druggist through 1924. By 1926, he had another druggist on staff while he ran a real estate business. By 1937, he did some interior renovating and took over the position as pharmacist, which he continued for many years.

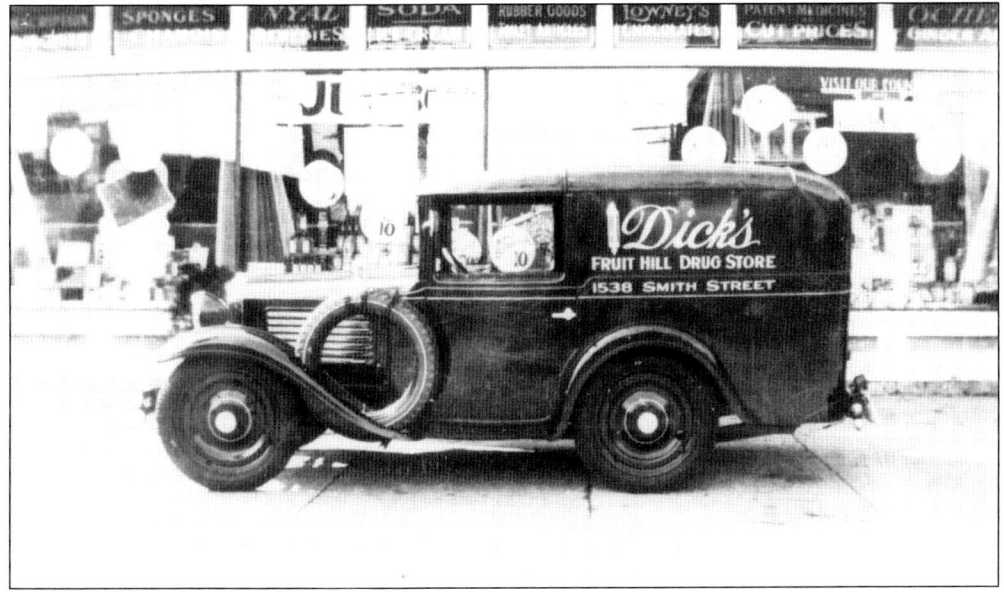

This 1954 photograph shows Dick's delivery truck on the sidewalk in front of the drugstore. This building became a liquor store for several years and now is Cal's Restaurant.

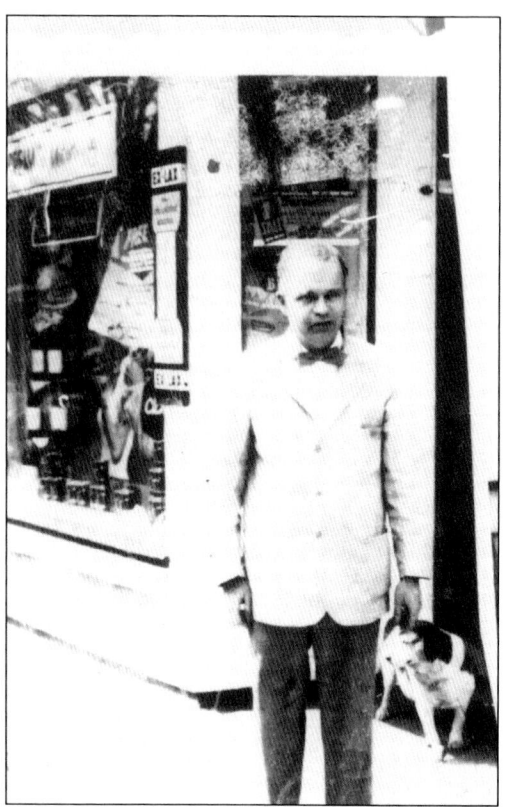

This c. 1940s photograph features Penny Dick, the co-owner of Dick's Drug Store and son of David "Pappy" Dick. The dog was named Joe-Pete. After many years as owners of the business, the Dicks moved to Florida where Penny passed away in 1995.

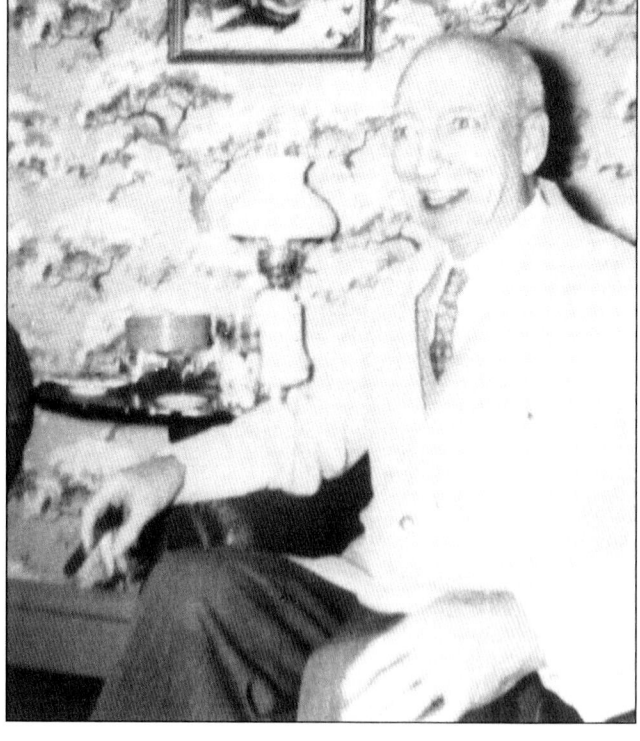

This 1953 photograph shows David L. Dick, the first owner of Dick's Drug Store which was built in 1914. Everyone knew him as "Pappy" Dick. A happy person who was always singing or humming to himself, Pappy was born in 1885 and died in 1961. In 1916, he also owned the Greystone Pharmacy in the Whitehall Building.

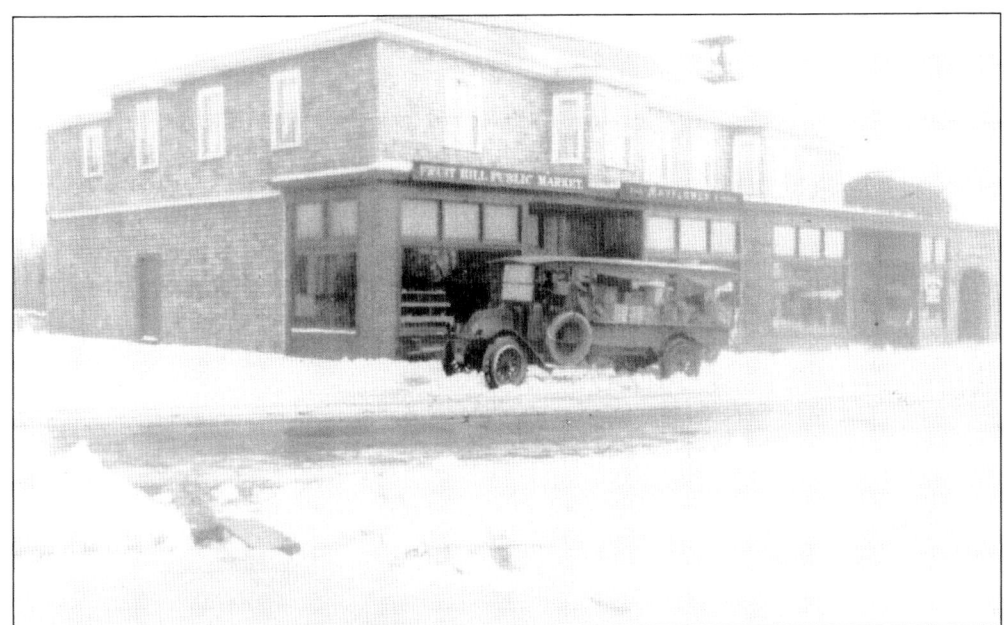

Here we have the David L. Dick building, which was built c. 1923. It housed several shops on the ground floor and a dance hall on the second floor. David Dick purchased these lots in 1922. Sometime in the early 1930s, the entire structure burned to the ground. Arson was suspected but never proved.

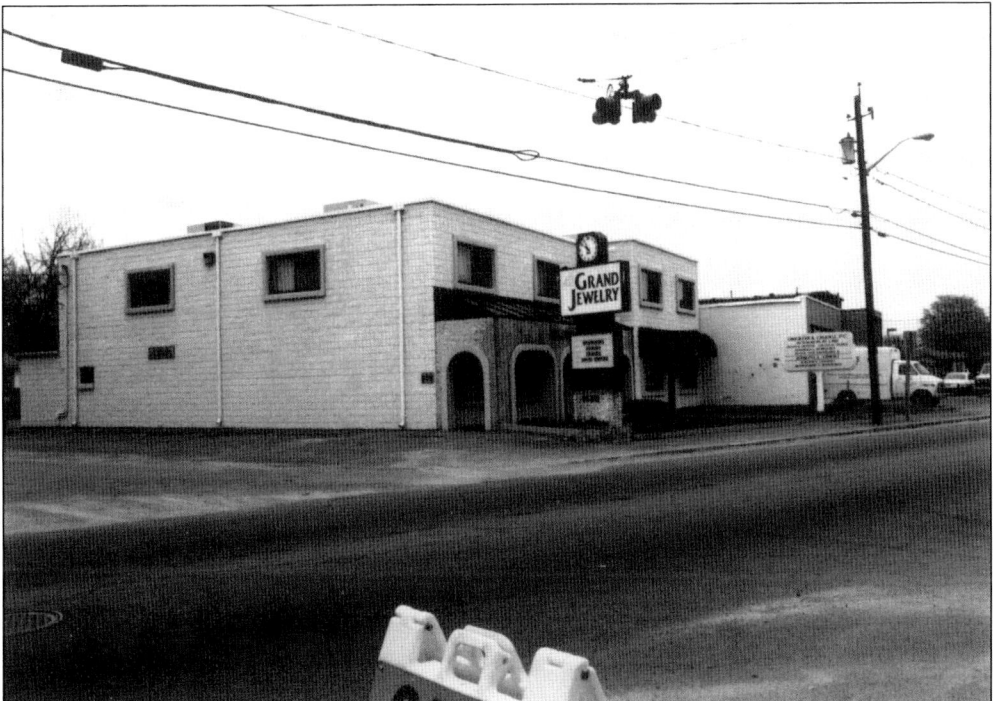

This is the corner of Smith Street and Homewood Avenue, which was the site of the David L. Dick building. After the 1930s fire, another similar structure with stores and a cafe was built. That building burned to the ground in January 1985. This is how the corner looks today.

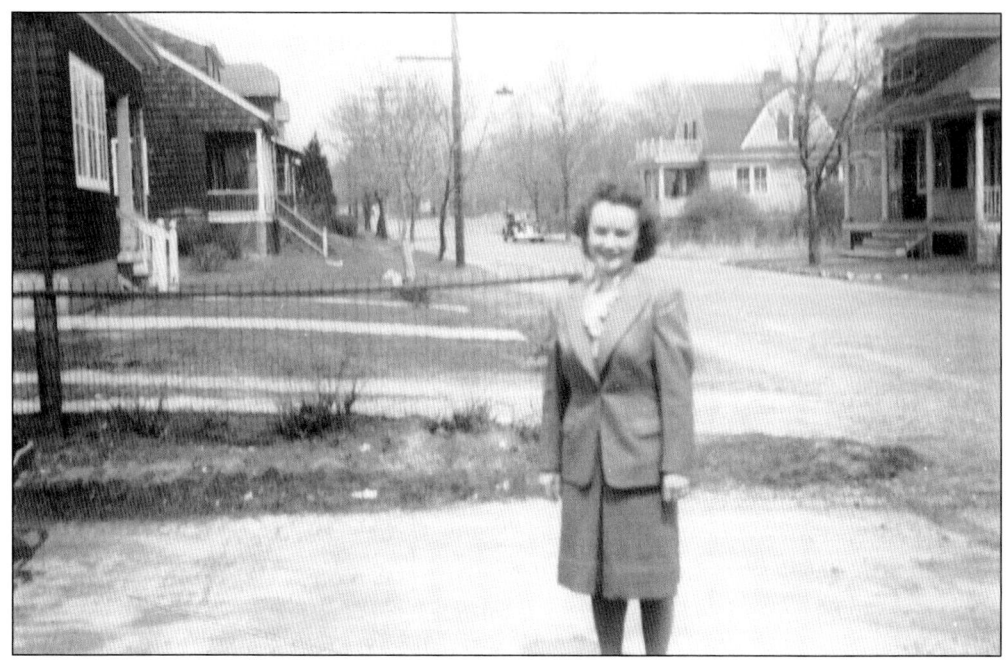

This scene looks up from 39 Homewood Avenue in the mid-1940s. The lady shown is Marianna Dickerson (Church). The second house on the right was the residence of Joseph Whalen, who eventually became the superintendent of schools in North Providence.

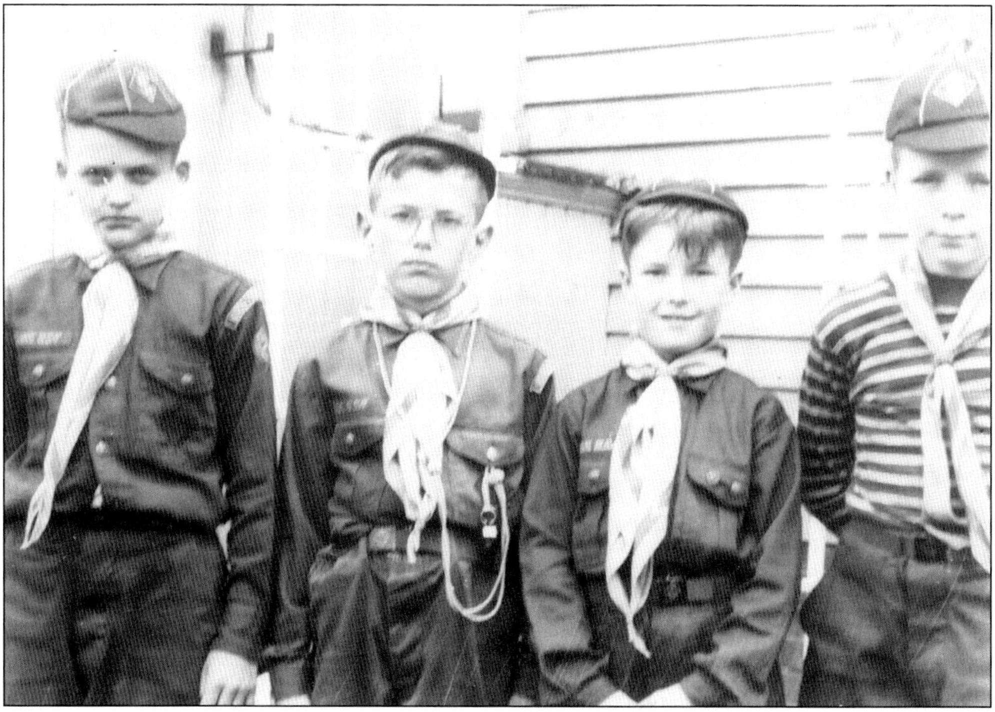

A group of cub scouts is in the backyard at 39 Homewood Avenue. They were members of the cub scout pack sponsored by the Saint James Episcopal Church c. 1943. From left to right are: David Peterson, Robert Donahue, Thomas E. Greene, and Paul Swanson.

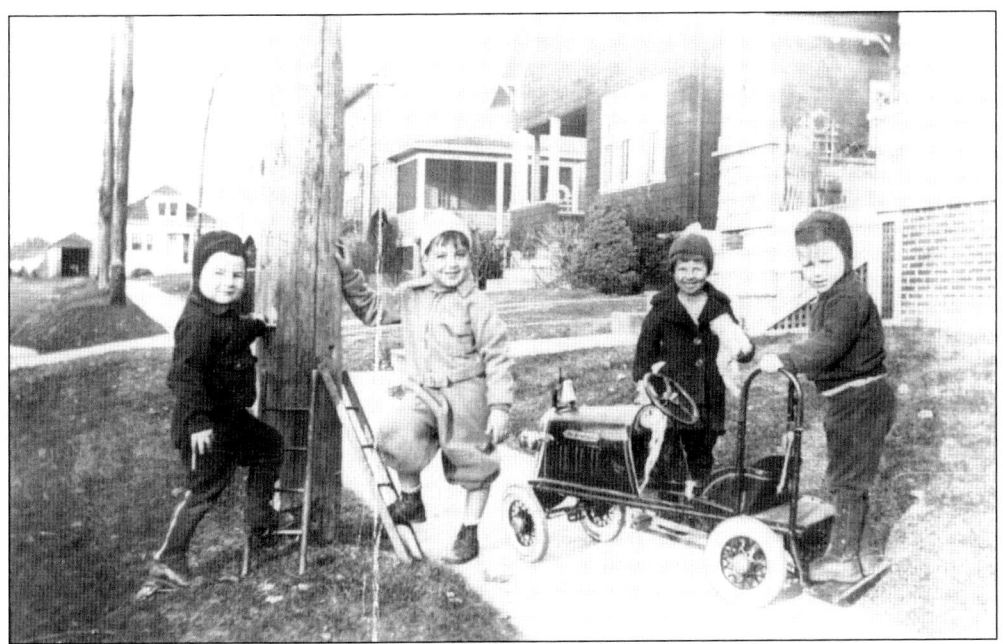

On Wellesley Avenue, which is a side street off Smith Street, there are four young children playing. This 1934 photograph shows, from left to right: Robert L. Black, Herb Desimone (who later became attorney general), and two unidentified friends, probably members of the Hall family.

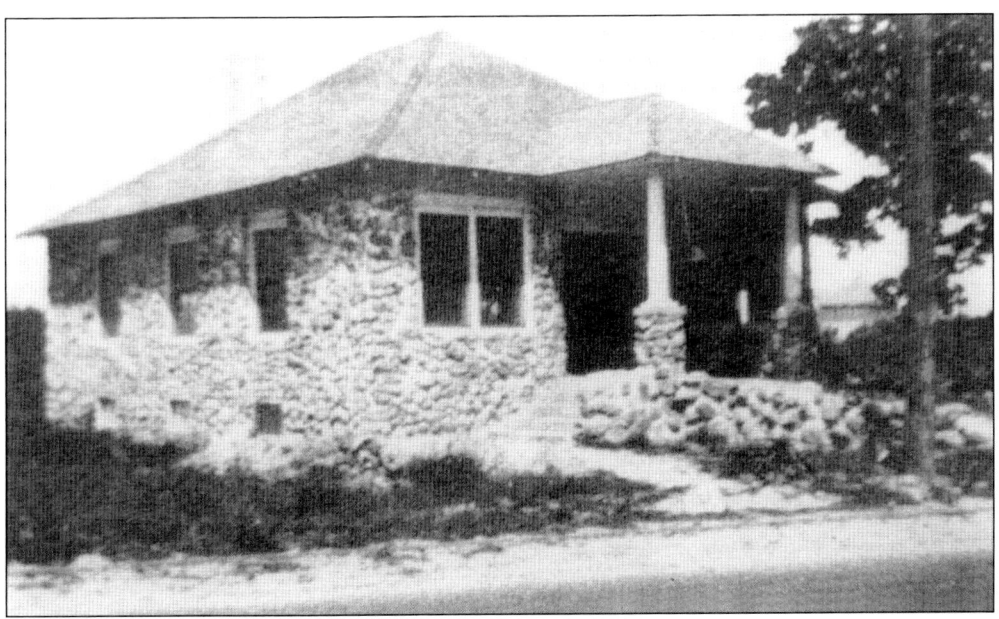

The Fruit Hill Bungalow was built c. 1925 and was headquarters for the Fruit Hill Volunteer Fire Company. The building was also used for dances and as a local meeting hall. At the time of the Dick's Dance Hall fire, the bungalow was also damaged severely. (*Observer* photograph.)

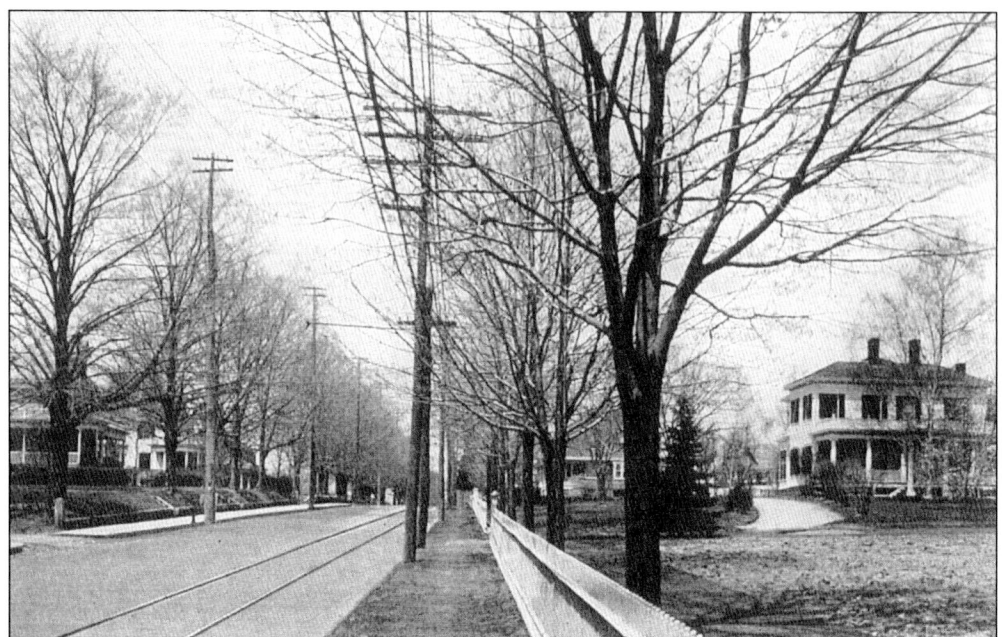

Above: This view looking into Fruit Hill along Smith Street was taken c. 1917. On the left is the entrance to First Street and then the George Lamberton house built in 1898 (now the Maggiacomo Insurance Agency). The next house was the home of George Whitaker, "Dean of Rhode Island Artists," built c. 1900 (now the site of the Janemor Apartments). On the far left is the Herbert Farnum house, built c. 1910 by Mr. Farnum, a cotton broker in Providence. The large white house on the right was the James Murphy house, built by William H. Corey in 1869. It is now the site of the Hamilton House Apartments. Below: Looking up Smith Street c. 1917, towards Fruit Hill, we see Longwood Avenue with the prominent Macrae home on the left. In the distance, few buildings are seen as compared with today.

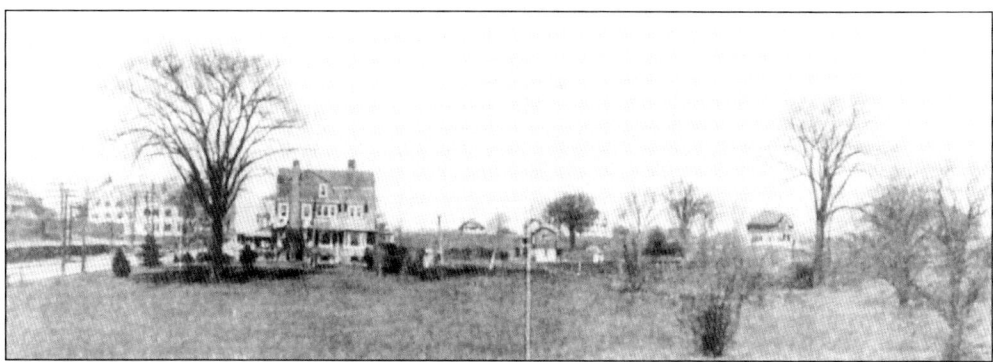

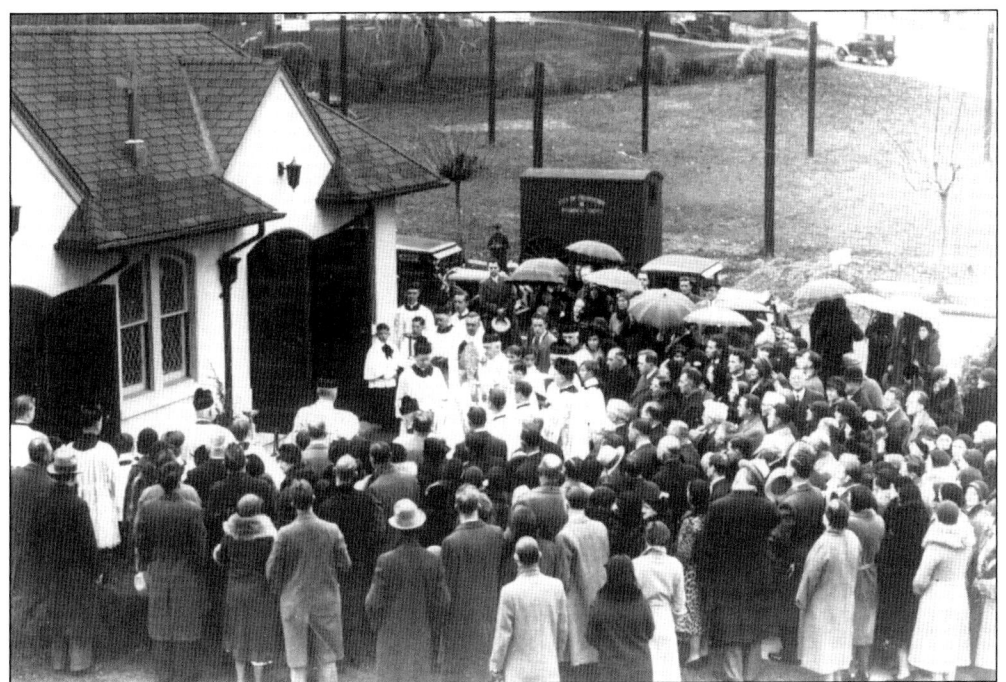

This was the dedication of the first Saint Augustine's Church on November 29, 1931. This was the site of the 1828 Fruit Hill School. In the background we can see Smith Street at the intersection of Olney Avenue

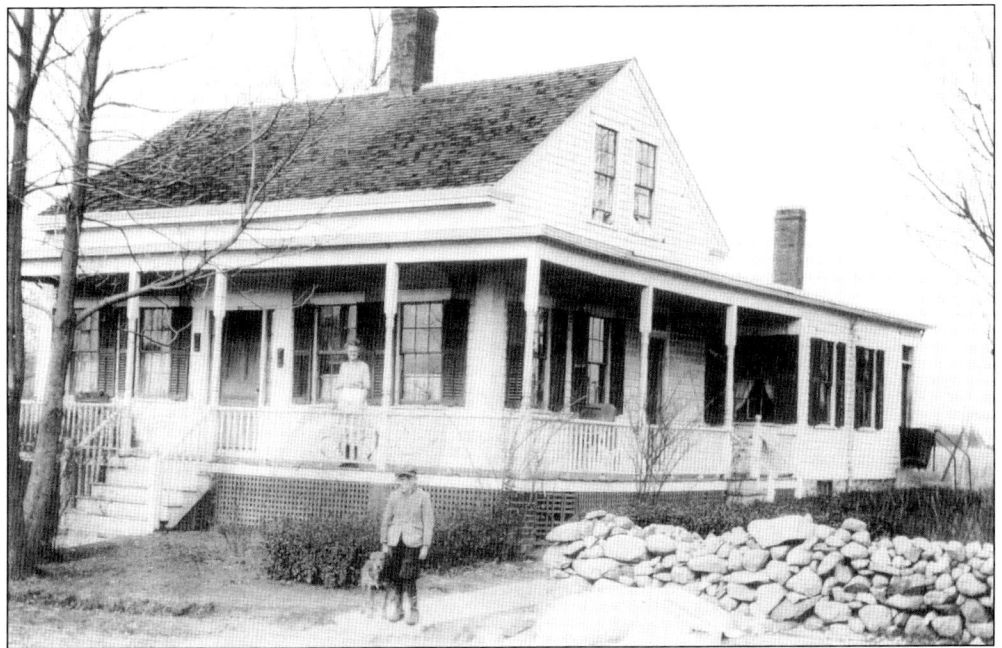

This is a 1924 photograph of 71 Sylvia Avenue, which was built in 1829. The house was owned at that time by James and Bridget McCarron. Pictured here are Mrs. Bridget McCarron and her son Hugh. This house was originally located at the intersection of Belvedere Boulevard and Smith Street where the Maceroni Funeral Home now is located.

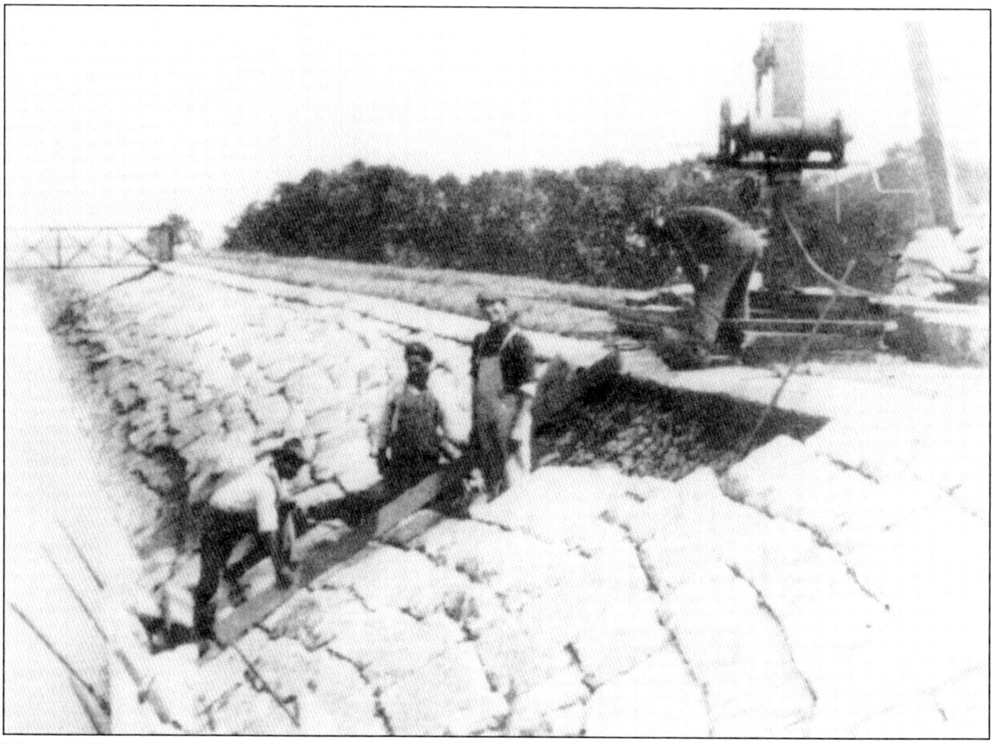

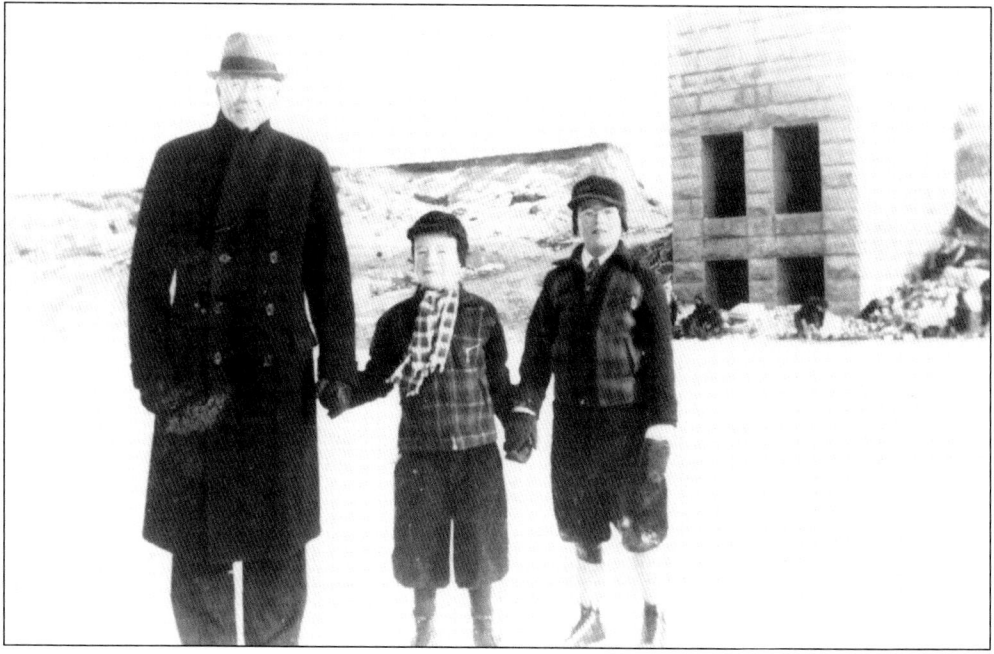

This 1890s photograph shows a work crew doing repairs on the High Service Reservoir at the present site of Fatima Hospital. The water source was built in the late 1880s. (*Observer* photograph.)

This 1940s photograph shows the Black family at the site of the abandoned reservoir. From left to right are: Alfred R. Black, William Black, and Robert L. Black.

Four

GREYSTONE

Greystone became a mill village in 1813 when Captain Olney Angell, Peleg Williams, and Mathewson Latham built a two-story stone textile mill equipped with twenty looms. This building was located on the right side of Greystone Avenue near the present Greystone Social Club. In 1817, Richard Anthony of Coventry purchased the mill, which he and his son continued until he sold it in 1835. At that time, James Westcott purchased the mill and enlarged it to three stories.

The mill had several owners until 1904 when Joseph Benn and Company purchased it as a storehouse and built a much larger brick mill on the opposite side of the street. The Benn Company of Bradford, England, were manufactures of alpaca and mohair who wanted to relocate here to escape the outrageous British import taxes on wool. They spent 2.5 million dollars establishing a model industrial community that included a new mill, mill housing, a social club, and the Whitehall Building, where an auditorium, shops, and quarters for overseers were located. Employees were recruited from England and soon numbered close to one thousand.

In 1913, a wooden four-room schoolhouse was built on Waterman Avenue This school was designed to be expanded to eight rooms as the student population demanded, which was a very advanced concept for its time.

Besides the Whitehall Building and mill complex, two other important structures were located in Greystone: the James Anthony house at 154/156 Waterman Avenue (built *c.* 1822) and the Richard Anthony house at 102 Waterman Avenue (built *c.* 1818), both of which remain standing today.

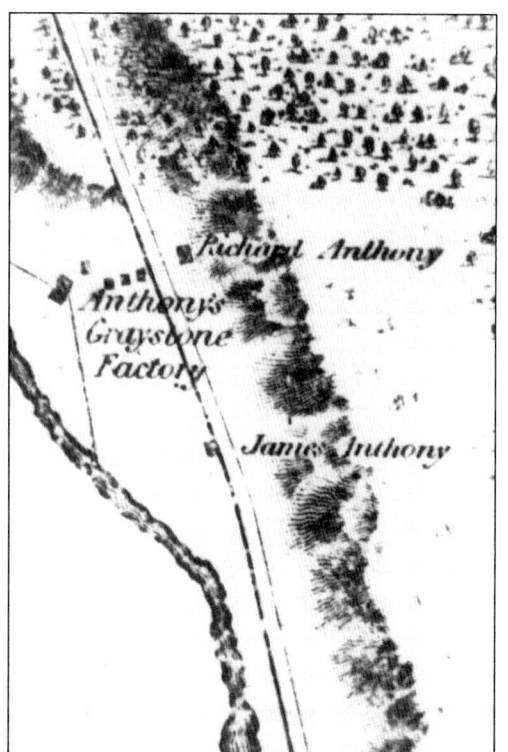

Greystone is shown here as it looked in 1835. Notice the spelling of the village name. It seems that cartographers did not always check this detail carefully before printing their maps. With the death of James Anthony in 1836 and the declining health of Richard Anthony (James's father), Richard was prompted to sell the Greystone mill. Richard died in 1840 and both father and son are buried at Swan Point Cemetery.

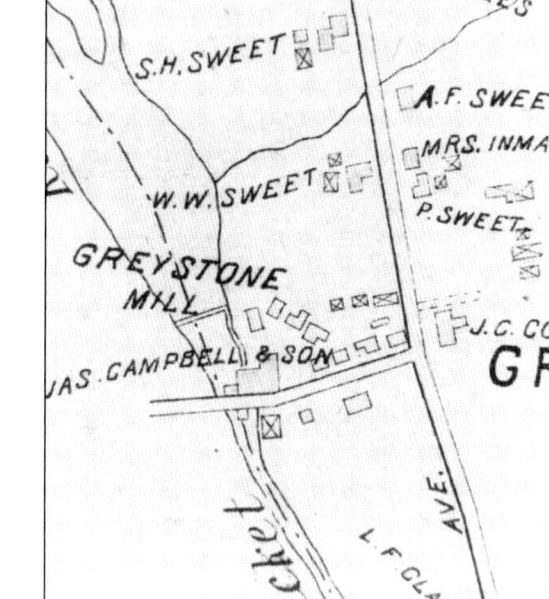

By 1895, the village had grown little. The mill had gone through several fires and was rebuilt twice. By 1882 it belonged to James Campbell and Son, who made shoddy (a waste products of textiles) for wool manufacturers.

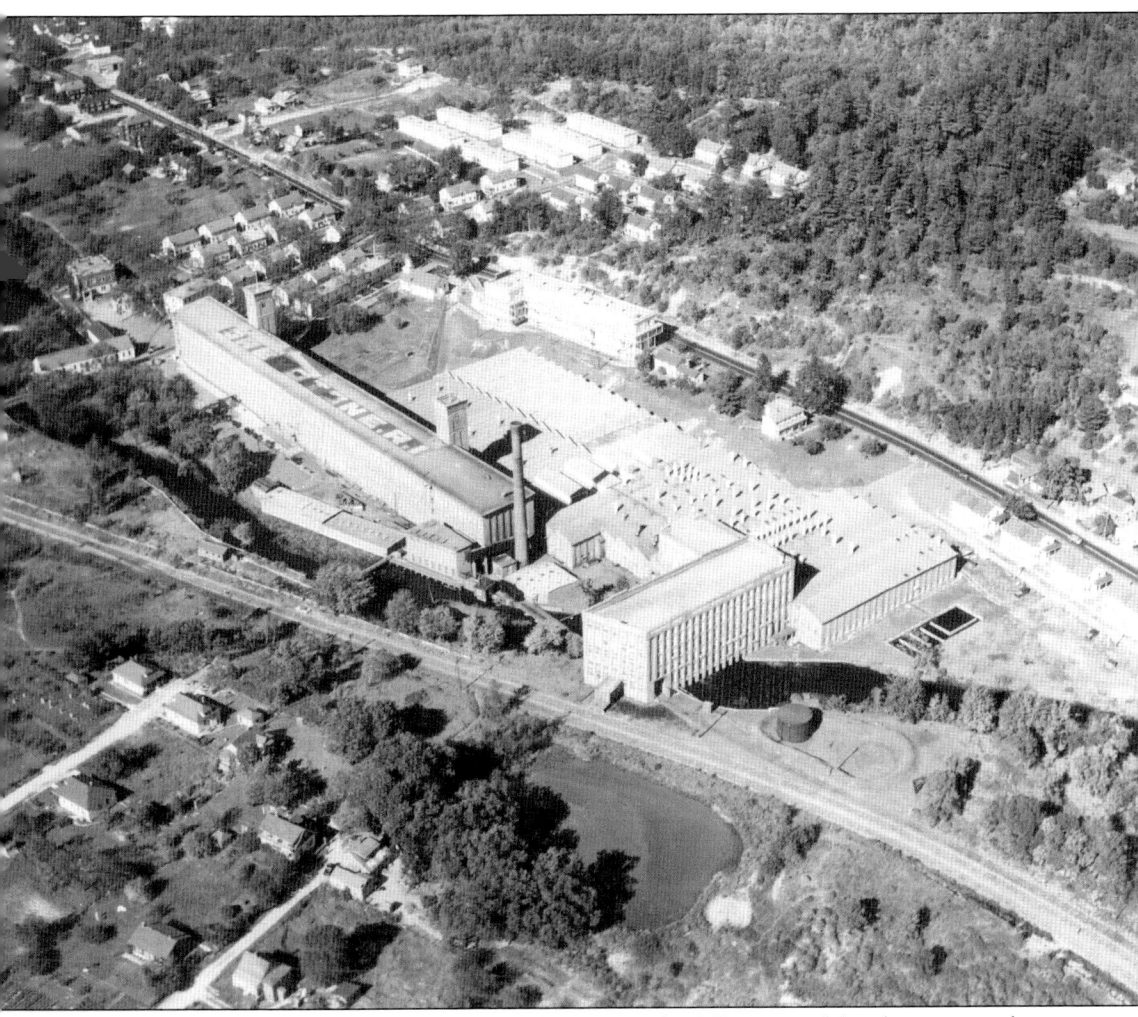

This birds-eye view of Greystone was taken in the 1930s. The full extent of development in the mill community can be seen. Directly above the mill is the Whitehall Building, which was built by Joseph Benn and Company. It is a three-story building. On the street floor facing Waterman Avenue were commercial stores, including a post office which was open until 1955. The second floor contained apartments for mill overseers.

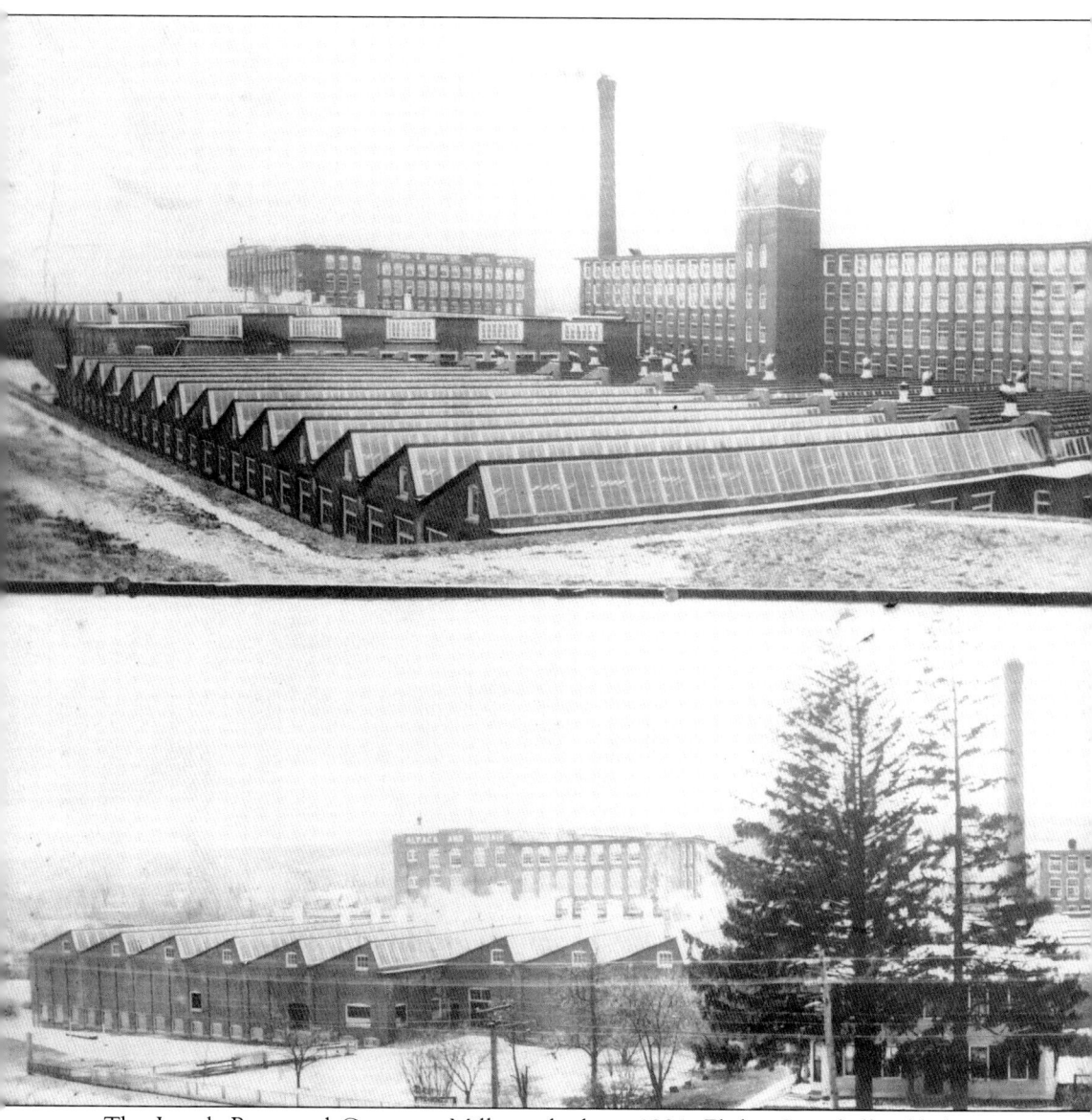

The Joseph Benn and Company Mill was built in 1904. Elisha Campbell sold this site to Joseph Benn and Company of Bradford, England; the British company manufactured mohair and alpaca and was relocating to escape British import tax on wool. In Greystone, they spent

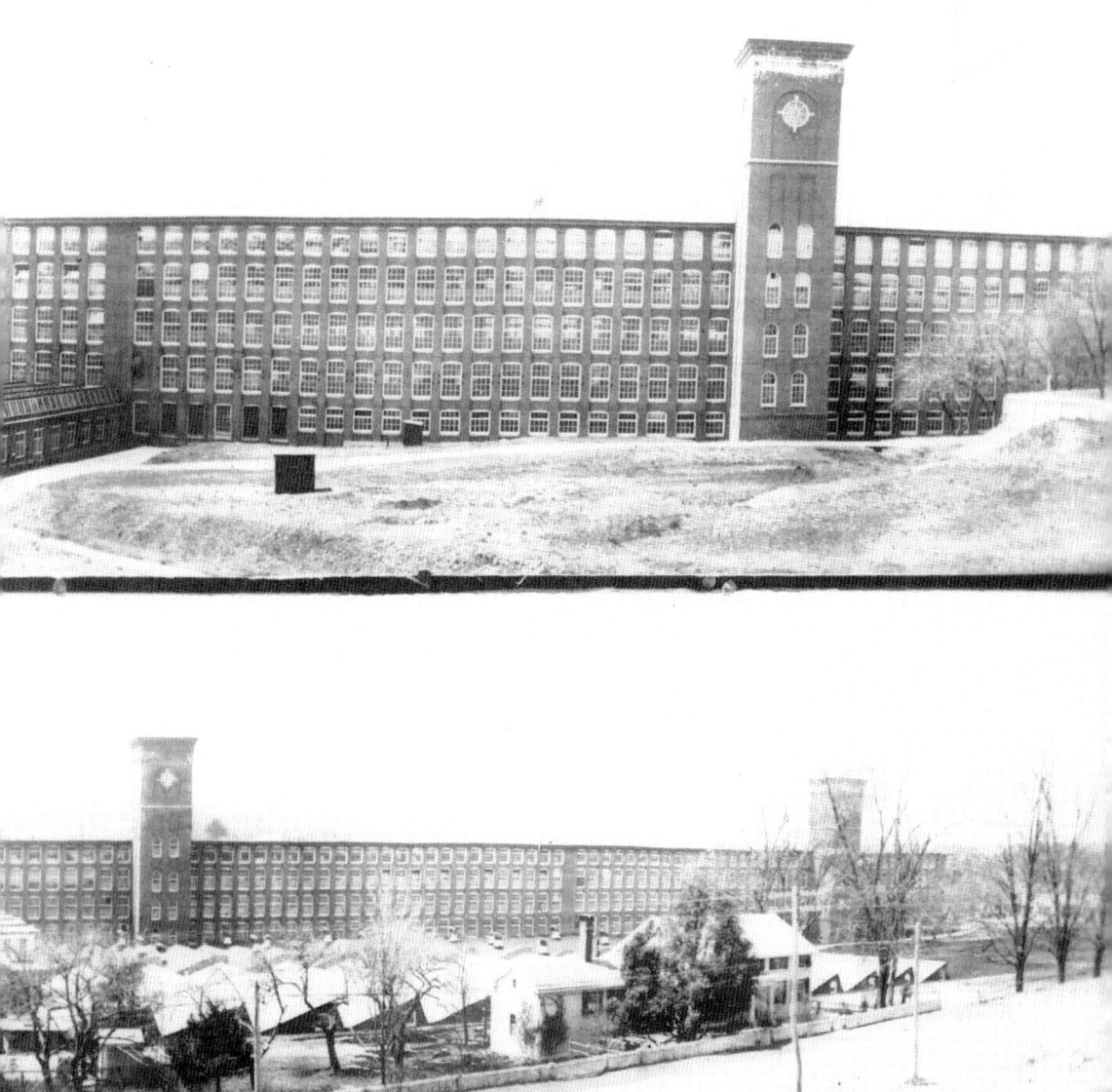

2.5 million dollars to establish a model industrial community with a new mill, mill housing, a social club, and the Whitehall Building, where an auditorium, shops, and quarters for overseers were located.

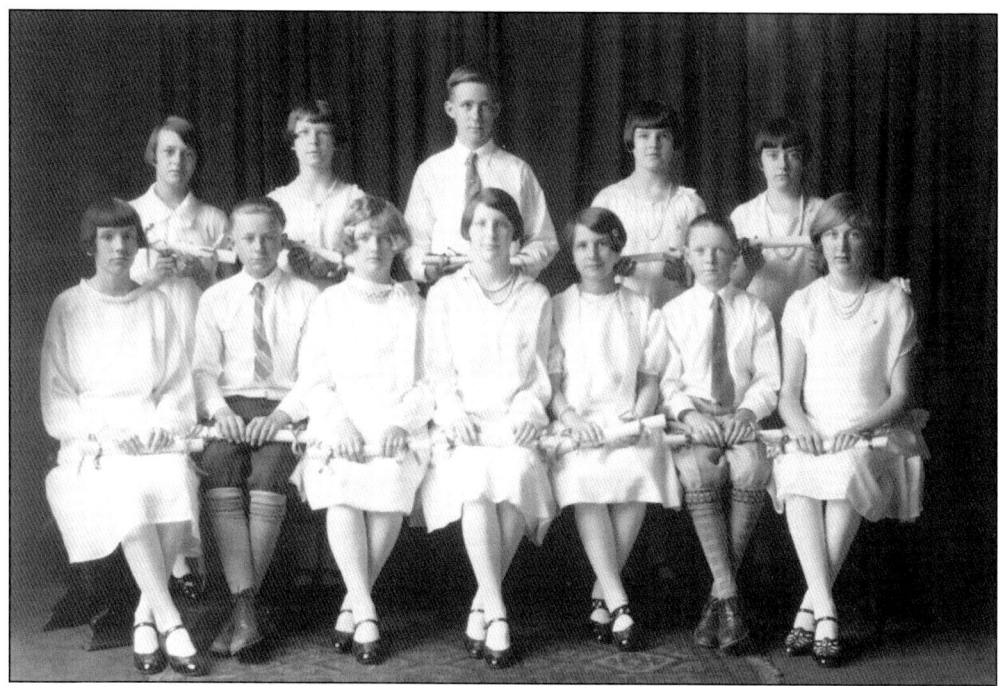

With the emigration of many people to work in the Joseph Benn and Company Mill, it became necessary to build a village school, which became a reality in 1913. This is the class of 1926. From left to right are: (front row) Margaret Williams, William Wilbur, Edith Gill, Alice Long, Florence Swain, Albert Charlwood, and Edith Burrows; (back row) Dorothy Sowden, Hilda Travis, George Smith, Ethel Sloan, and Edith Firth.

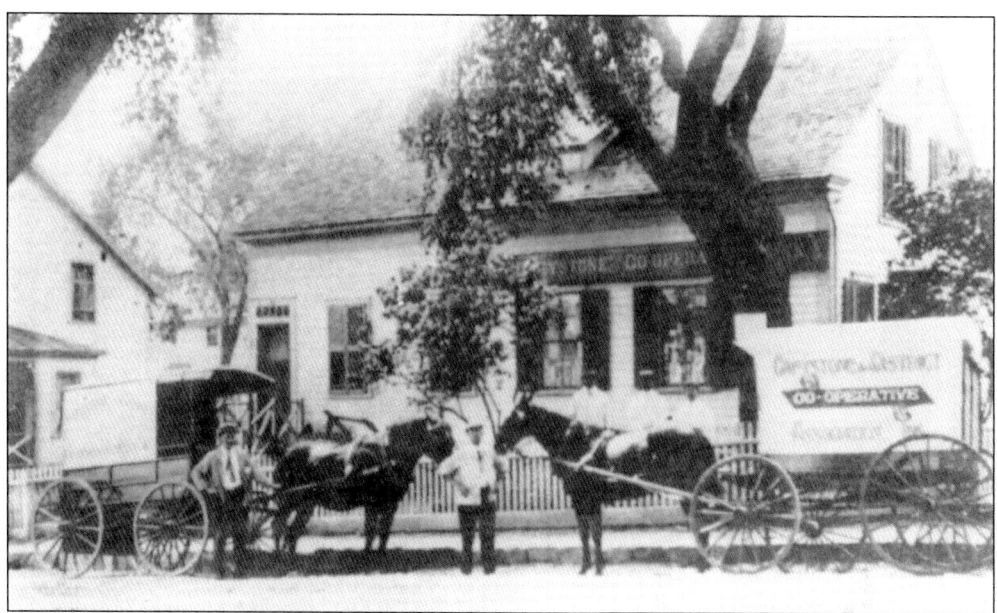

The start of a working day with the delivery men and their wagons at the Greystone Co-Operative Association is shown here. (*Observer* photograph.)

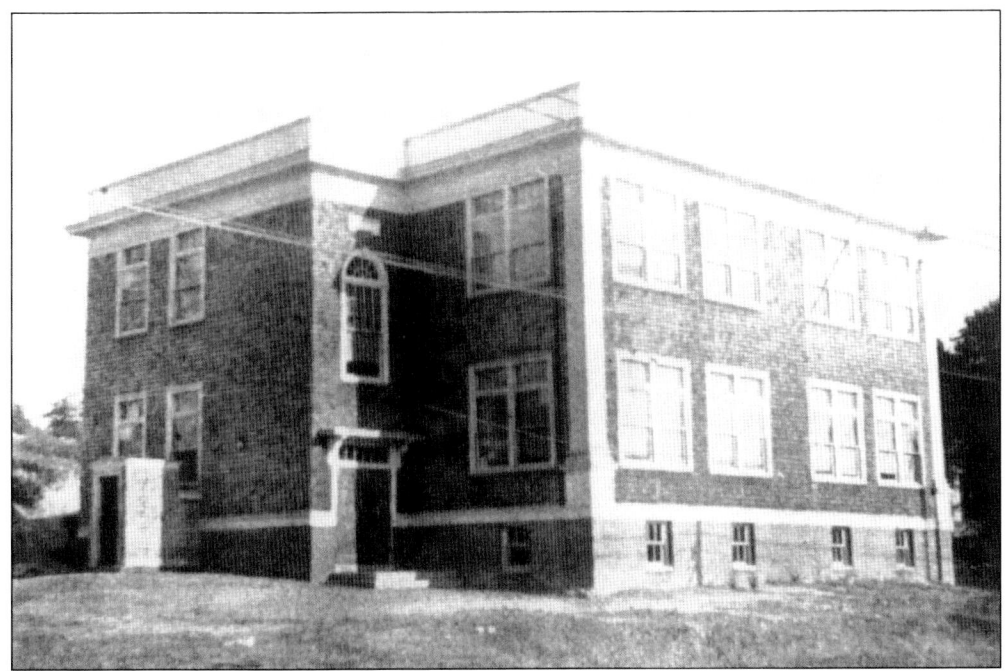

The Greystone School, a two-story, four-room building, was built in 1913 to educate the increasing English mill employee population. There was a plan to increase the school to eight rooms at minimal cost. The woodwork in the school was of North Carolina hard pine. This building cost $11,500 and the architect was Burrett S.D. Martin of Providence.

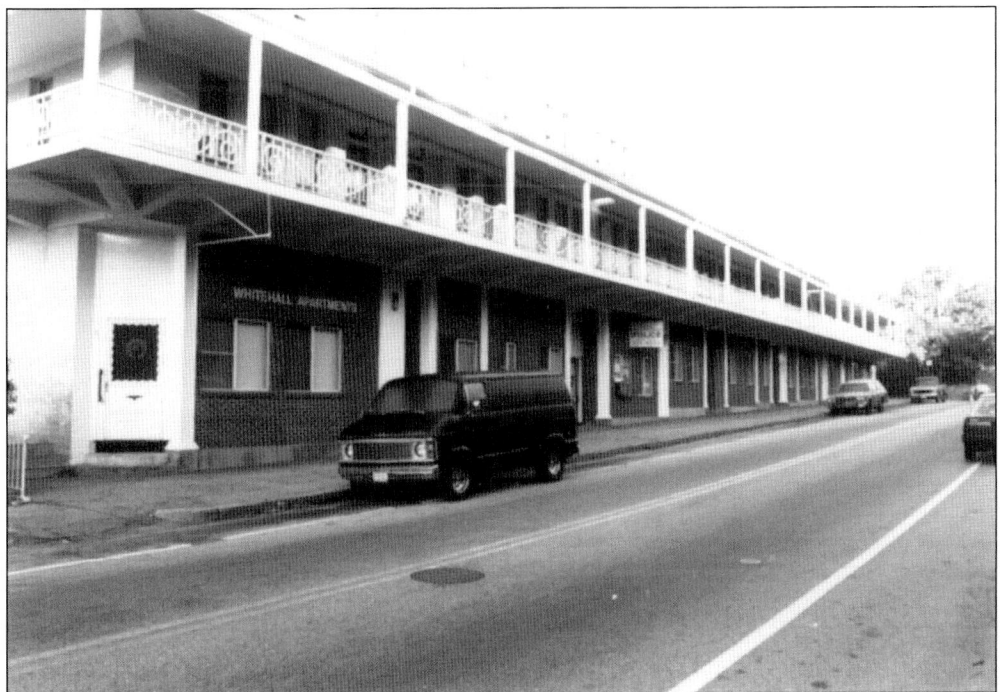

The Whitehall Building is seen here in 1955. It was built by Joseph Benn and Company in 1911.

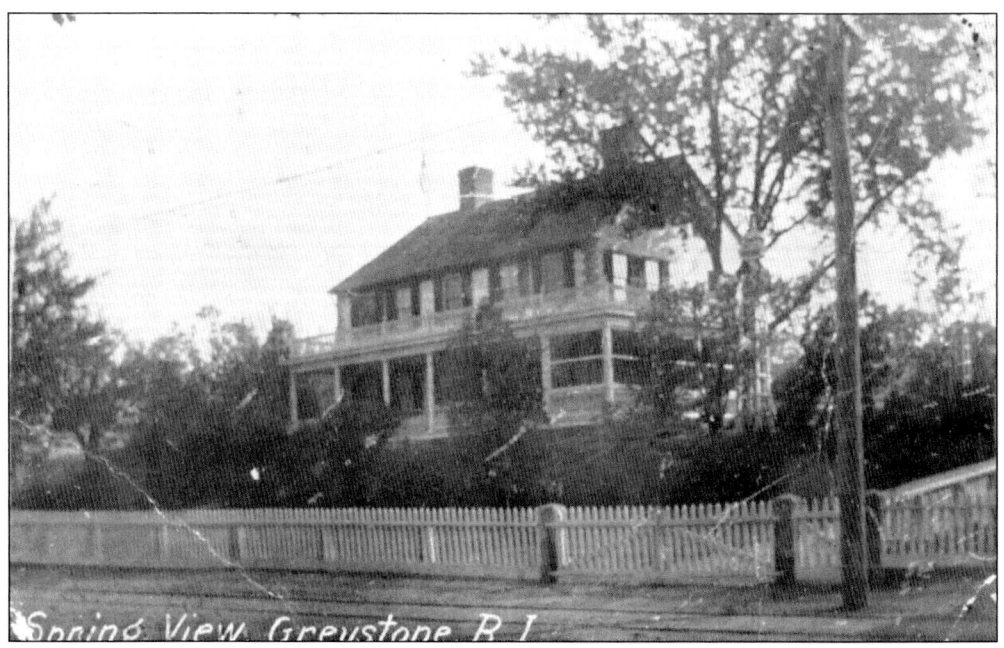

The Richard Anthony house at 201 Waterman Avenue dates to c. 1822. In 1816, Richard Anthony bought a mill and started his business. By 1822, he built this house. It has two large interior chimneys that supply ten fireplaces and two brick ovens. The porch was probably added toward the end of the nineteenth century.

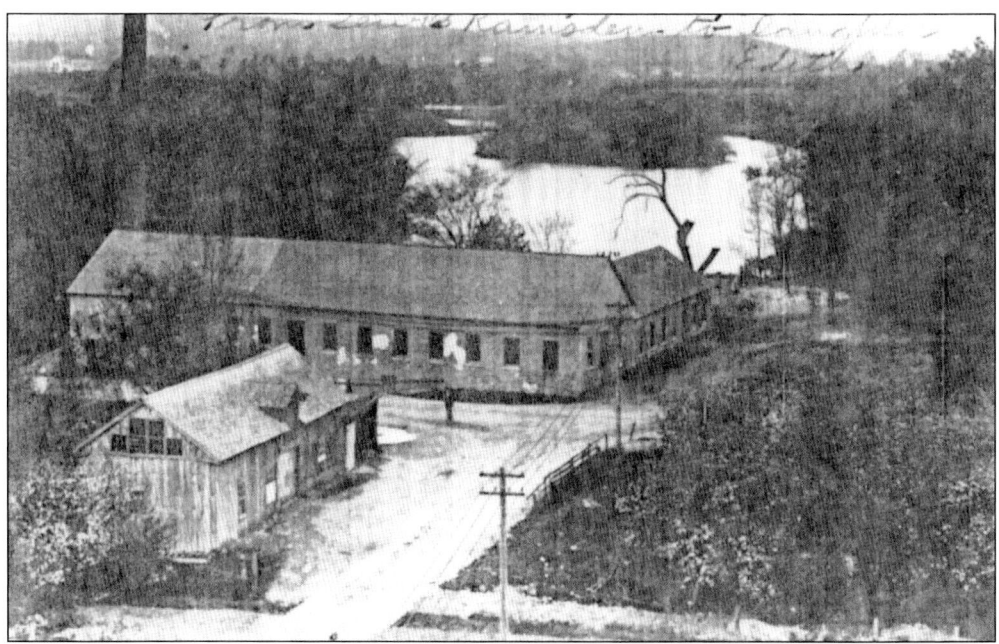

The first Greystone mill was built in 1813 by Captain Olney Angell, Peleg Williams, and Mathewson Latham. In 1816, Richard Anthony purchased it for the manufacture of cotton cloth. In 1835, it was again sold to Joseph Westcott and enlarged to three stories. It was modified in 1872 and 1877 after enduring fire damage over the years.

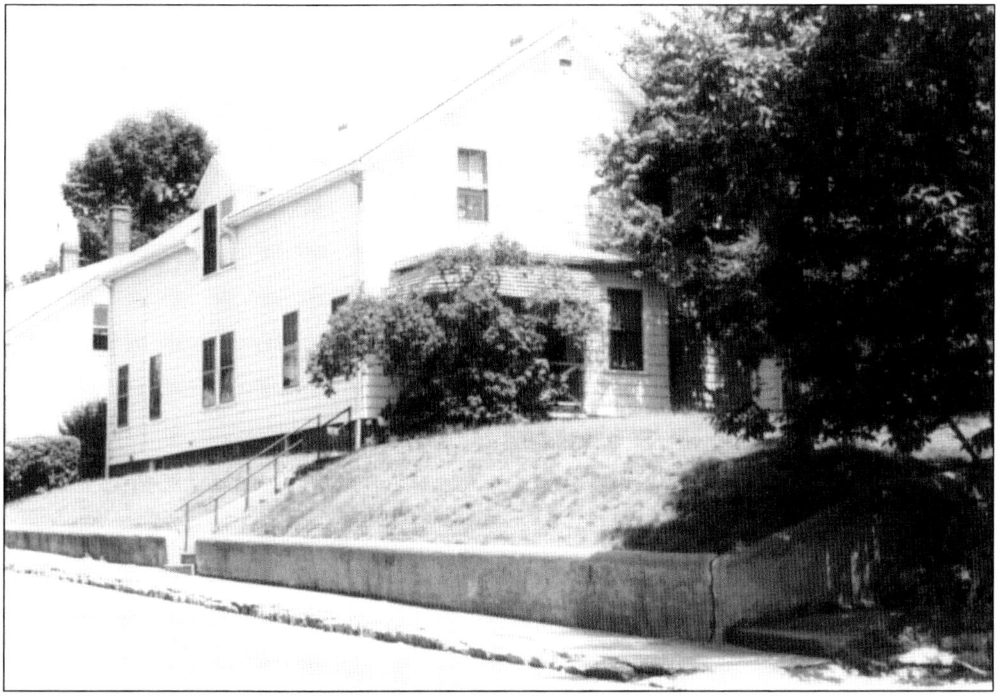

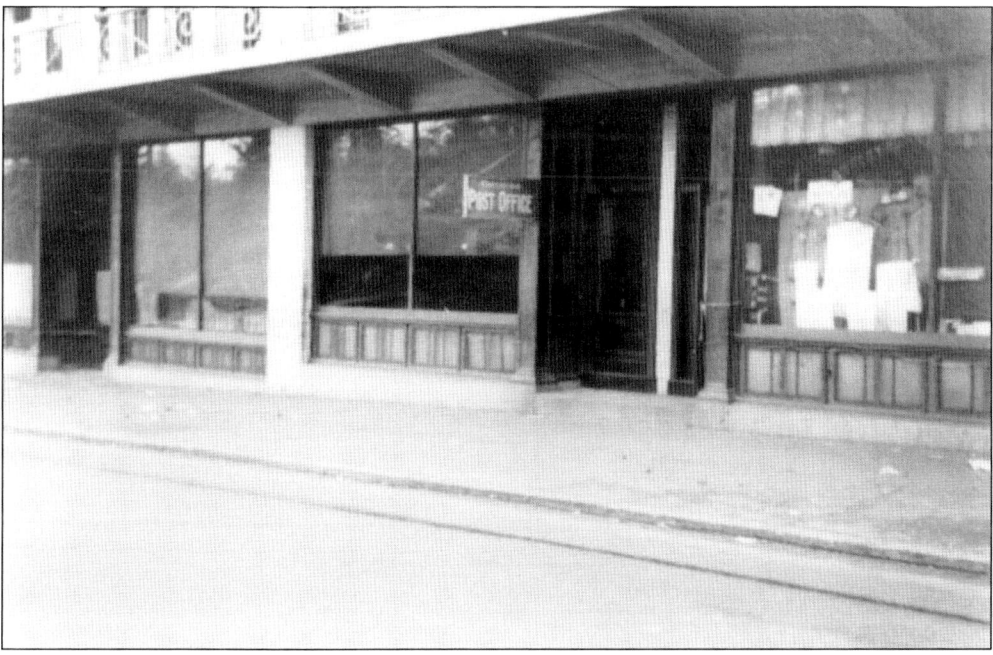

After the mill takeover in 1904 by Joseph Benn and Company, many more people lived in the village. On December 20, 1905, Frederick Webley applied to the U.S. Post Office for a Greystone office. On January 22, 1906, the post office was established at 2 Greystone Street.

In 1911, Joseph Benn and Company built the Whitehall Building. By 1912, the post office was moved to that site as seen in this photograph. Fred Webley was the postmaster until he died in 1914. The Greystone Post Office continued until August 31, 1955.

The Greystone Social Club was built in 1906 by Joseph Benn and Company. This was a center of social activity during the heyday of the mill. There were water carnivals, swimming contests, and ice polo matches on the adjoining river.

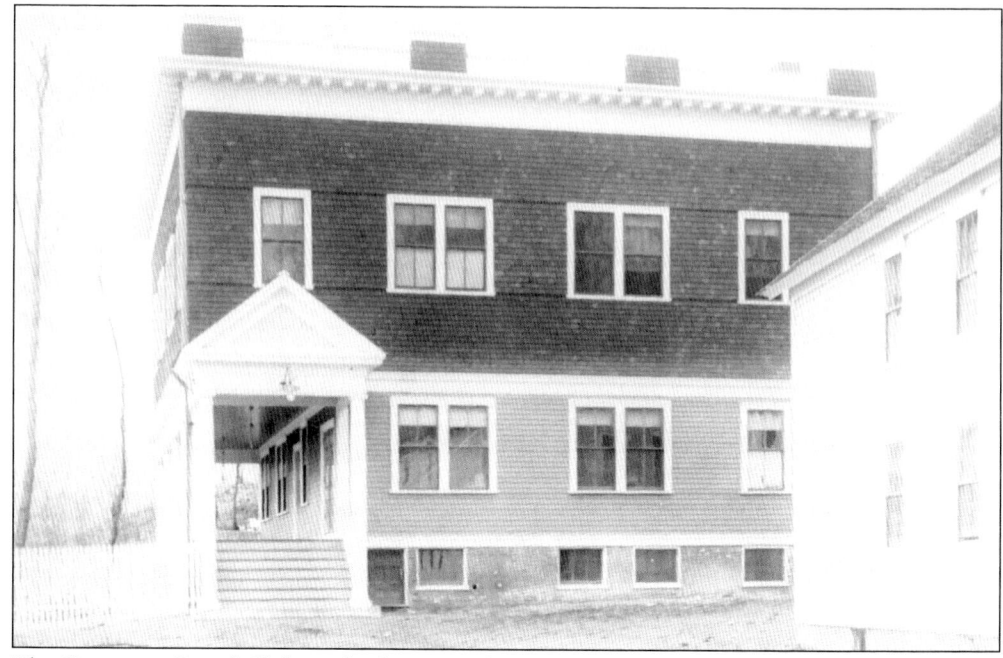

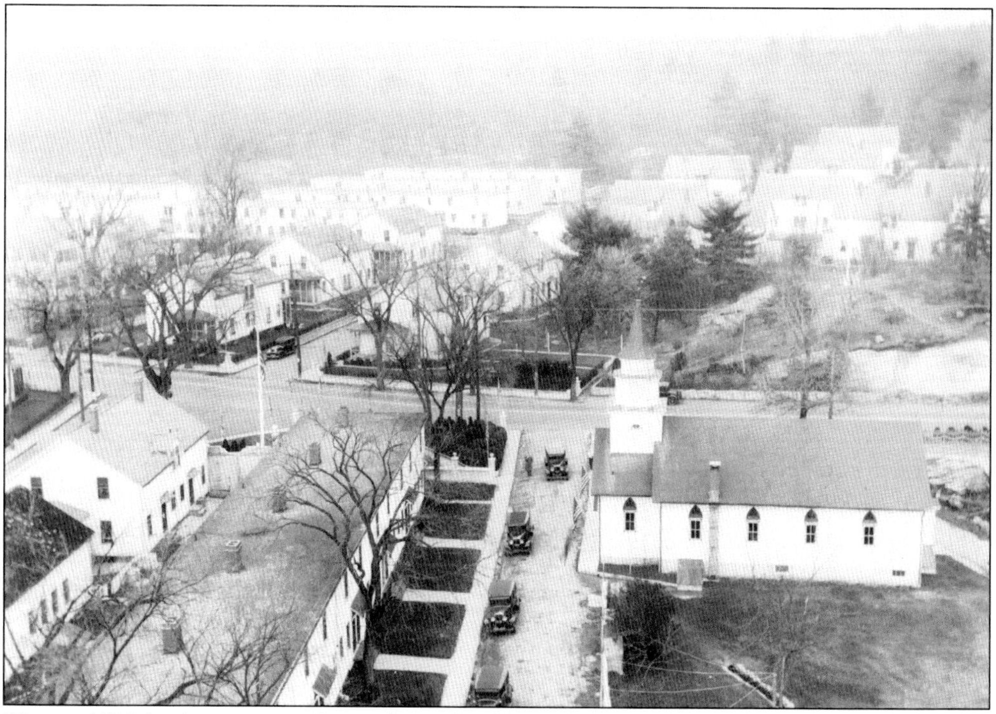

This c. 1920 birds-eye view shows the mill village with various company-built housing. To the right on Oakleigh Avenue is the Greystone Primitive Church, built in 1904 by the mill company.

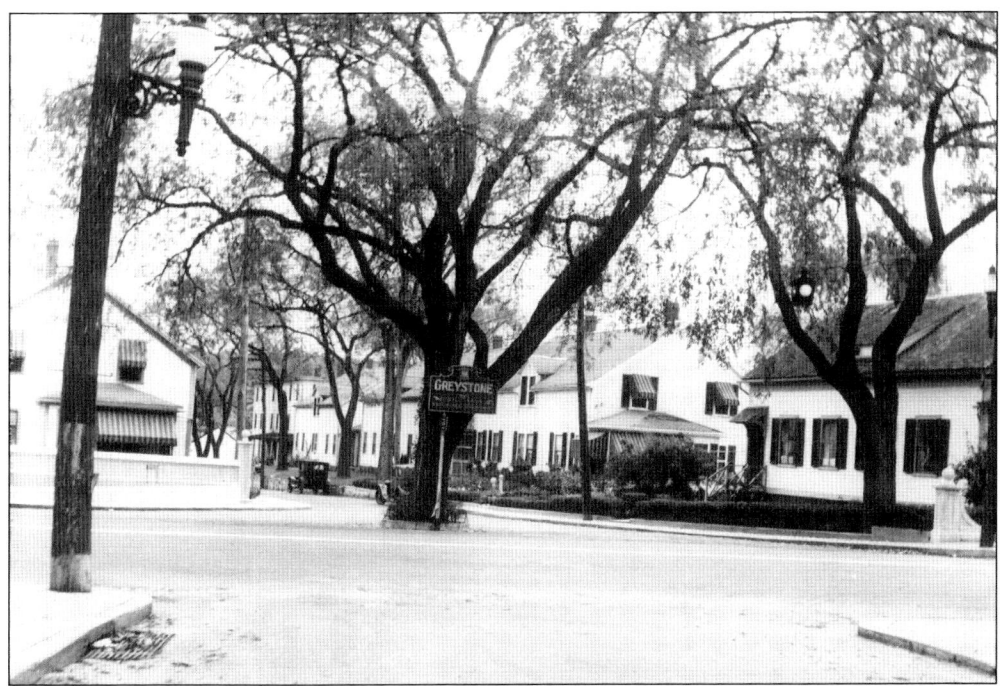

The village center was located at the intersection of Waterman Avenue and Greystone Avenue. Mill housing can be seen along the street. The sign identifies the village and gives directions to Centerdale, Providence, Esmond, and Woonsocket.

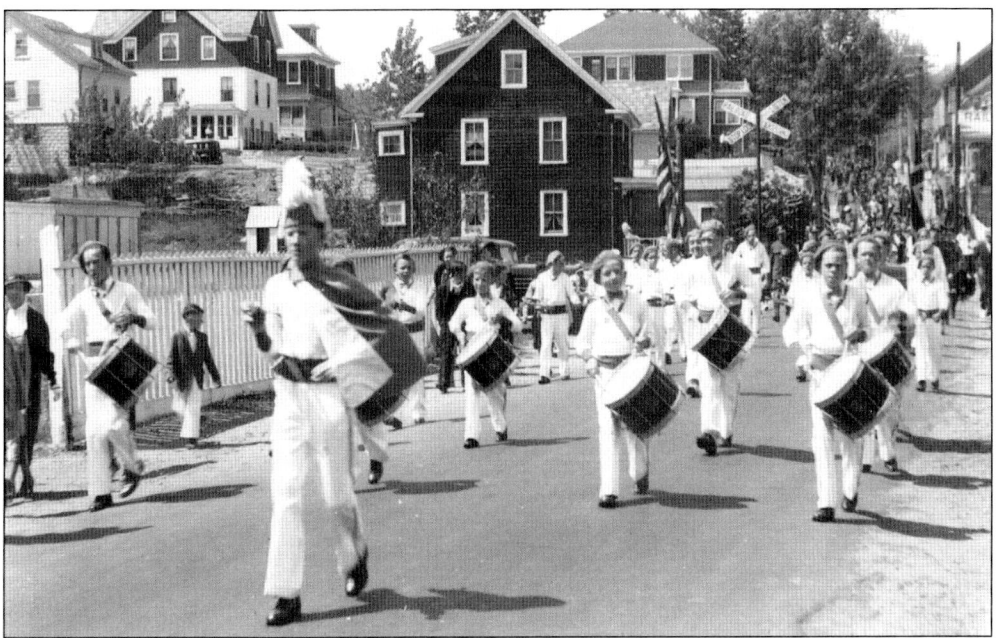

The Greystone Drum and Bugle Corps marches down Greystone Street from the Johnston side of the village.

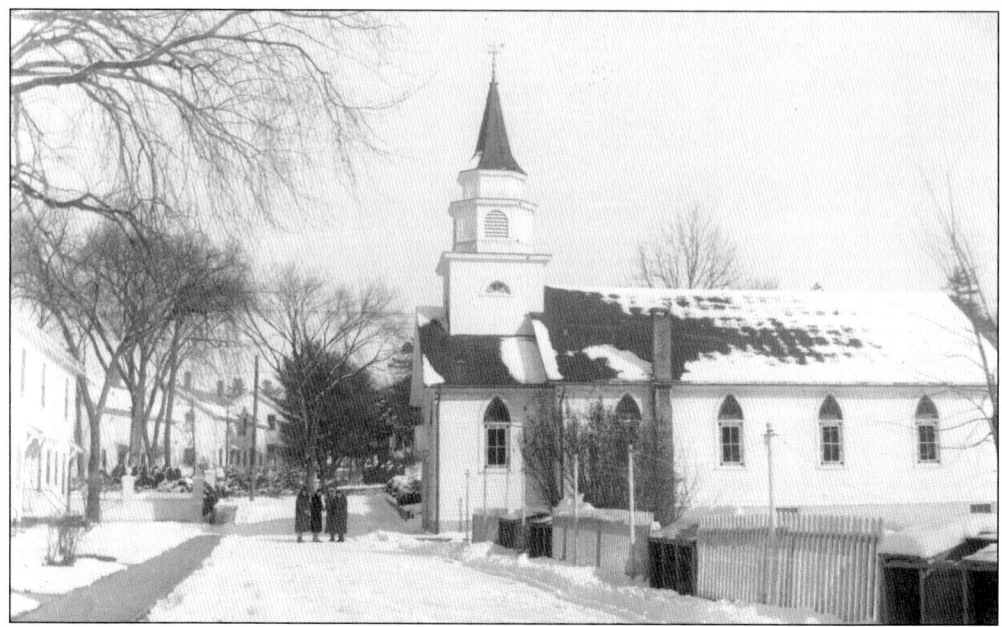

In this Oakleigh Avenue scene, the 1904 Primitive Methodist Church is on the right.

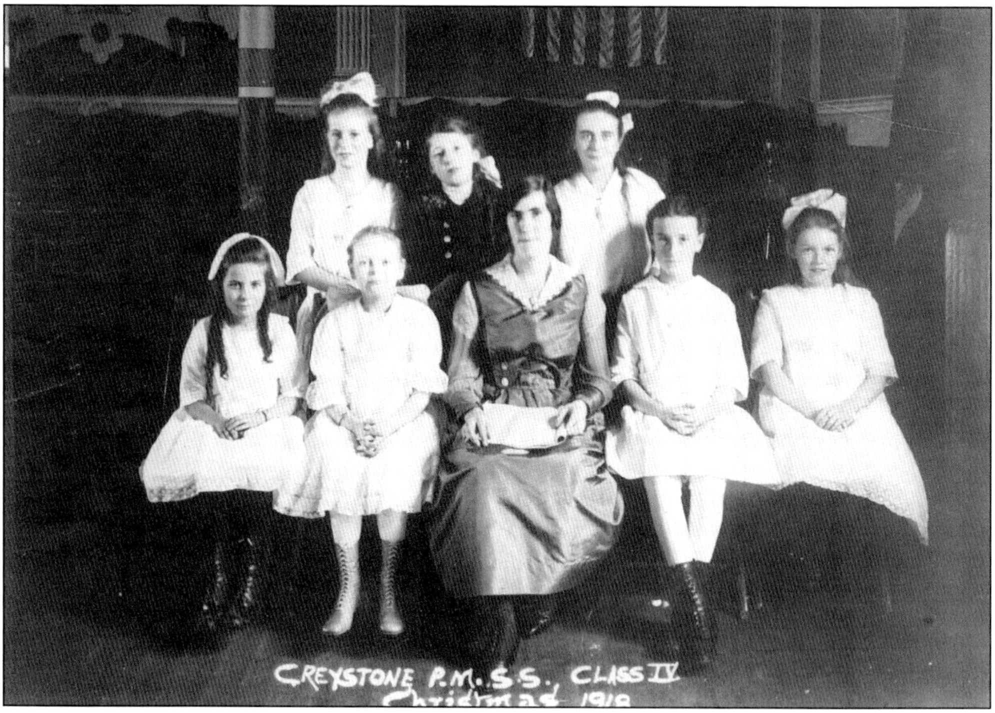

A Sunday school class at the Primitive Methodist Church is pictured on Christmas in 1918. From left to right are: (front row) Doris Hardcastle, Mabel Robinson, Lillie Wilkinson (teacher), Annie Norne, and Ethel Gill; (back row) Lillie Firth, Nellie Clements, and Ida Barker.

Five

LYMANSVILLE

The area known as Lymansville was first settled by Benjamin Whipple, who built a house c. 1674 on what is now Metcalf Avenue. The farm that the Whipple family owned extended from the Woonasquatucket River to the site of Saint James Episcopal Church on Fruit Hill Avenue.

Epenetus Olney (1675-1740) settled c. 1702 in the area where Falco Street is now located. That house remained standing until 1898 when it was demolished. The only remaining evidence of the Olney family is a cemetery at the end of Falco Street.

As North Providence moved into the nineteenth century, the rural farming flavor of this area began to change. On November 9, 1807, Daniel Lyman of Newport purchased an 80-acre farm off Fruit Hill Avenue from William F. Megee, who had purchased the property from Richard Whipple, great-grandson of Benjamin Whipple. In 1809, Daniel Lyman purchased the rights to build a dam and farm along the Woonasquatucket River. In the summer of that year, he built and established the Lyman Manufacturing Company. As was the practice, a mill village for his employees was also constructed. Daniel Lyman died in 1830 and the ownership passed to his son, Henry Bull Lyman.

In 1828, the Lymans gave a lot at the corner of Metcalf and Fruit Hill Avenues for a schoolhouse which educated the children of the Lymansville and Manton areas until c. 1850 when a larger school was built at Manton, then called Triptown, part of North Providence until 1874.

August A. Sack took over as president/treasurer of the Lymansville mill in 1884 and started construction on the present brick building. A larger mill meant an increased number of employees. This created the need for a local post office which was opened in 1896 and discontinued in 1909. By the 1890s, the increased population necessitated another village schoolhouse which was built on Packard Avenue in 1892.

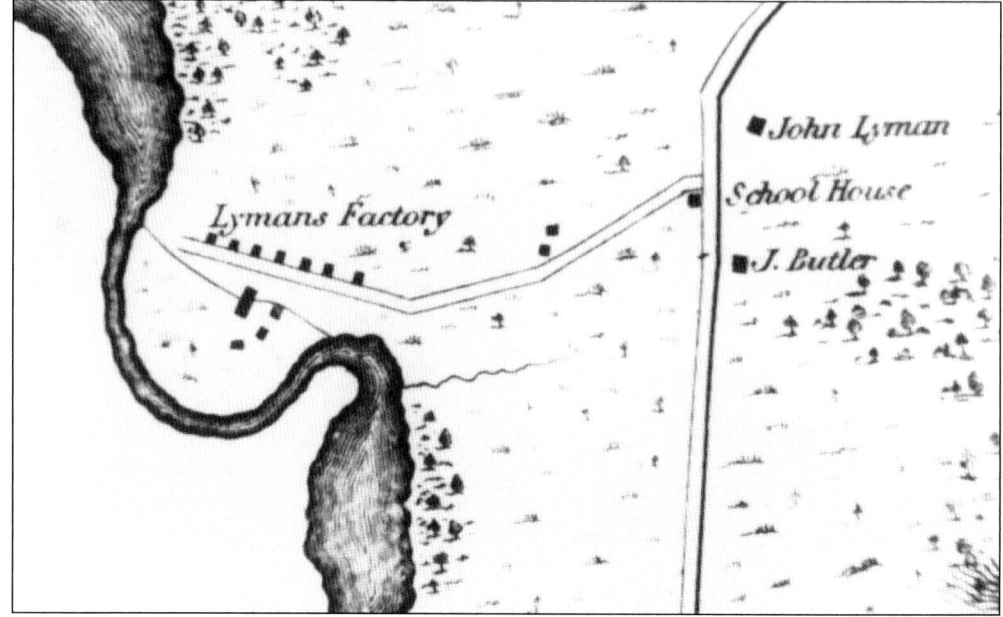

This 1835 Lymansville map shows the John Lyman House (now the Rhode Island College Alumni House) and the former J. Butler House (now the RIC president's house) on Fruit Hill Avenue. The Lyman Manufacturing Company is shown with its mill houses and the village school on Metcalf Avenue.

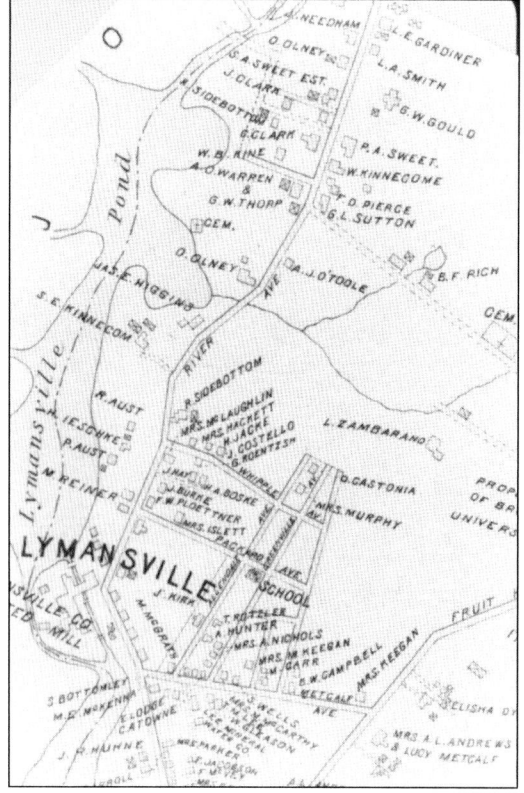

This 1895 map shows significant development since 1835. By this time, the old wooden mill had been replaced in 1885 by a brick mill, the Lymans were all deceased, and Augustus Sack was now the mill owner.

Daniel Lyman (shown here in an artist's portrait) was the originator and owner of the Lymansville mill. The village took its name from him. He established the Lyman Manufacturing Company in 1809. He died at his home on October 16, 1830.

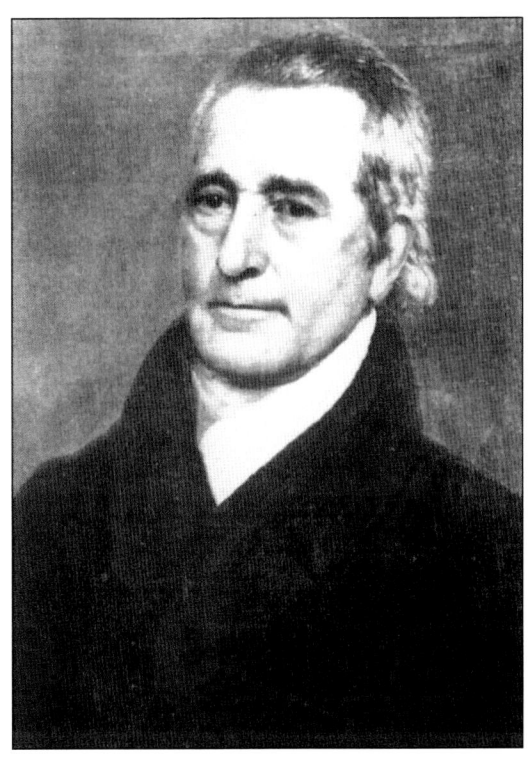

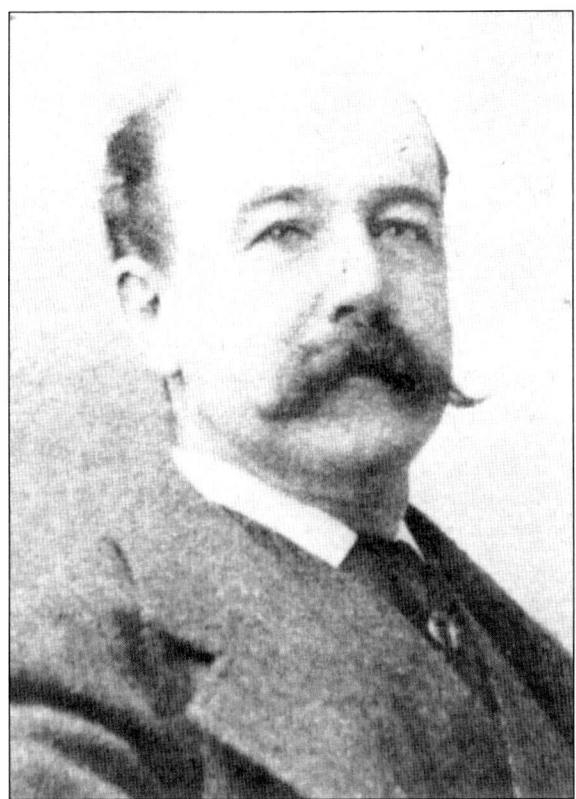

Daniel Wanton Lyman was a state senator from North Providence in 1876 and again in 1879 and 1880. Because of his special interest in the state militia, he bequeathed a sum of money to the town to build a Civil War monument. This was built at the intersection of Fruit Hill and Olney Avenues. (*Observer* photograph.)

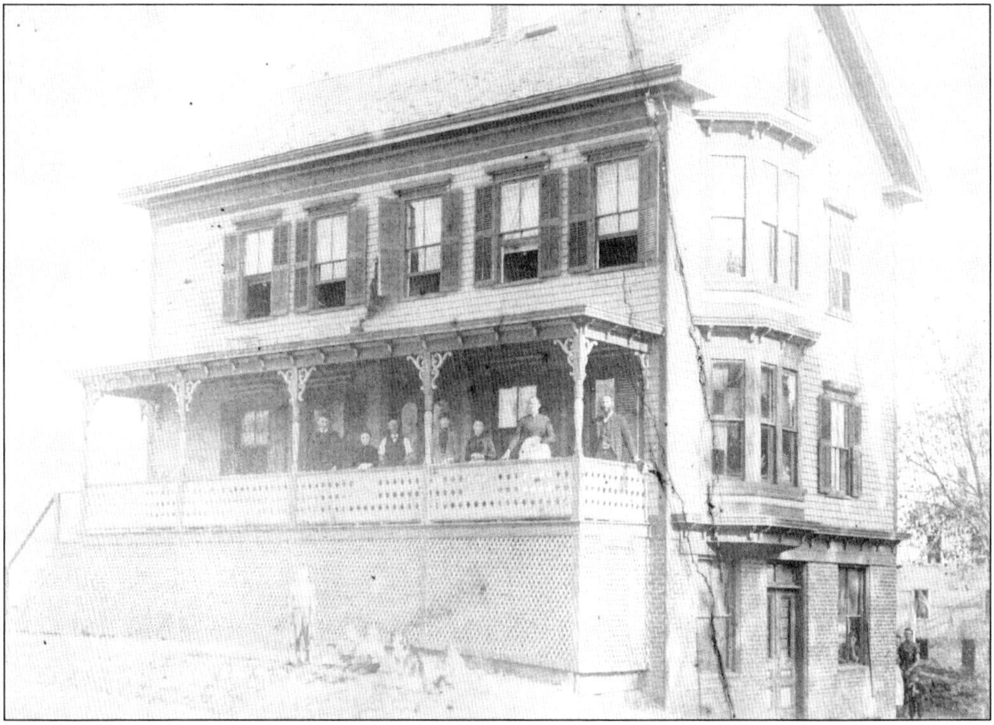

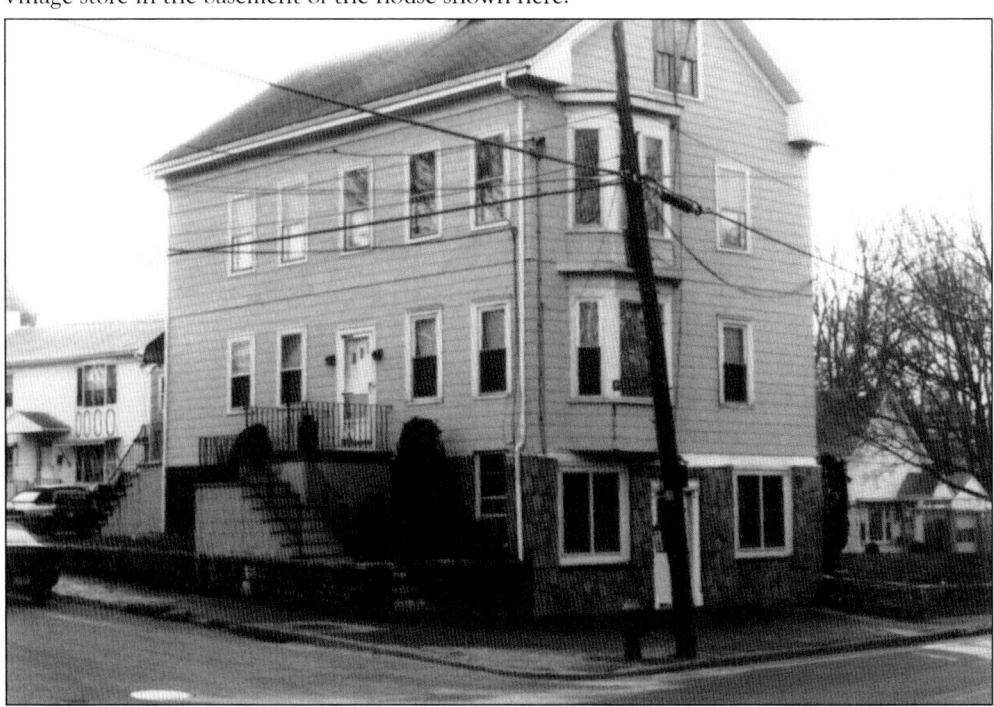

The Michael McKenna house is at the corner of Metcalf and Woonasquatucket Avenues. It is pictured above c. 1880 and below in 1995. The family is pictured on their porch, which is now gone. In the early twentieth century, the family owned a pharmacy in Centerdale as well as a village store in the basement of the house shown here.

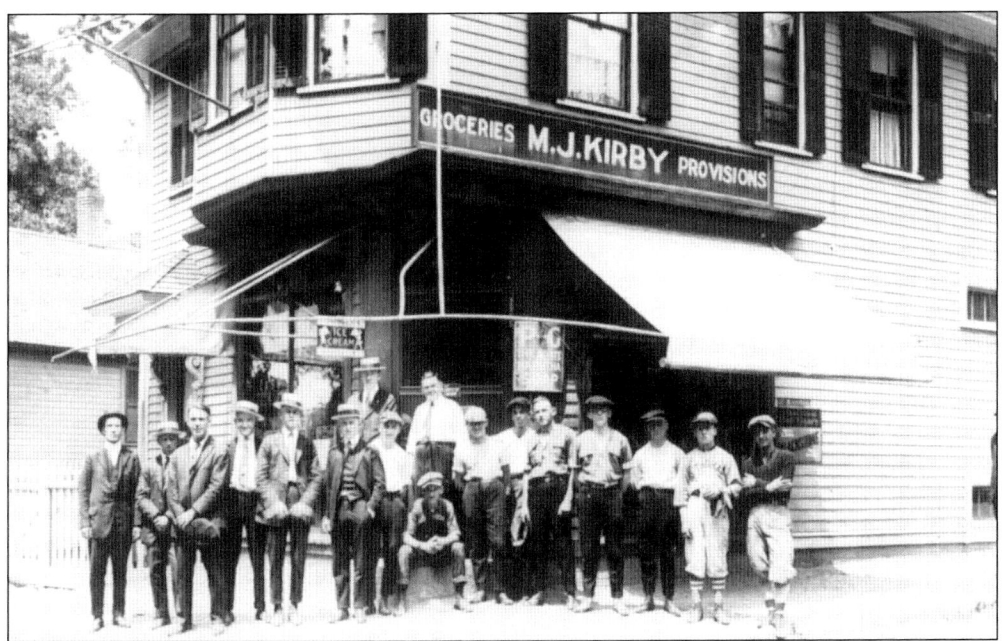

A group of neighborhood people gathered in front of the Kirby Store c. 1910. This store and home were located on the corner of Metcalf and Woonasquatucket Avenues. Michael J. Kirby purchased this lot in 1908 and built the store and tenement. The 1910 North Providence Directory lists the store at 127 Woonasquatucket Avenue and Kirby's home at 9 Metcalf Avenue.

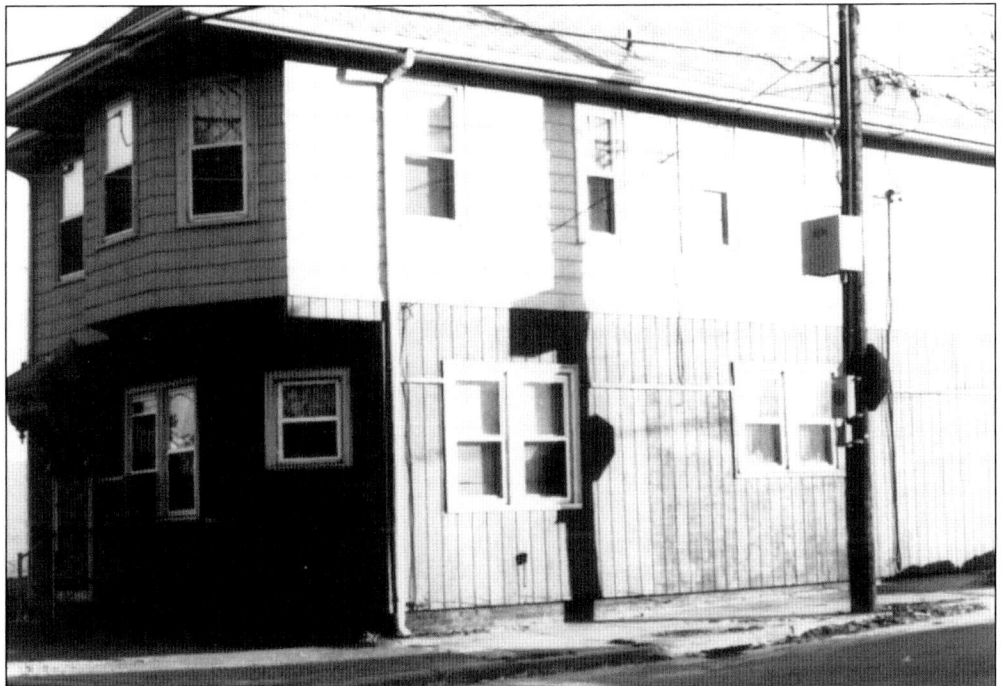

This is the site of the M.J. Kirby Grocery store as it looks today. The business is long gone and the building is now used for apartments.

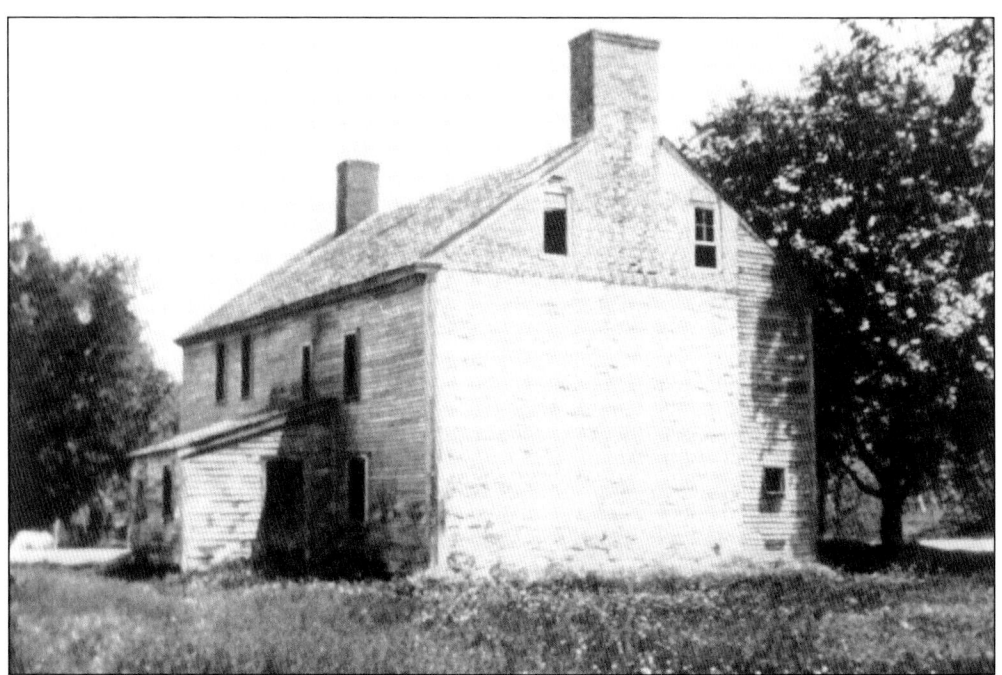

This is the Epenetus Olney house, which was located in the vicinity of Falco Street. It was built c. 1702 and was constructed according to the Rhode Island "Stone-ender" architectural design. Epenetus, born in 1675, married Mary Williams, a descendent of Roger Williams. This house was demolished in 1898.

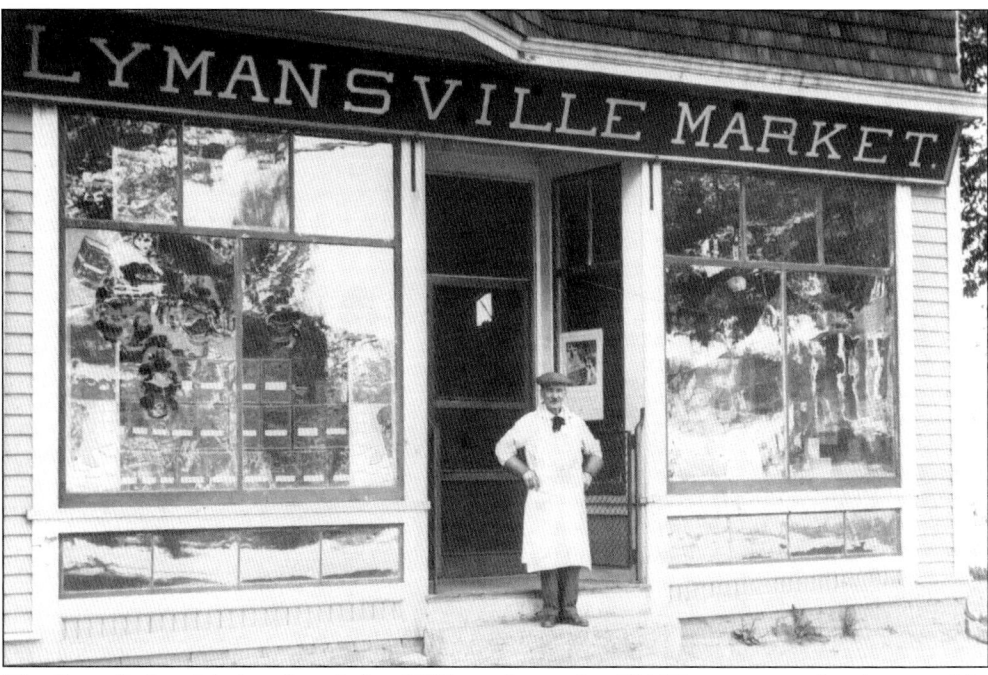

The Oscar P. Aust Market, founded in 1895, was located at 256 Woonasquatucket Avenue. Mr. Aust stands here in front of his market. From the mid-1920s through the early 1930s, it was called the Lymansville Market. Finally, Aust replaced the sign with one that read "Aust's Market."

TO CONTRACTORS.

Proposals are invited for the erection of a two-room frame school house at the corner of Packard and Greenville avenues, in the village of Lymansville, North Providence, R. I.

Plans and specifications can be seen at the office of William R. Walker & Son, Architects, 27 Custom House street, Providence, R. I.

All proposals to be sealed, endorsed "Proposals for building school house at Lymansville," and delivered at the office of the architects on or before 12 m. of SATURDAY, March 26, 1892.

The committee reserve the right to reject any one or all proposals submitted.

By order of the Building Committee,
A. L. ANDREWS, Chairman.

m17   J&B3t

This newspaper clipping shows the beginning of the construction process of the Lymansville School in 1892.

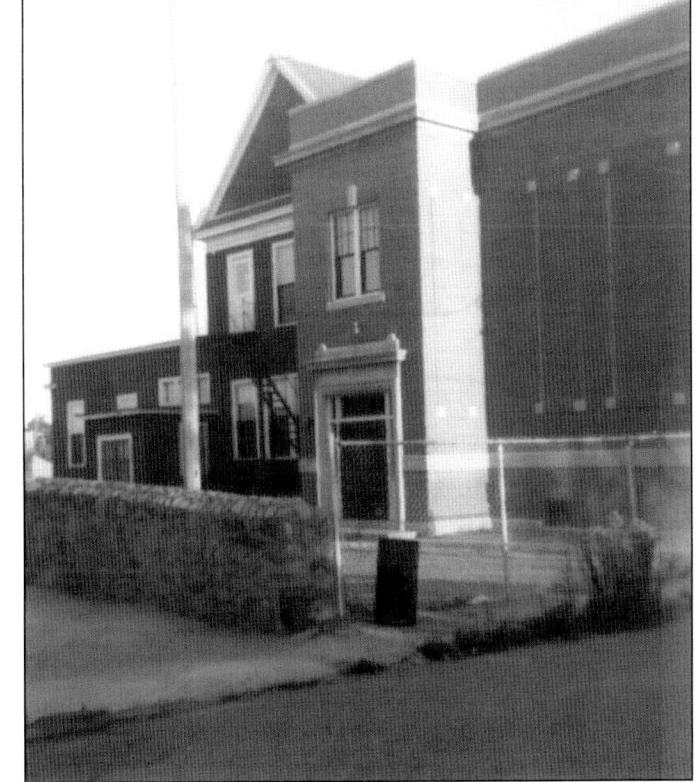

This 1961 photograph of the Lymansville School shows the first (c. 1892) wood school and its 1928 brick addition. Both schools were located at the corner of Greenville and Packard Avenues. Now the site is a vacant lot used for gardens by the Lymansville Neighborhood Association.

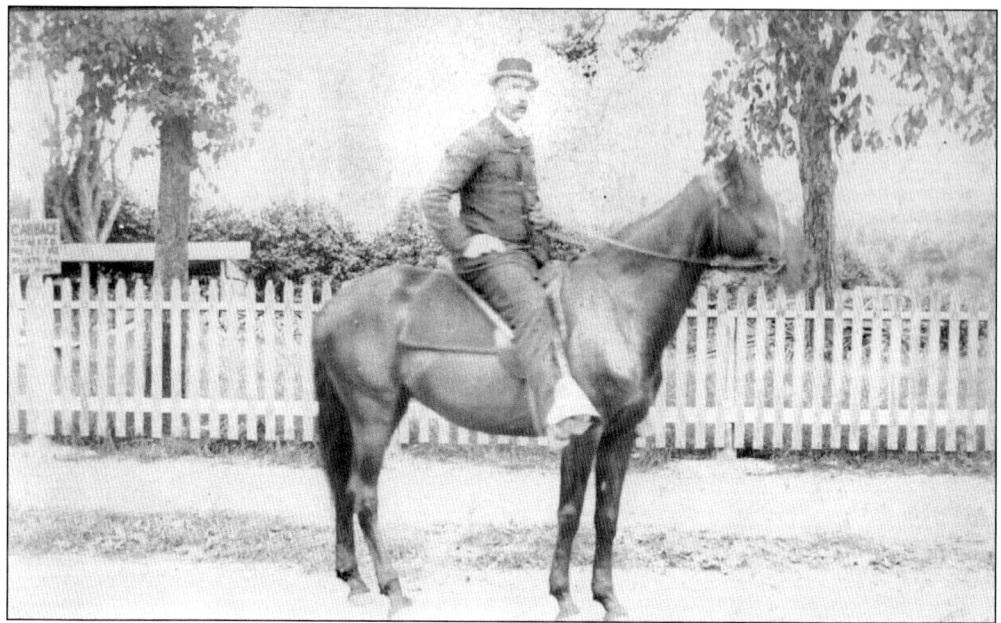

This scene shows Sanford Kinnecom, town sergeant for sixteen years. Notice the advertising sign to the left behind the fence. Kinnecom was born in Allendale in 1863. In addition to his service as town sergeant, he was a member of the state legislature and a disbursing officer for the attorney general. When not occupied with these jobs, he was a painter and wallpaper hanger.

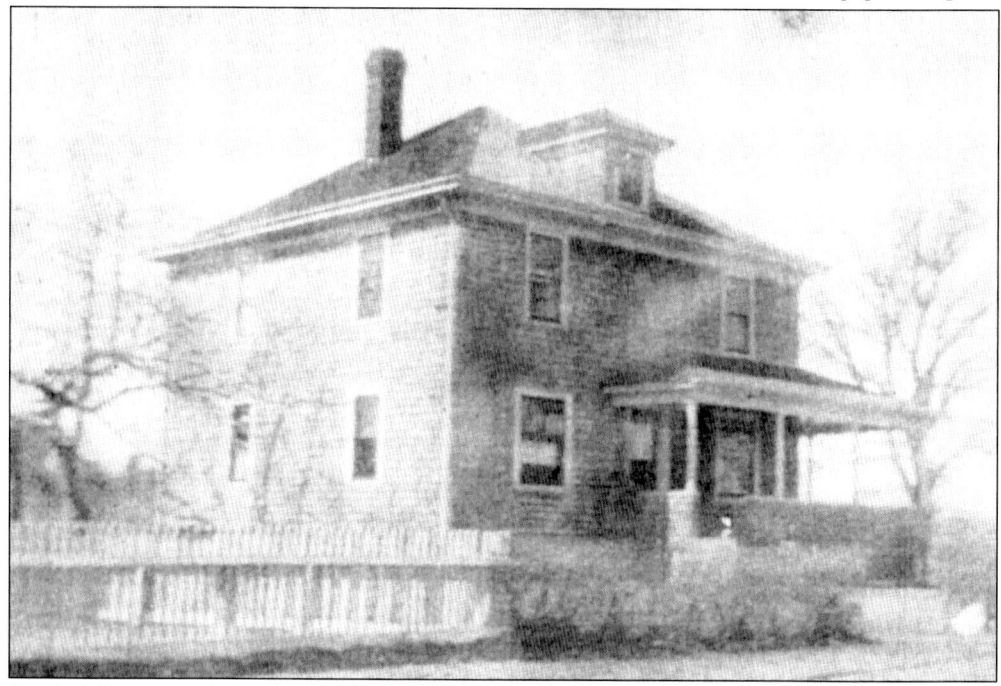

Sanford Kinnecom's family had lived off Woonasquatucket Avenue for many years. He was a direct descendent of Epenetus Olney and Roger Williams through Epenetus's wife Mary (Williams) Olney. His house at 296 Woonasquatucket Avenue is pictured here. It was partially burned in 1992 and is presently being renovated.

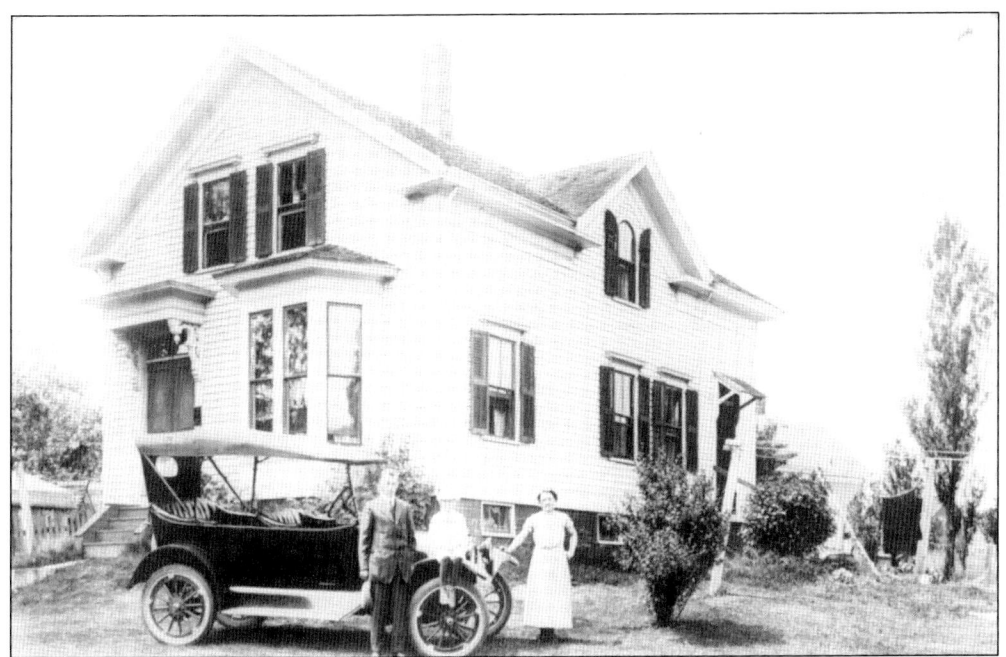

This home is now located at 28 Metcalf Avenue. Earlier in the century, it was listed at 16 Metcalf Avenue. The house was built c. 1885 by Mary Keegan. In 1900, the property was sold to Margaret Maher and her husband. This photograph dates c. 1910-1915 and shows members of the Maher family.

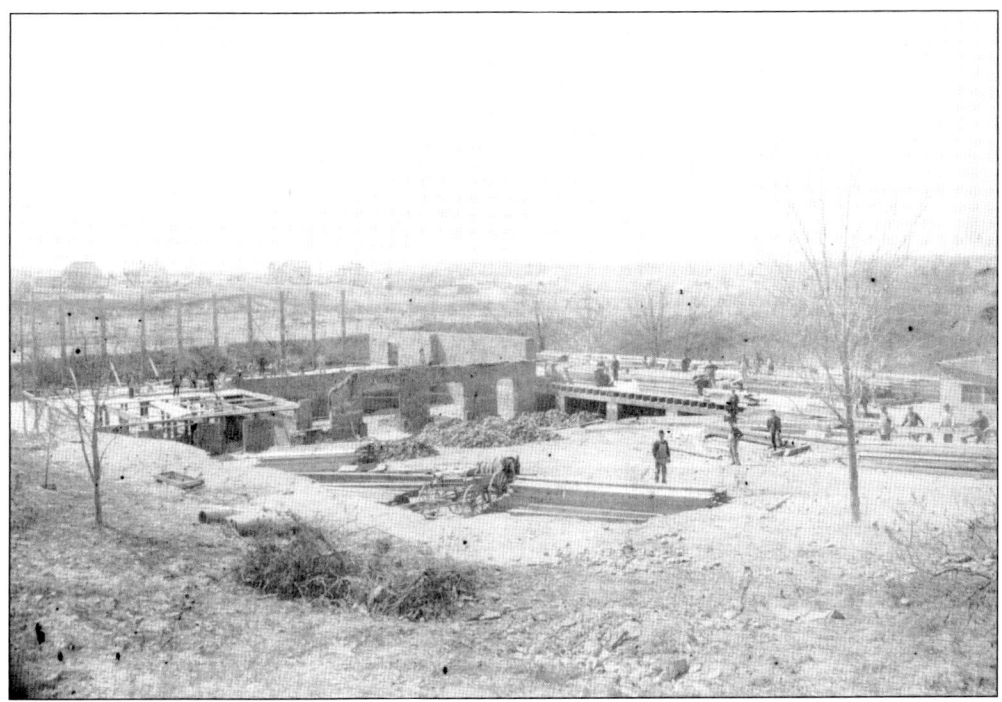

In 1884, August Albert Sack took over the leadership of the Lymansville mill. He immediately began to build a modern brick factory. This photograph shows the c. 1885 construction.

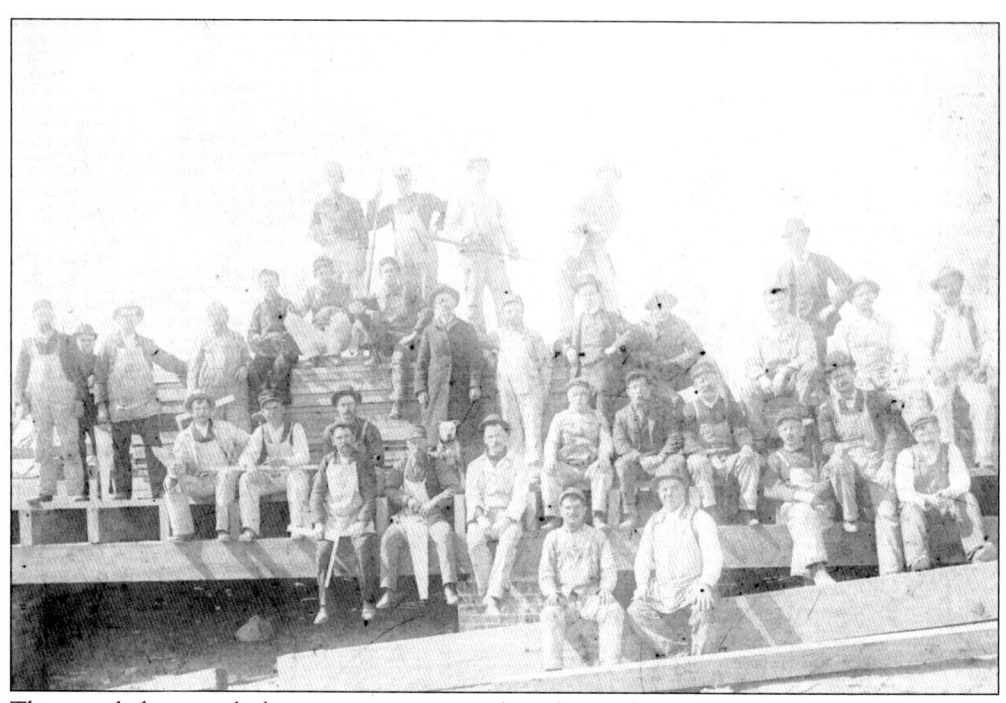

This posed photograph shows construction workers during the new mill construction c. 1885.

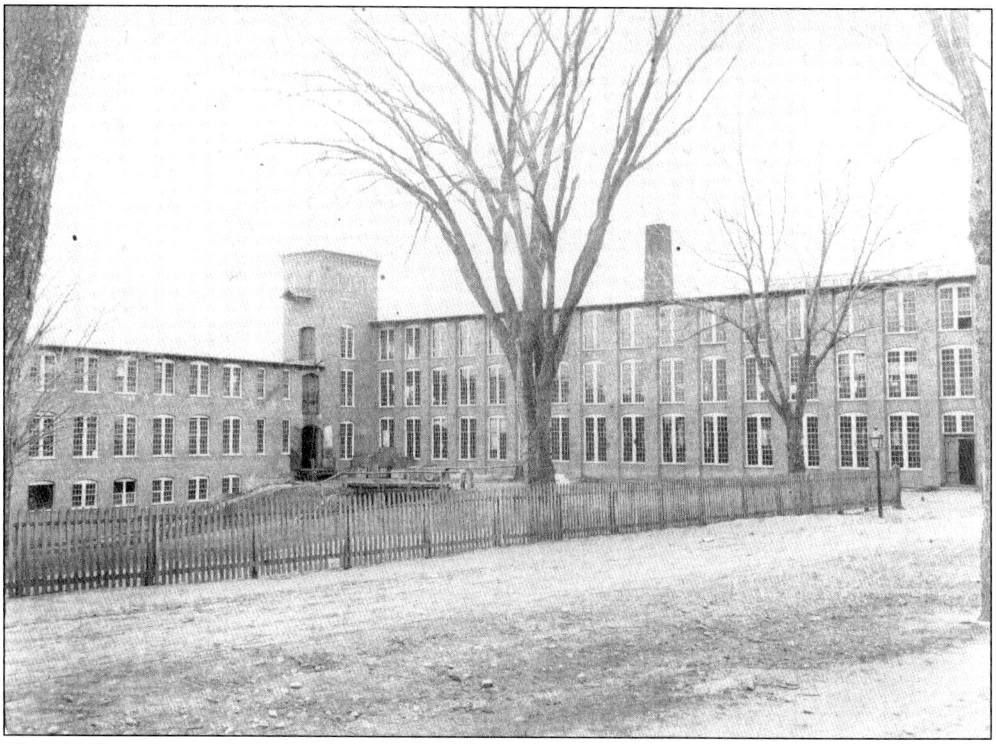

This 1890s photograph shows the completed Lymansville mill. Notice that Woonasquatucket Avenue was a dirt road and there were no electric wires. There was, however, a kerosene post light.

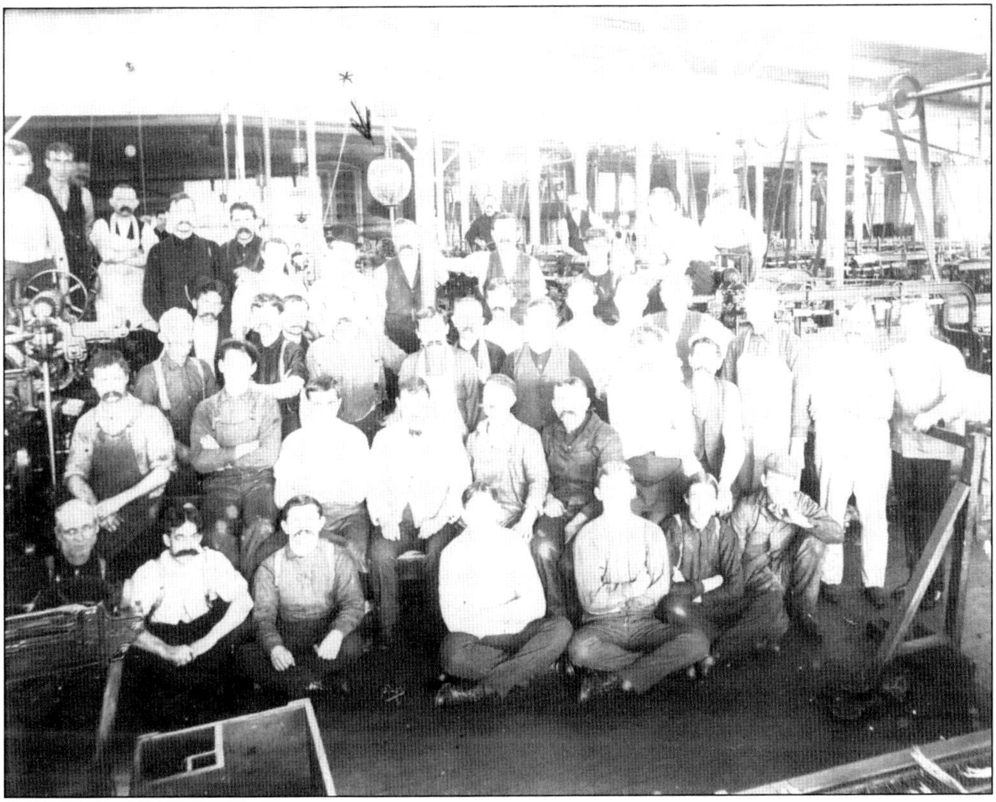

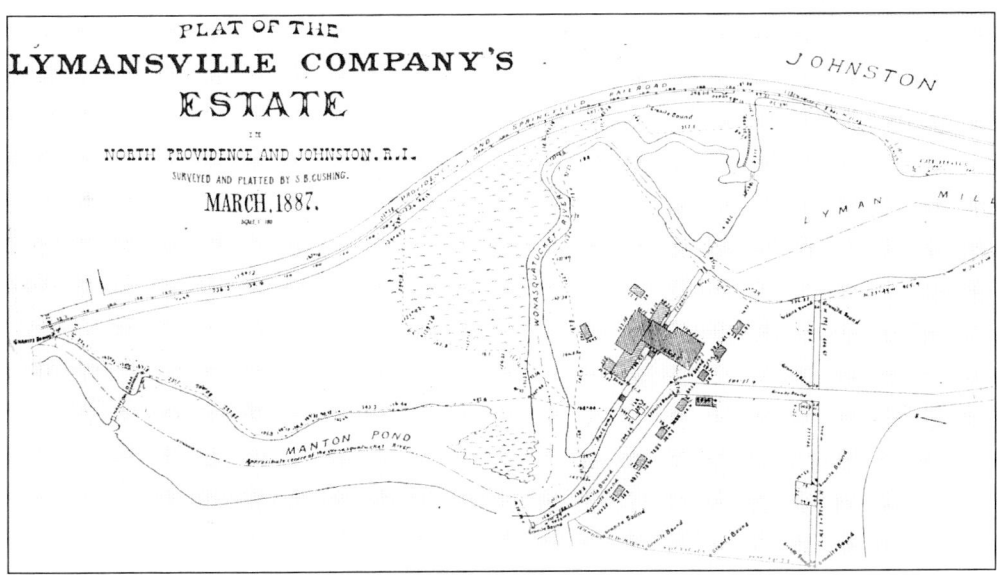

This 1890 scene depicts the interior of the Lymansville mill. This was the weave shed. Arc lights allowed for adequate visibility.

Here we see a map of the Lymansville Mill Company property shortly after the new mill was erected. Mill houses along Woonasquatucket Avenue were present in 1887. Only two remain today.

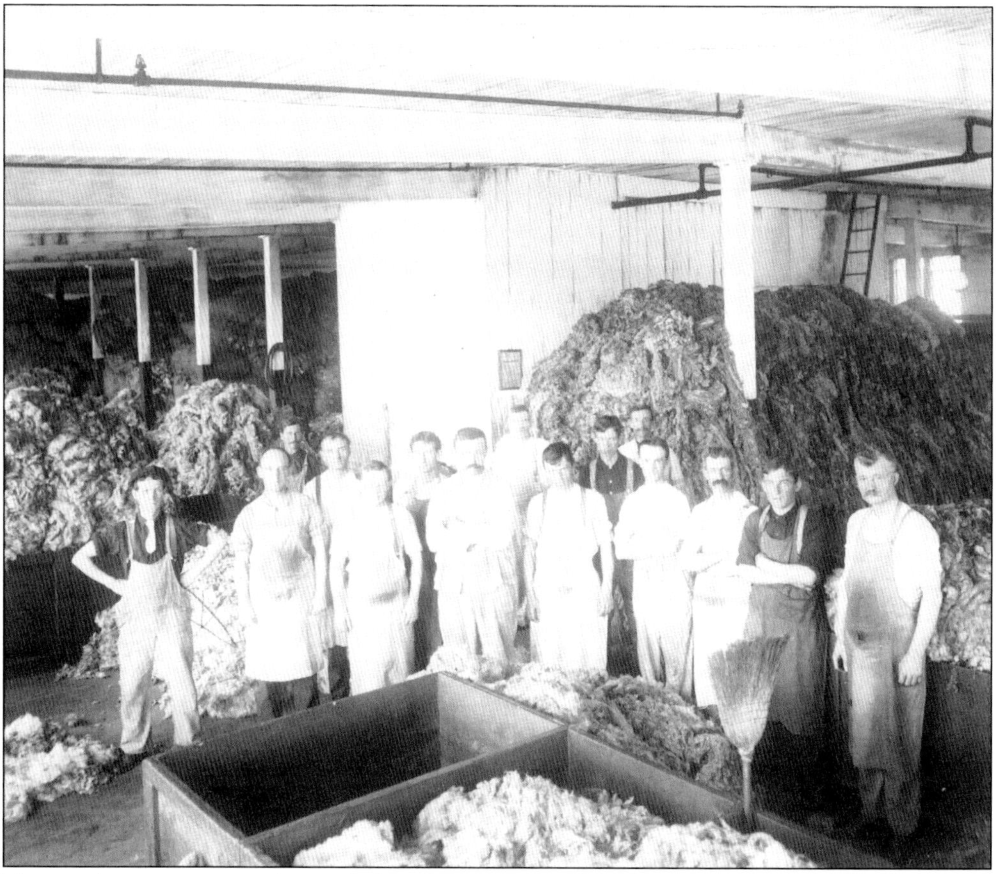

The wool sorting room is depicted above in a c. 1890 photograph of the mill's interior, and the Lymansville mill is seen below from various angles as it looked in 1887.

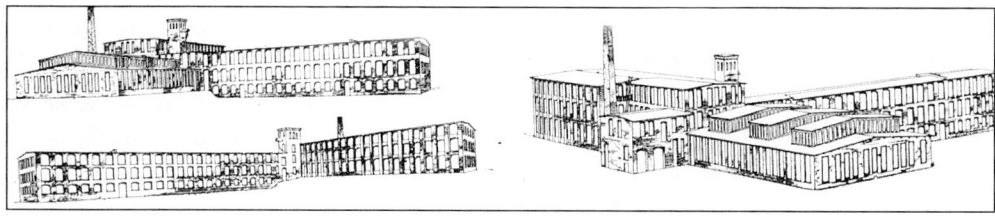

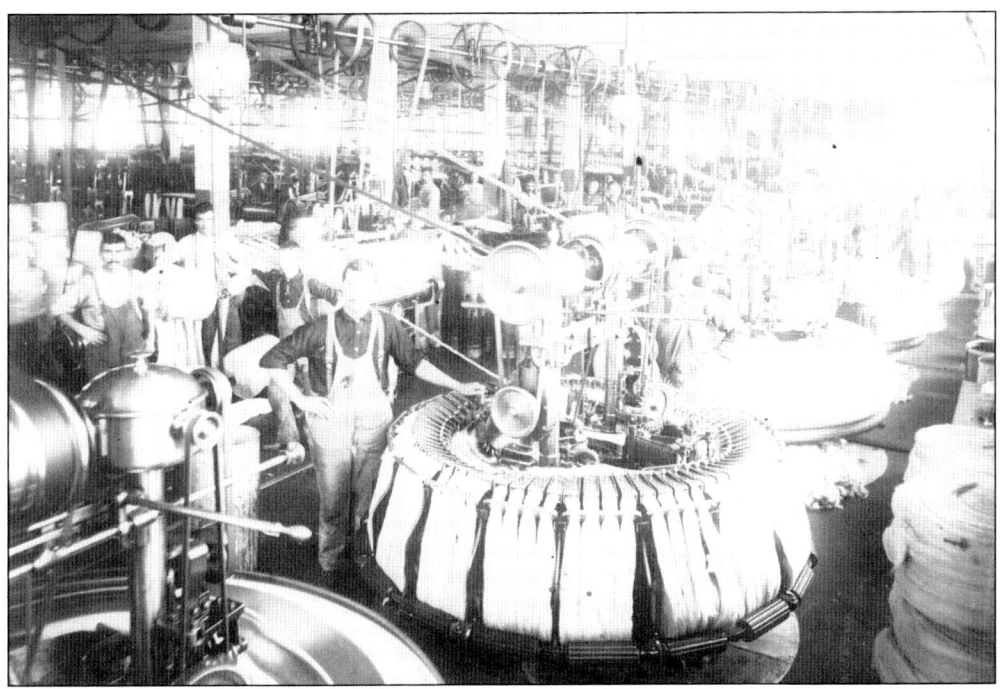

This c. 1900 photograph shows the interior of the mill. Notice the arc lights.

LYMANSVILLE CO.

SERGES
CHEVIOTS
SUITINGS

MILLS AT LYMANSVILLE

PROVIDENCE

R. I.

Here we see an example of advertising for the Lymansville mill that appeared in the 1910 North Providence Directory.

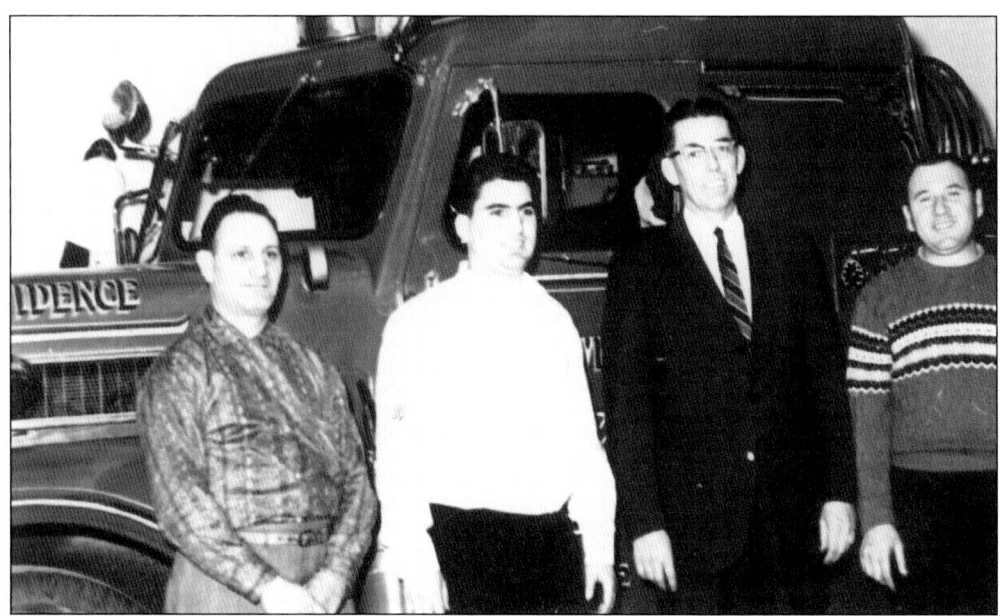

Lymansville, like other villages in the town, had volunteer fire-fighting groups early in the twentieth century. In 1896, there was a Hose #1 at 133 Woonasquatucket Avenue. Shown in this c. 1960 photograph are, from left to right: Joseph Carnavale, Kenneth Chille, an instructor from the East Providence Fire Department, and Anthony Caccia.

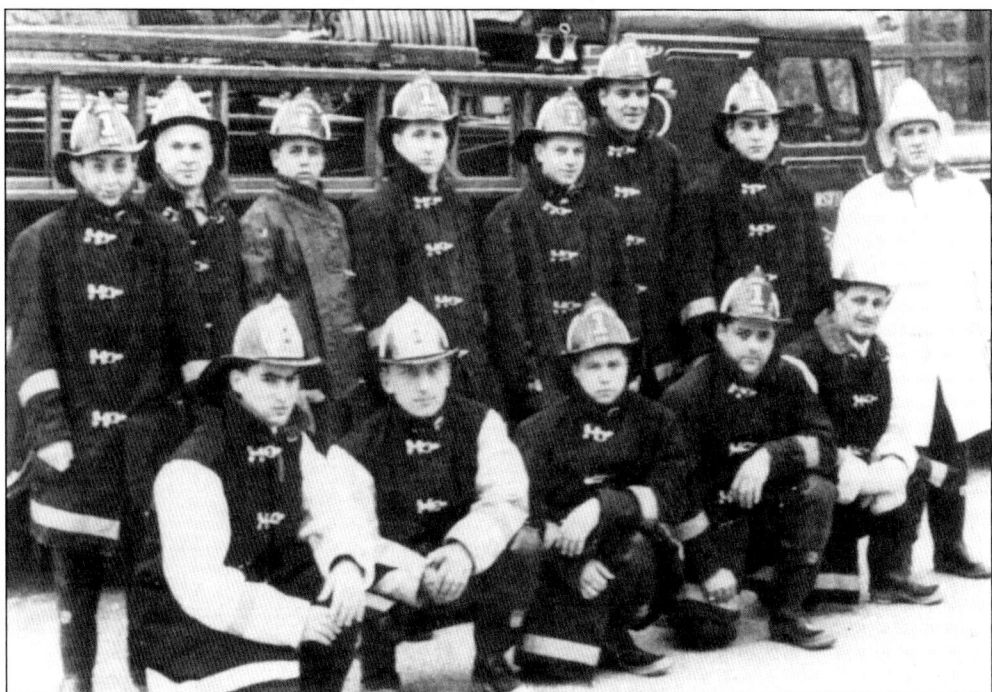

This fire department photograph of February 1962 shows Angelo Rotondo, James Payette, Anthony Cardarelli, Nick DeChristofaro, Vincent SanAntonio, Anthony Carbone, Mike Balassone, Joe DeRosa, Driver/Engineer John Parisi, Lieutenants Ken Chille and Joseph Carnavale, Captain Henry Parisi, and Chief Anthony Caccia. (*Observer* photograph.)

Six

MARIEVILLE

Marieville was not established as a village until *c.* 1885 when the Canadian, Italian, and Belgian immigrants arrived. The name was taken from the village of Marieville in the township of Monnoir in Quebec, Canada, the birthplace of many of the earliest residents.

The entire area was originally owned by the Randall family. By the late eighteenth century, William and John Randall had built houses on the east side of what we now call the Old Louisquisset Pike not far from the Lincoln town line. By the mid-nineteenth century, one of the Randall descendants, Julia A. Miner (nee Randall) was the owner of all the Randall land to the Providence line and east toward Pawtucket.

Julia, who was a good businesswoman, had the land below Mineral Spring Avenue surveyed and platted in 1876 and named it the "Plat of the Heirs of William Randall." Samuel Hedley, a real estate developer, bought many lots for re-sale. One of the earliest, if not the first house built was purchased by Jean Baptiste Brillon in 1894. Construction of this house began *c.* 1885. Jean's direct descendent, Richard Brillon, lives in the house today. Another prominent name in Marieville is Plante. Godfrey Plante lived at what is now numbered 160 Vincent Avenue as early as the 1890s.

By the late 1880s, there was a need for a school in this area and construction on the building was started immediately. An 1895 land ownership map shows two schools west of Charles Street. We have been told that one was a "portable school" which handled the overflow of students.

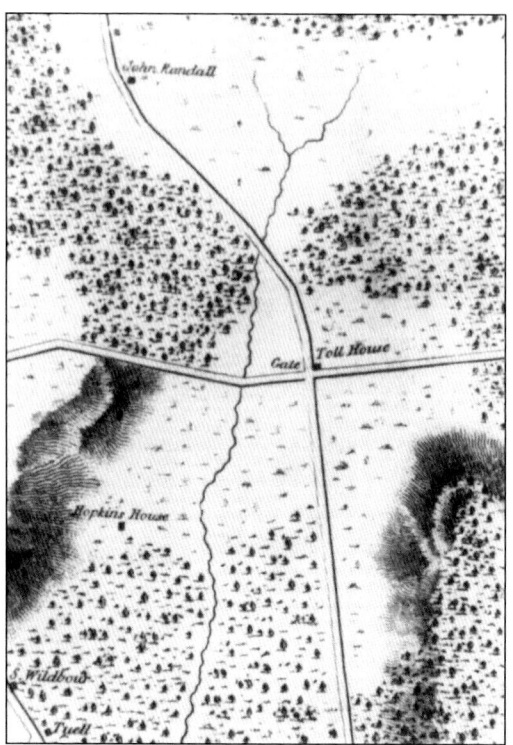

This 1835 map of Marieville shows the William Randall (1782) and John Randall (1793) houses on the Louisquisset Pike, the toll house and gate at the four corners, and the William Hopkins house (1830), located at the present 1 Tingley Lane.

In 1883, Julia A. Miner began to sell lots in the lower Marieville area. This 1895 map shows how development had progressed in twelve years. The person taking the survey when this map was published apparently didn't realize the correct spelling was "Marieville." In fact, town council records of that time used the "Maryville" spelling. Some old family names like Senecal and Plante are still known in the village.

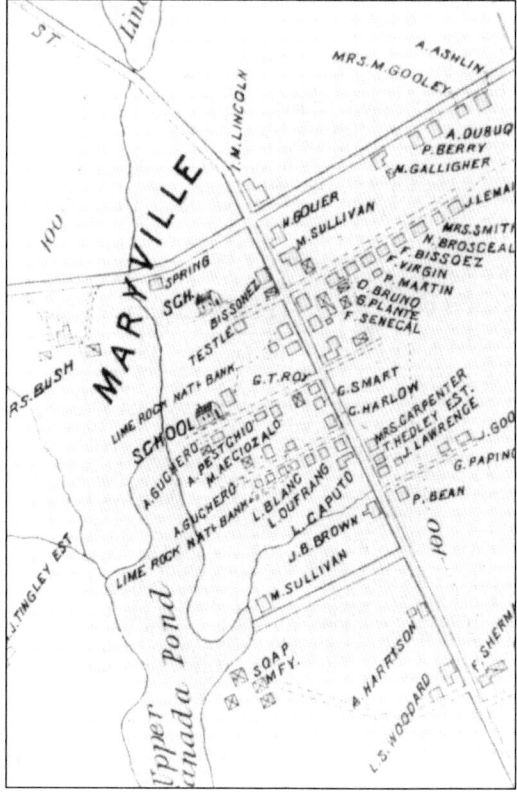

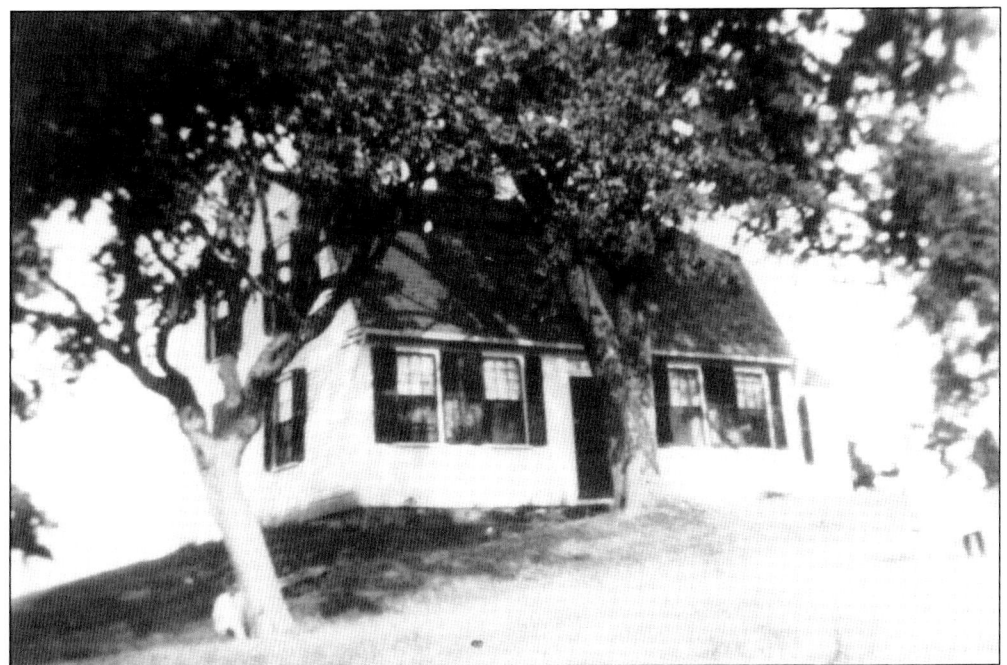

This 1913 photograph shows the 1782 William Randall house at 1367 Louisquisset Pike. William built the house in the eighteenth century and lived there until the 1830s. The last lineal descendent to own the house was Deborah Burton. A late-nineteenth century descendent developed and sold lots in what is now Marieville village.

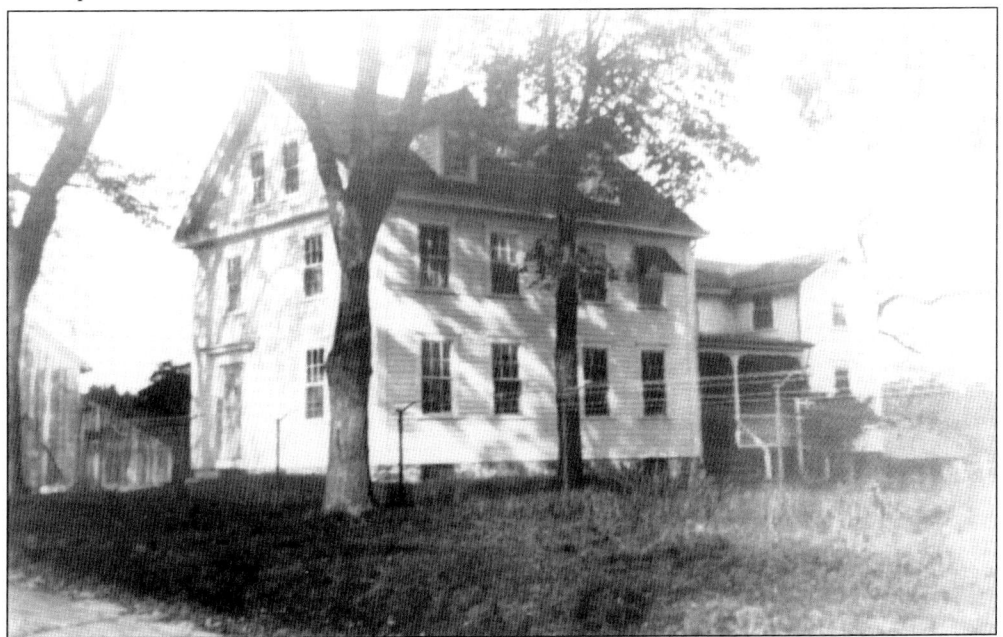

This house and barn at 1 Tingley Lane was built by William H. Hopkins c. 1830. The site was previously home to the Stephen Sweet dwelling, which was built in 1770. Shortly before 1830, that house burned to the ground and William H. Hopkins built a new house which has descended through the Tingley and present Callaghan families.

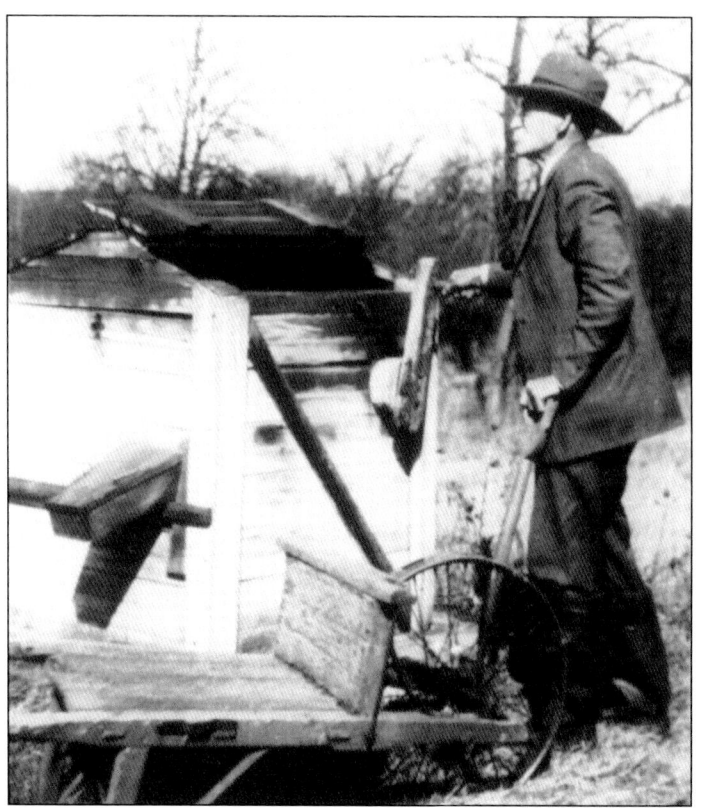

Xenophon Tingley, born the son of Hartford J. Tingley in 1844, is standing at his water well on the estate at 1 Tingley Lane. The Tingleys were well-educated people who apparently loved Greek names because they named their son Xenophon Demosthenes Tingley.

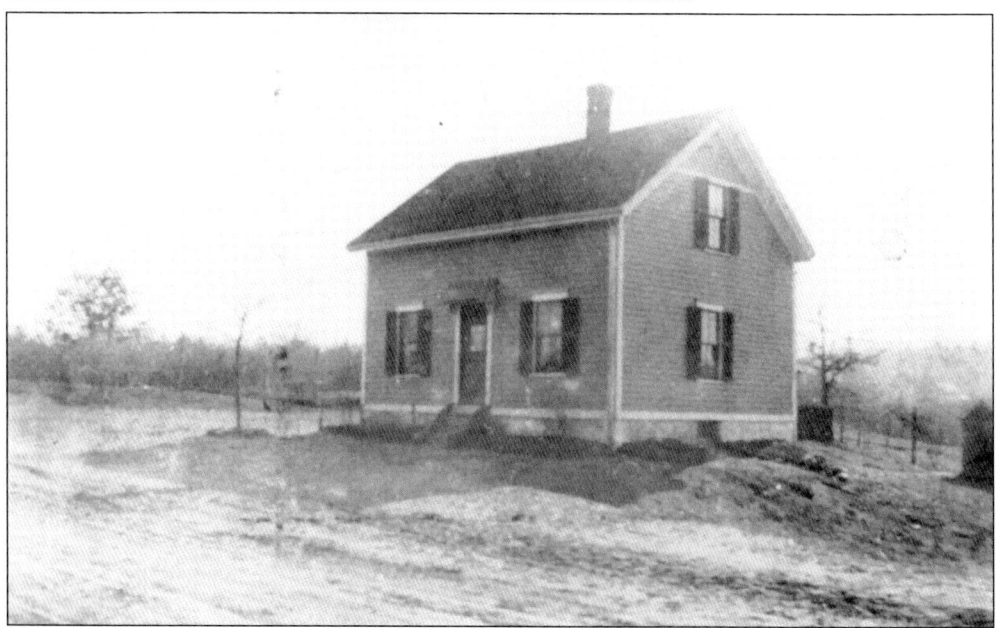

This house located at 1002 Charles Street was probably photographed at the turn of the twentieth century when Charles Street was still a dirt road. The house was built by Samuel Hedley in 1885. In 1894, Jean Baptiste Brillon, an immigrant from Marieville, Canada, bought the house. His direct descendent, Richard Brillon, still lives in the home.

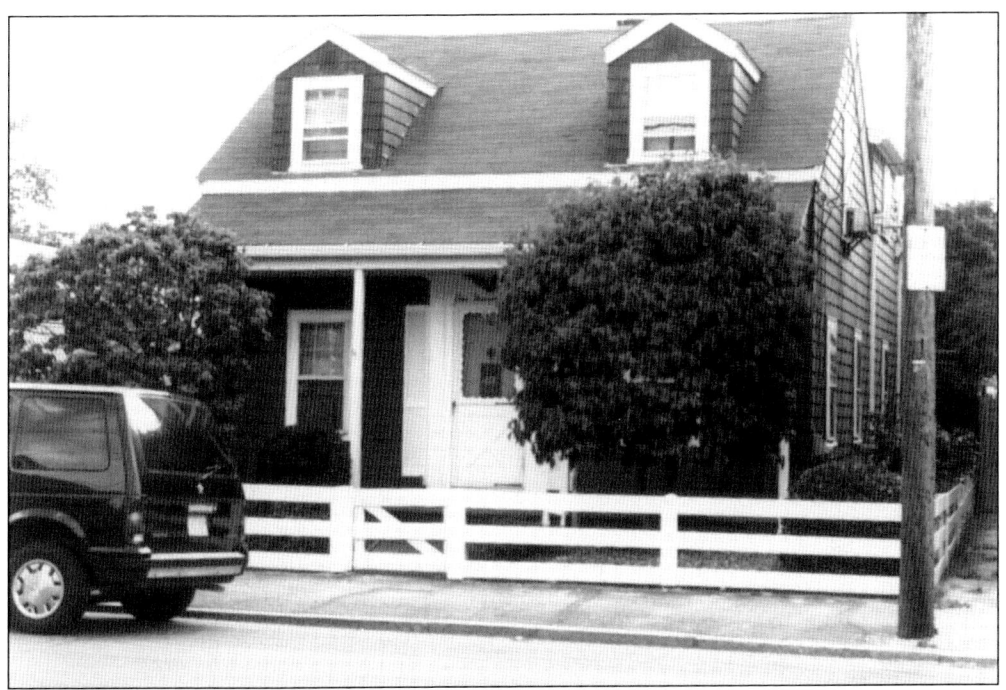

The residence of Mr. and Mrs. Richard Brillon at 1002 Charles Street is shown here as it appears today.

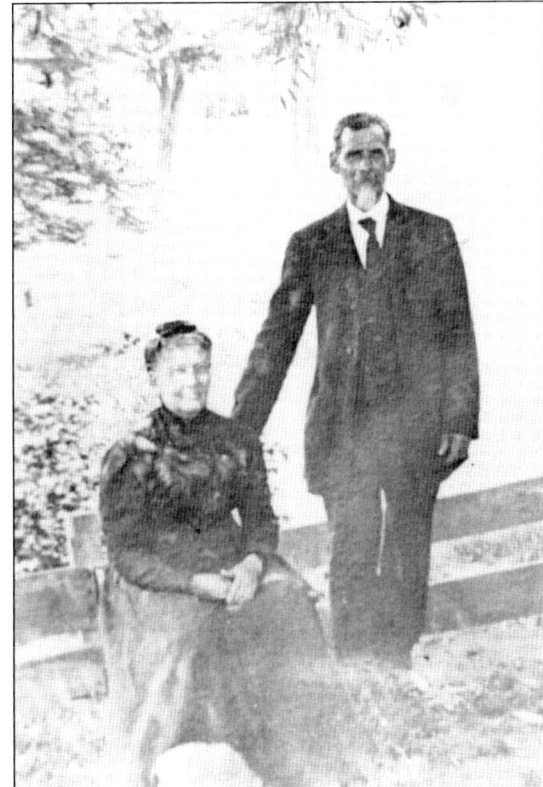

Jean Baptiste and Selina Brillon were the first in a long line of Brillons to live in Marieville. Jean Baptiste emigrated in the late nineteenth century from Canada to find better opportunities in the United States.

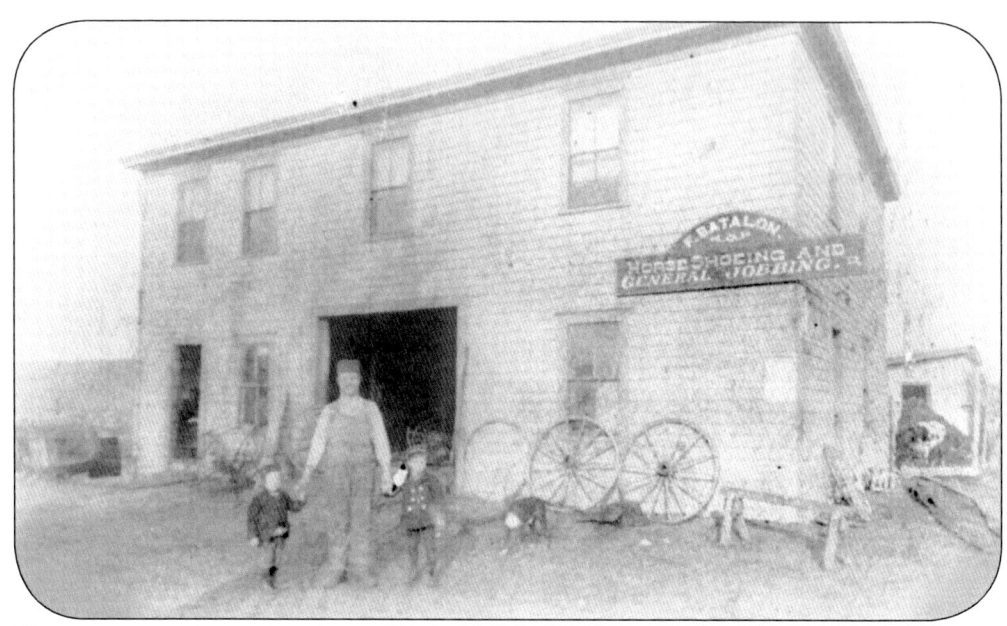

This structure is located at the northwest corner of the intersection of the Louisquisset and Mineral Spring Pikes. Francis Batalon opened a blacksmith shop here c. 1906. The business continued until 1926 when Francis converted it to an ice cream and milk business, which continued until 1939. In the photograph is Francis Batalon with two of his children.

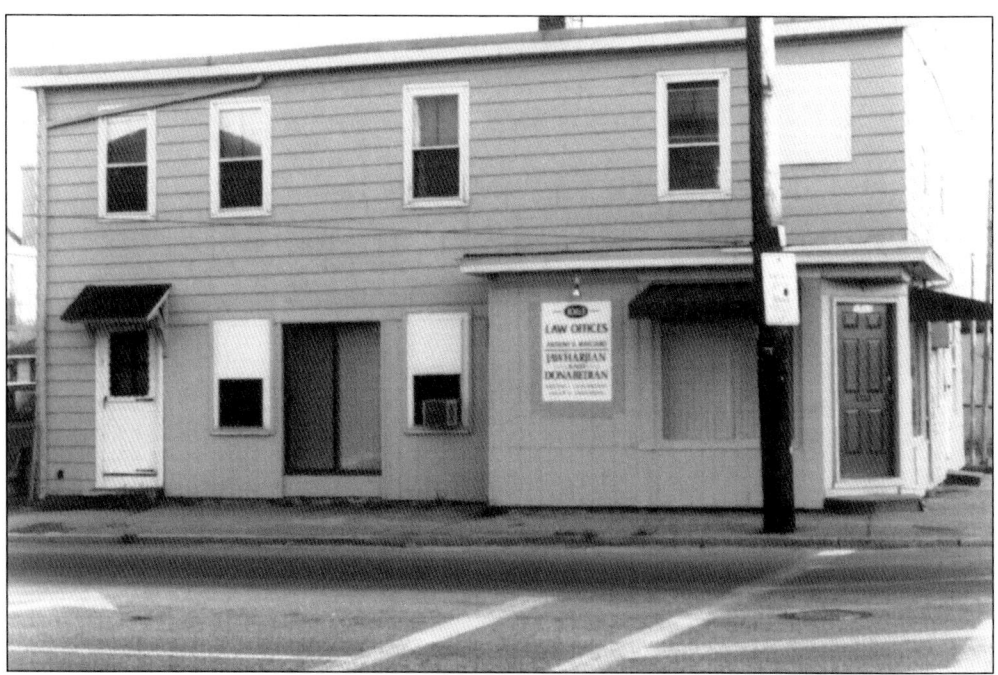

This is the Batalon blacksmith shop as it appears today.

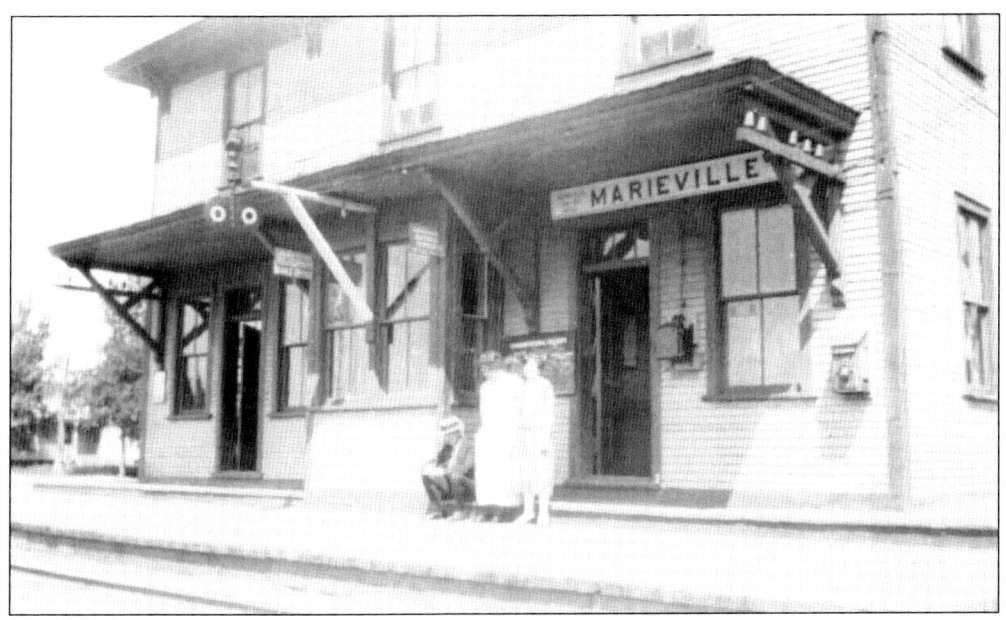

This scene was taken in the village of Marieville, Canada, from which the French residents of Marieville, North Providence, emigrated in the late nineteenth century.

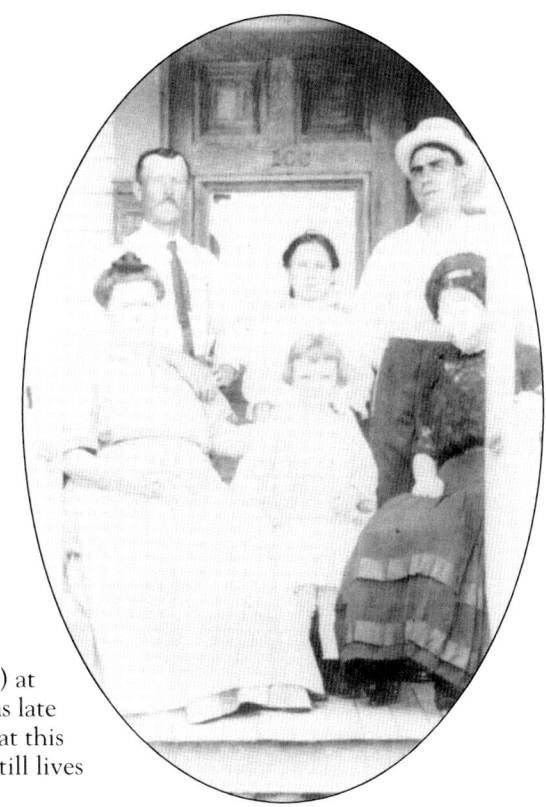

This family scene depicts Godfrey Plante (left) with his third wife Exeline (Fournier) at 106 Vincent Avenue, where Plante lived as late as 1913. The 1895 map shows a G. Plante at this location. His descendent, Gilbert Plante, still lives in Marieville.

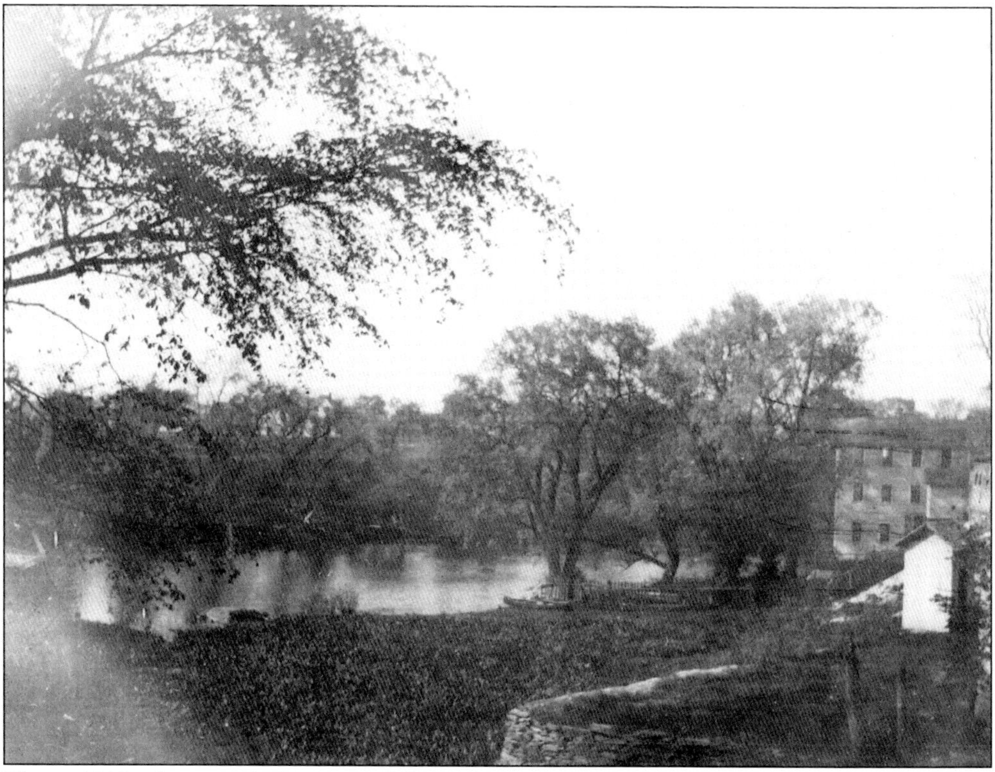

This c. 1900s photograph shows Randall Pond. An 1870 map of the area indicates a pond to the west of Charles Street with an ice house operation run by an S. Randall.

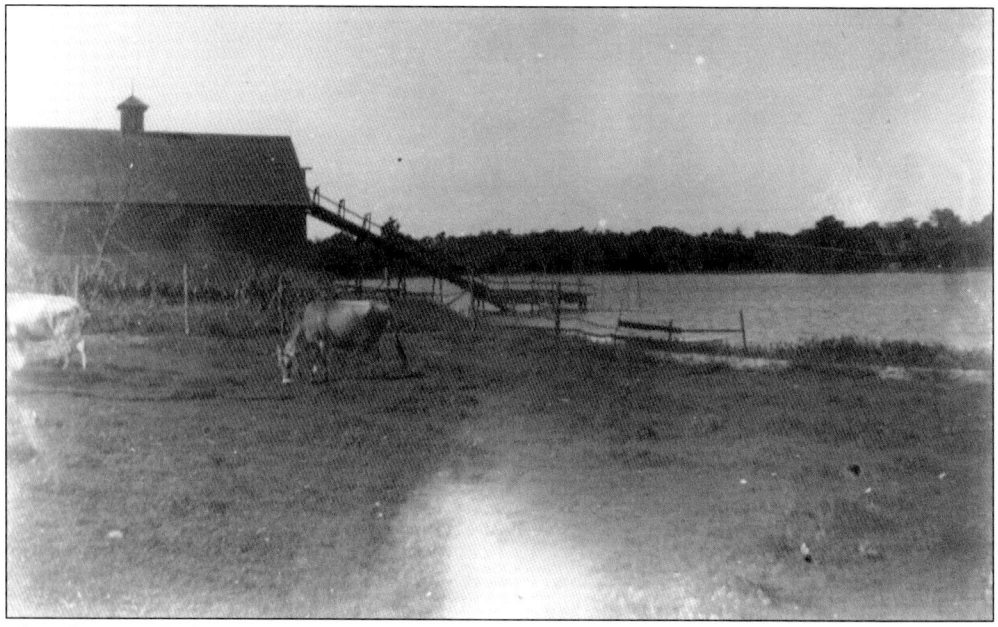

This photograph shows an ice-gathering ramp on the same pond. This body of water was named "Upper Canada Pond" on an 1895 map. What remains of this pond can be seen to the east while driving on Route 146 today.

This home was located at 1083 Mineral Spring Avenue which is the present site of the Church of the Presentation. It was built by Godfrey Plante Jr., the son of Godfrey Plante, an original settler. Godfrey Jr. was a carpenter. The structure was at that location in the 1920s but was later moved to Manchester Farm Road.

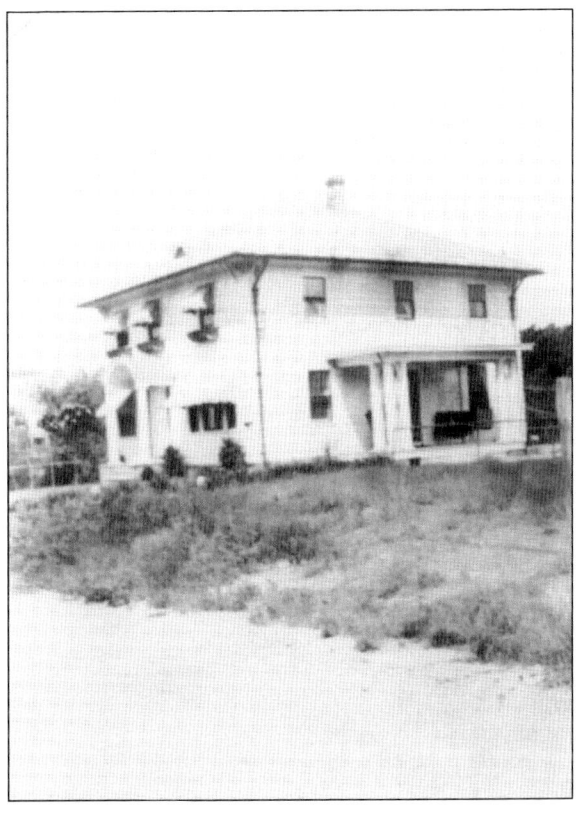

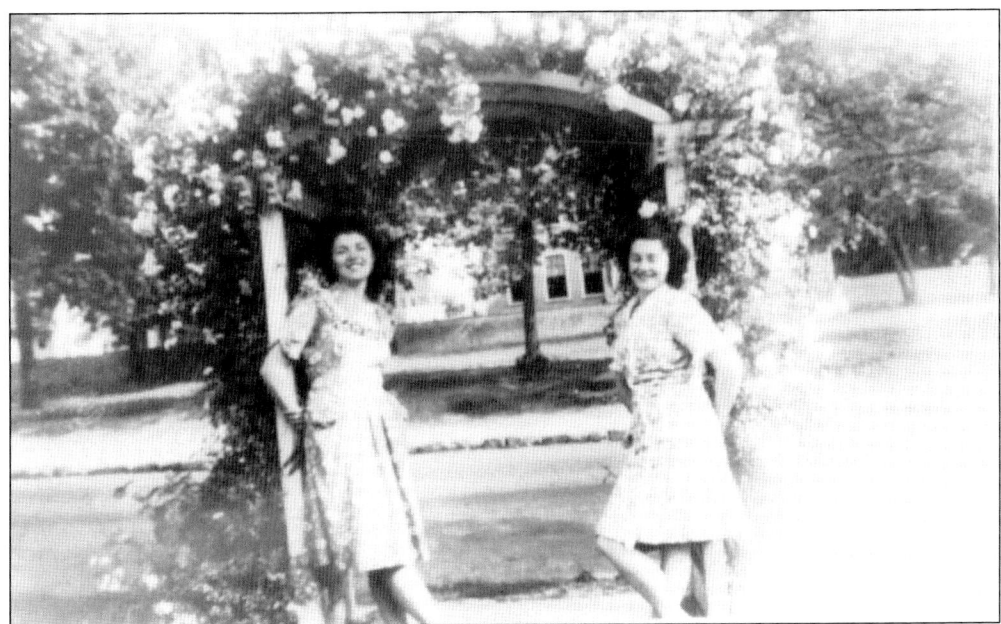

From left to right in the arbor are Olive ? and Yvette Plante. In the background is what was called "The Grove" and the old Marieville School. The girls are standing where the Church of the Presentation now is located.

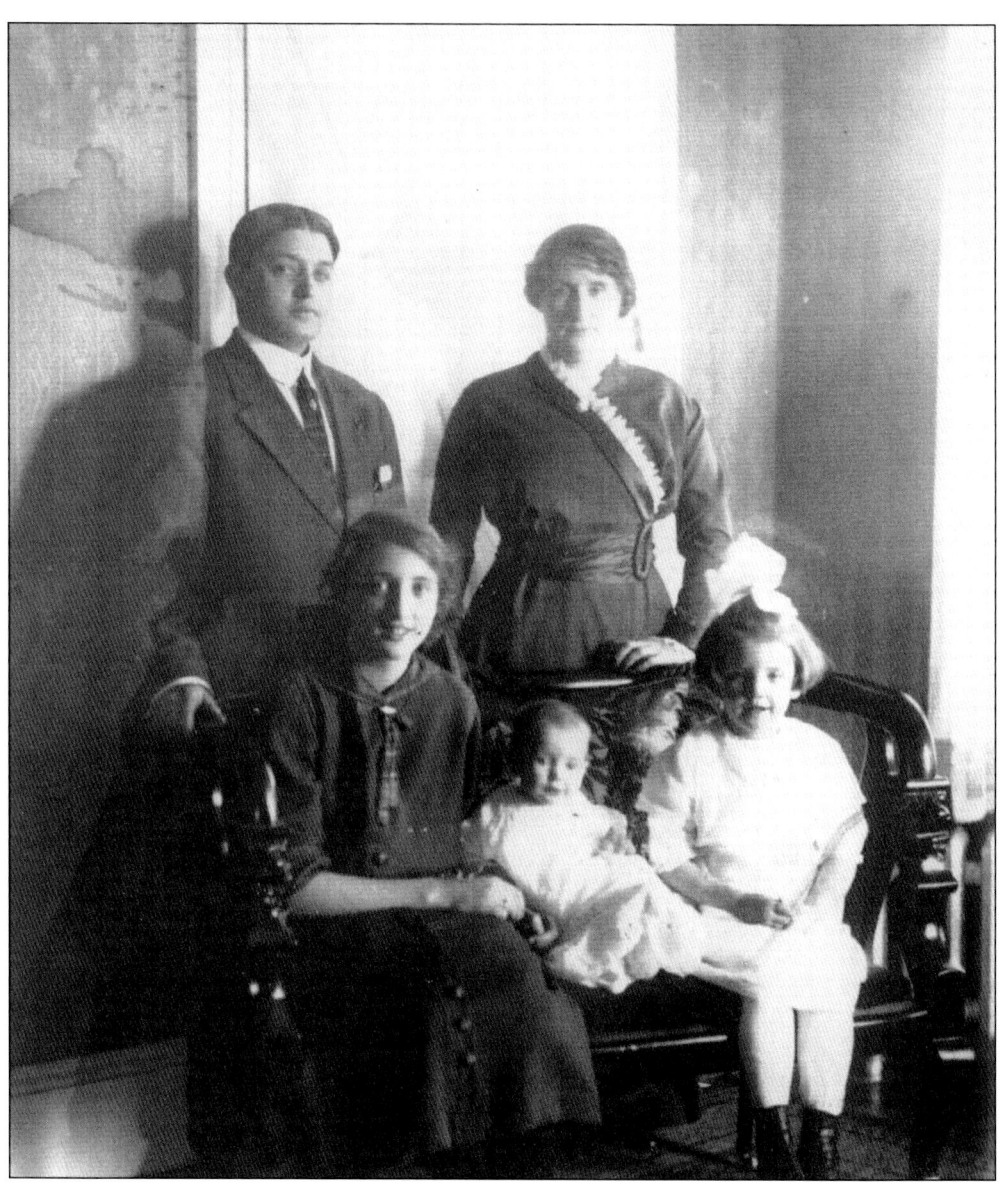

Another prominent family was that of the name Senecal. In the late nineteenth century, Pierre Senecal settled in Marieville. One of his descendants is pictured here with his family. From left to right are: (front row) Hope, Dorothy, and Mary Senecal; (back row) Alderic and Sarah Antoinette Senecal. Sarah was known as "Nettie." The family home was located at 982 Mineral Spring Avenue. Hope was the last to live in the house, which she sold a few years ago. Alderic Sr. was a prominent businessman in Marieville for many years.

The Hotel Squantum at 925 Mineral Spring Avenue is shown in 1913 with Alderic Senecal, proprietor. The location of the hotel, listed as Marieville, was actually just east of Power Road within the limits of Pawtucket. The present address is 877-879 Mineral Spring Avenue. The advertisement with this photograph reads, "Newly Furnished Rooms-Special Attention Given To Private Parties-Garage Attached."

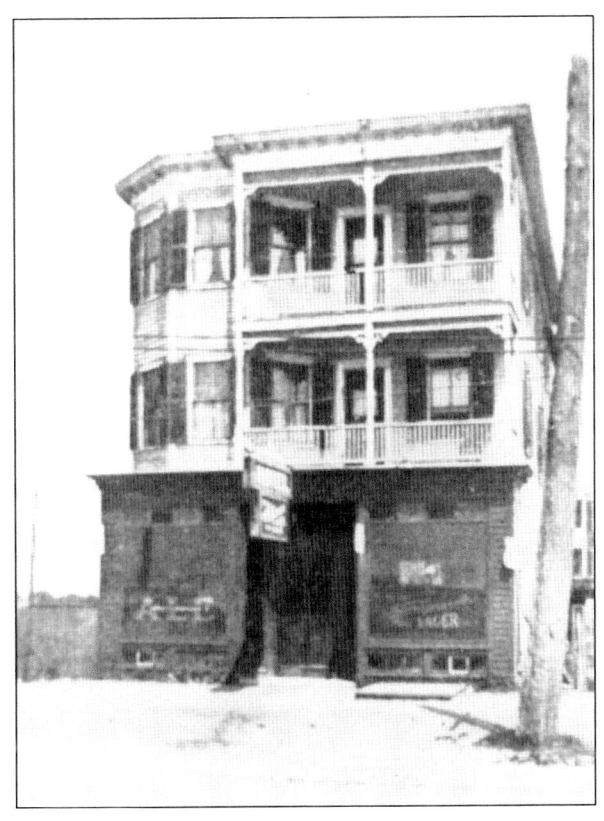

The Mineral Spring Pharmacy at the southwest corner of Charles Street and Mineral Spring Avenue is shown as it looked in 1913. William G. Morin, a registered pharmacist, was the owner. This building as well as the adjoining buildings are shortly to be demolished to make way for a Walgreen's pharmacy.

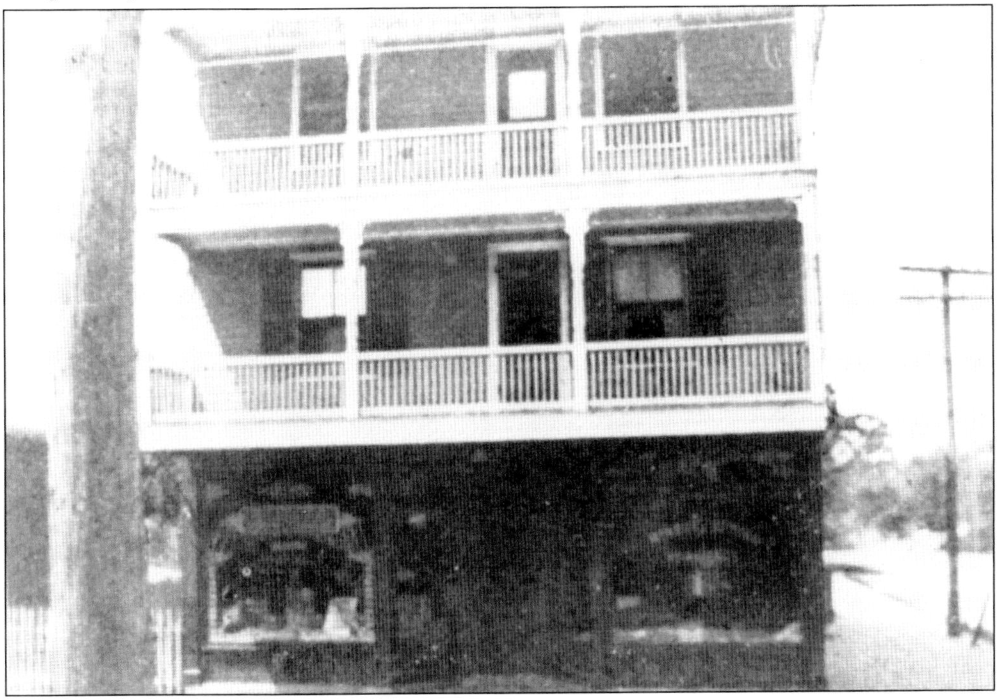

MARIEVILLE COAL AND WOOD YARD
ARTHUR GOOLEY, Proprietor
Wood Sawing a Specialty   Furniture Moving
Dealer In
COAL AND WOOD
Also LIGHT EXPRESSING OF ALL KINDS
924 Mineral Spring Avenue, Marieville, R. I.

S. JENNELLO & SON
CONTRACTORS
ALL KINDS OF MASON WORK AND
GENERAL JOBBING PROMPTLY ATTENDED TO
7 Oregon Ave., Fruit Hill
Tel. Con.   P. O. BOX 167, CENTREDALE, R. I.

ANTONIO JANNETTA
Orchestra and Band Leader
MUSIC FURNISHED FOR ALL OCCASIONS
PICNICS A SPECIALTY
6 OBED AVE., MARIEVILLE

DEXTER LIME
Plastering Hair
PLASTERER and STUCCO WORKER
ADOLPH JODOIN, 122 VINCENT AVE.
'Phone Pawt. 1030-Y   MARIEVILLE, R. I.

ODENA COTE
STONE and BRICK MASON
ESTIMATES FURNISHED   TELEPHONE CONNECTION
PLASTERING AND WHITEWASHING
927 Charles Street, North Providence, R. I.

MAX BIZON
Dealer in
French Sausages and Blood Pudding
68 Vincent Ave., Marieville, R. I.

This advertisement touted five Marieville merchants in 1913. The village had become very prosperous by this time. Notice that four out of the five proprietors' names are French, reflecting the ethnic majority of the community. A survey of Marieville *c.* 1913 revealed that there were Italian, Irish, Belgian, and French people living in the village.

This 1910 Alderic Senecal advertisement promoted his market and cafe, both located in the same building. This building eventually became the Hotel Squantum *c.* 1913.

ALDERIC SENECAL

Senecal's Grocery & Market
Meats and
Provisions
Grain and
Flour
921 Charles Street
MARIEVILLE

SENECAL'S CAFE
Ales, Wines,
Liquors and
Cigars
925 Mineral Spring Ave.
MARIEVILLE

Seven
WOODVILLE/GENEVA

During the eighteenth century this area was composed primarily of farms with at least two saw mills built along the West River. Early in the nineteenth century, mills began to be established along the Douglas Pike from Twin Rivers to the Providence line. In 1814, Wilbur Kelley built a two-story stone factory and a stone gambrel-roof dwelling to the east of the present Route 7 on a tributary of the West River. A grist mill was established in 1834 below the Wenscott Reservoir and Otis Angell built a stone factory on the West River c. 1846, which James Hilton was using as a bleachery by 1868.

The man for whom Woodville was named, John B. Wood, built a factory in 1846 at what is now known as the Woodville four corners. He manufactured "coconut dippers." This mill passed c. 1852 to Clark and Gideon, manufacturers of cotton, and finally to the Dempsey brothers, who ran a bleaching and dyeing operation. Before it burned in 1882, it employed one hundred workers and ran on steam power. A mill was also opened at Geneva in 1827 by Edward S. Rhodes and sold to David Heaton and Martin K. Cowing in 1832.

The oldest house still standing is located north of the Geneva mill on the east side of the Douglas Pike and is the residence of Mr. and Mrs. Robert Miner.

In the nineteenth century a Poor Farm was established. It was located on the northeast side of the Douglas Pike and could be reached by going past the Hilton Bleachery or from Angell Road. The building was part of the Angell Farm c. 1700 and was demolished in 1880.

The first schoolhouse in Woodville, the North Providence Academy, was established in 1809 at the site of the present Stephen Olney School. In 1815, a stone schoolhouse was commissioned by the same subscribers to be built by John Angell. A new wooden school was built c. 1845 on Mineral Spring Turnpike and in 1890 a two-story wooden school was built on the Douglas Pike. Finally, in 1926, a brick building was erected on the original 1809 location; this building still stands with additions.

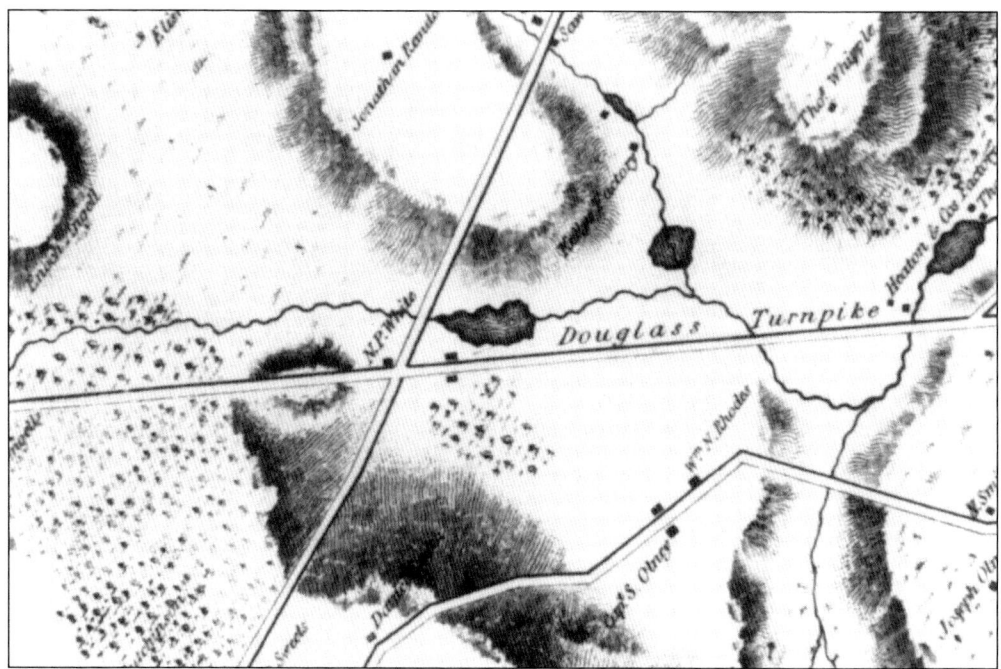

This 1835 map shows the sparsely-settled Geneva/Woodville area. The Jonathan Randall House (c. 1701), the William N. Rhodes house (c. 1705), the Thomas Whipple house (c. 1719), the Hezekiah Olney house (c. 1776), the Heaton and Cowens factory (c. 1827), and the Nicholas White house (c. 1824) are shown on this map.

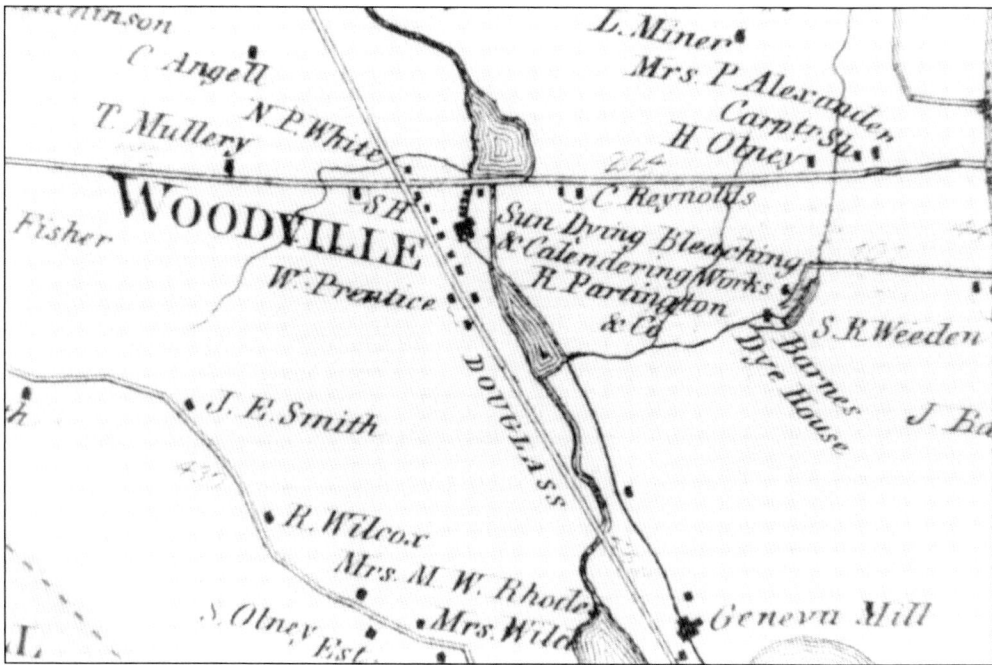

This 1870 map shows the extensive growth that had occurred since 1835. In 1846, John B. Wood opened a factory to manufacture "coconut dippers." Mr. Wood's name was given to the village. The public school was now located on the southwest corner of the pike intersection.

This map shows the area in 1895. The schoolhouse at the southwest corner of the pikes was built in 1845 to replace the stone schoolhouse.

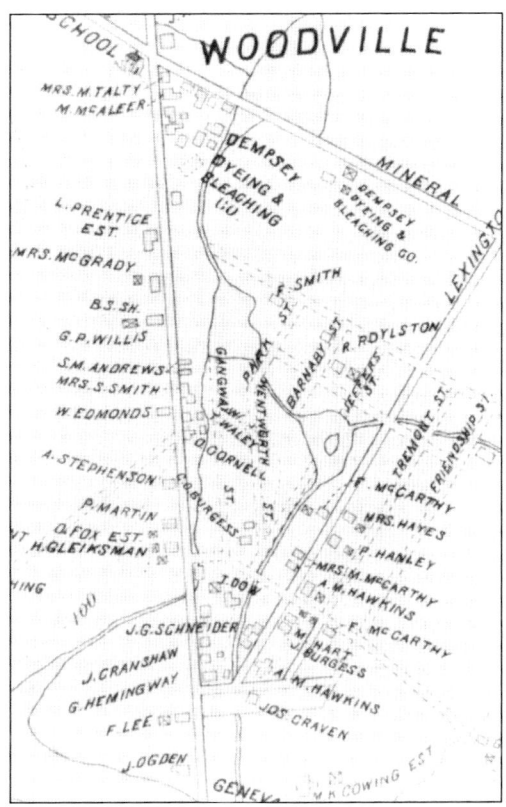

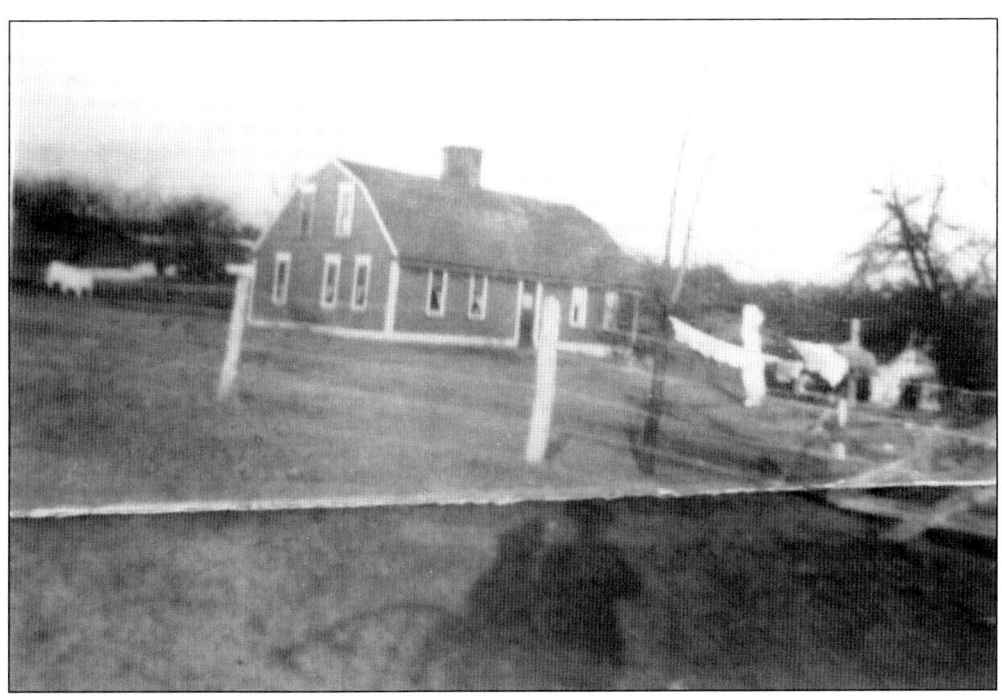

This is the Jonathan Whipple house on Lexington Avenue. It was built c. 1701.

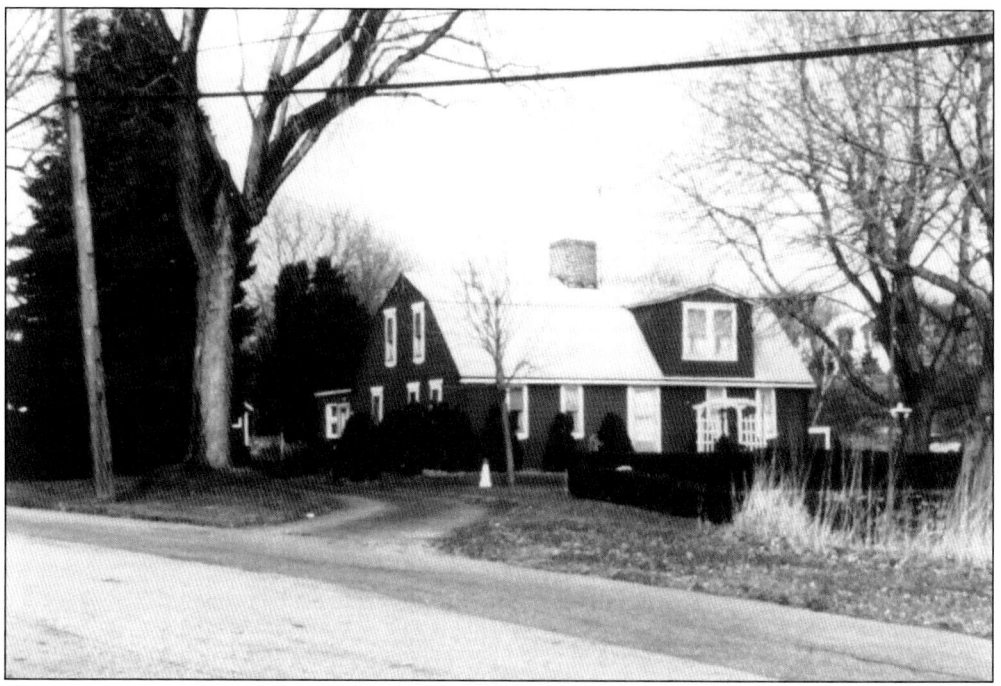

This is the Jonathan Whipple house as it looks today, except that it now has a light color siding.

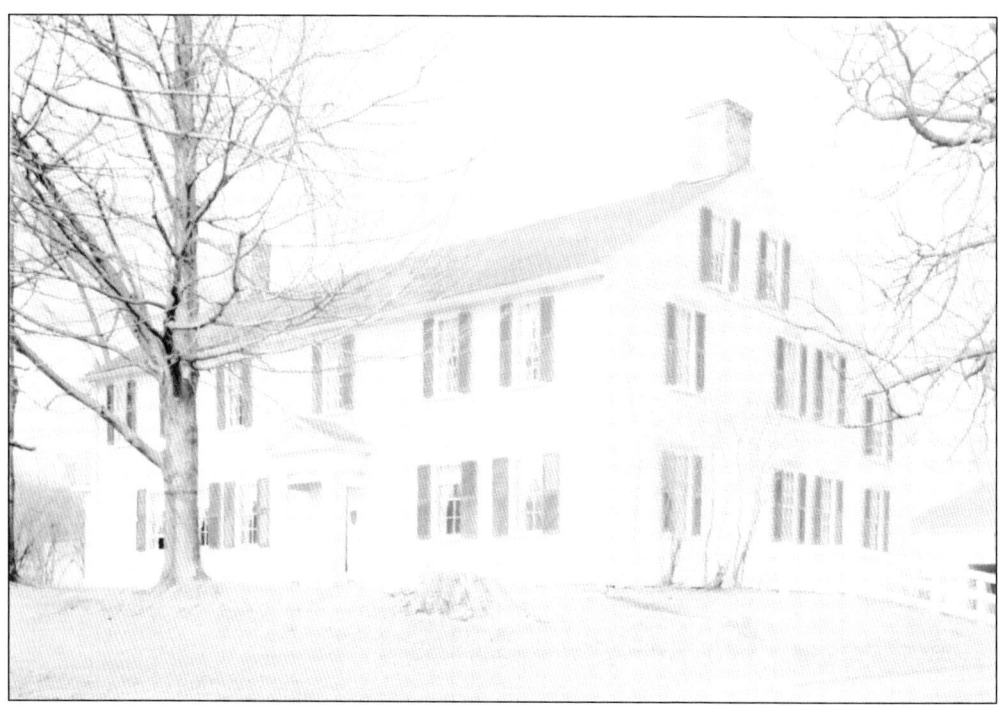

This home was built c. 1705 by Joseph Smith, a descendent of John Smith, the Providence miller. It is located on Smithfield Road and until the 1970s was occupied by a direct line of Jenckes family descendants.

This is a side view of the Joseph Smith house (built c. 1705). You can see the original stone end with later enlargements made in brick above it. This construction is typical of most late seventeenth- and early eighteenth-century homes constructed according to the Rhode Island "Stone-ender" architectural design.

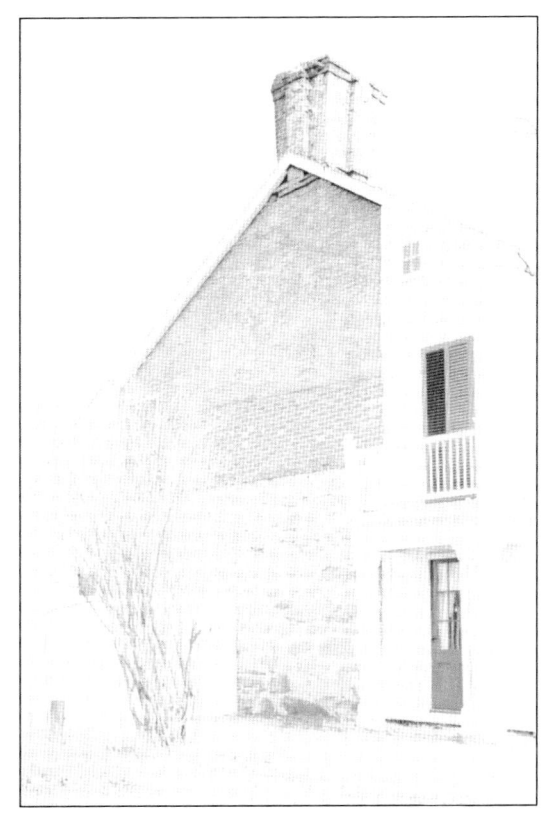

On the other side of Smithfield Road is the Captain Stephen Olney house, which was built, according to the Olney genealogy, in 1806. Captain Olney was a famous Revolutionary War hero. When LaFayette visited Rhode Island in 1824, he ran to Captain Olney in a crowd and embraced his good friend. The present owner of the house, Henry McCutcheon, is seen here in the yard.

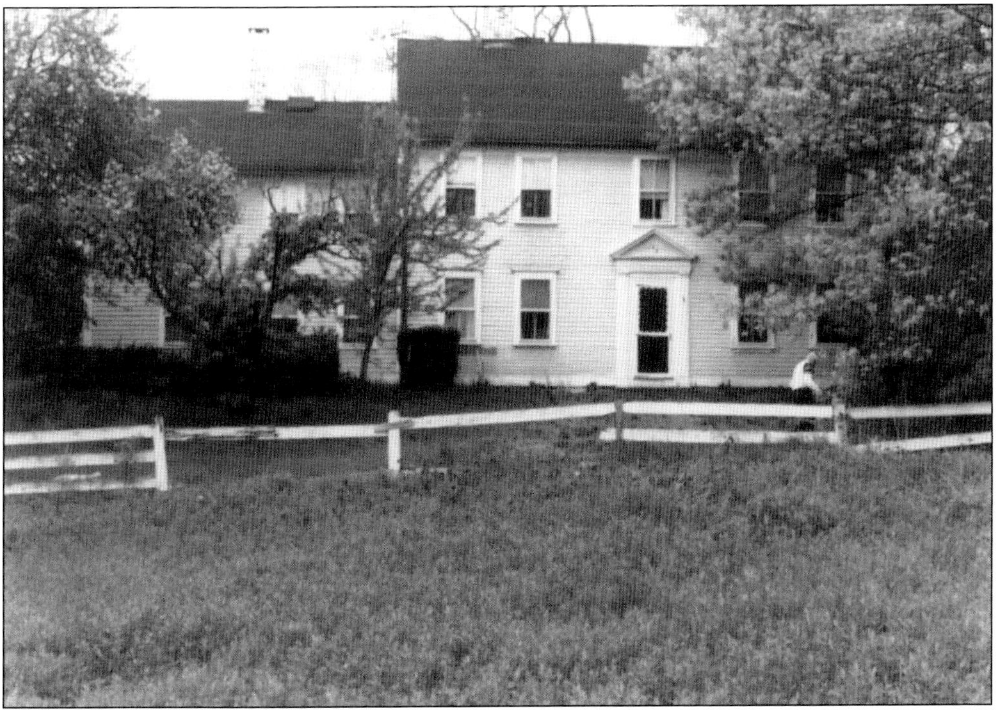

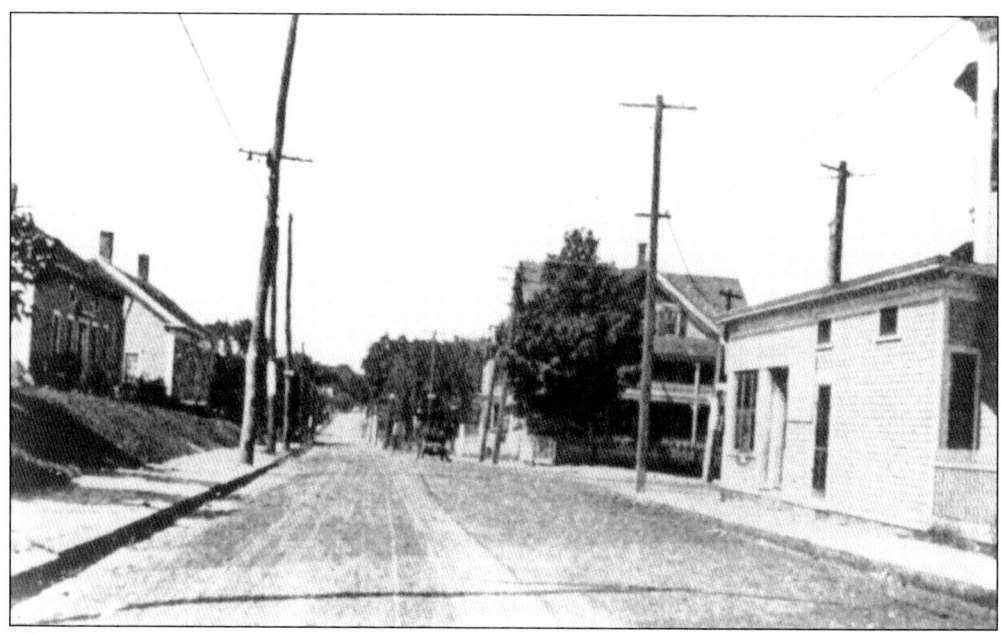

This is a 1919 view up the Douglas Pike from the intersection of Branch Avenue and the Douglas Pike.

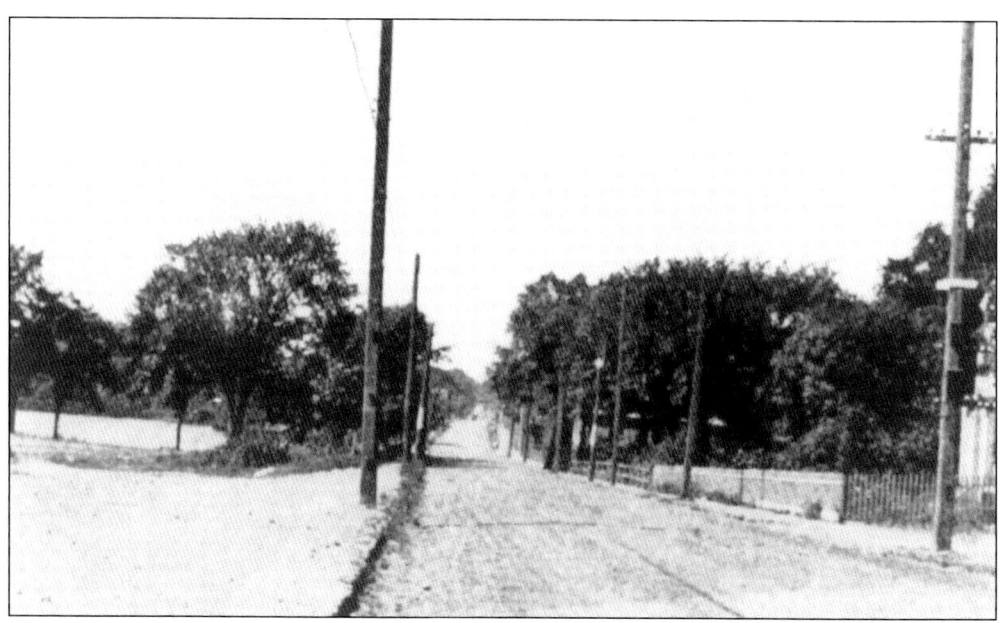

This 1919 view was taken from just before the Geneva mill, which would be on the right. To the left is the Geneva Pond.

This image of Captain Stephen Olney was printed in the Olney genealogy. Steven was the sixth generation in a line from Thomas Olney, an original settler and contemporary of Roger Williams. Olney made his reputation as a hero when he was chosen to lead the attack column at Yorktown.

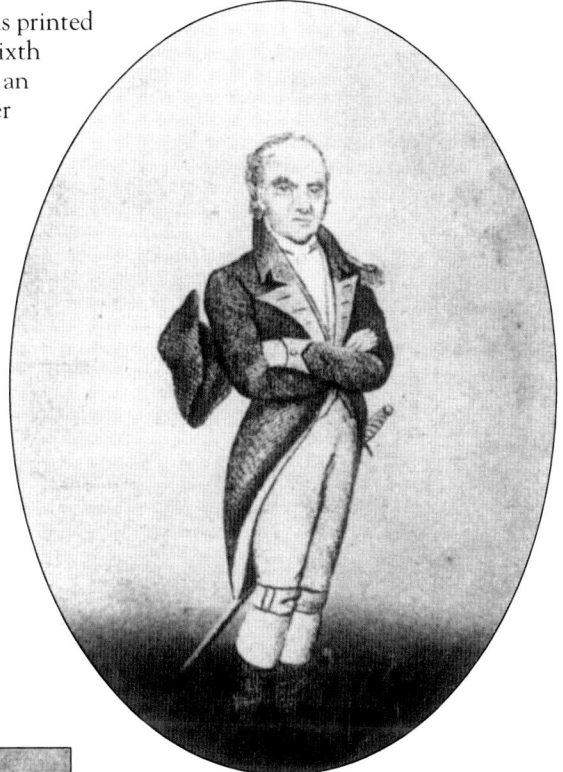

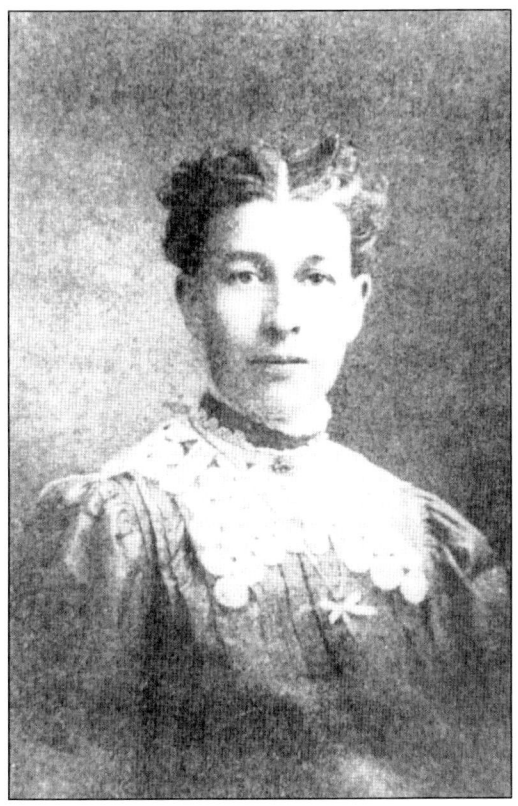

Mary Elizabeth Olney was the last lineal descendent of Captain Stephen Olney to live in his 1806 house on Smithfield Road. She was born in 1864 and died in 1952 after many years as a prominent North Providence citizen. She taught in the public school system, was a member of the Daughters of the American Revolution, and was a staunch prohibitionist.

OMNIBUS NOTICE.

On and after Monday, September 2d, 1867, an Omnibus will run from

Woodville to Providence

Making Two Trips Daily,

AS FOLLOWS:

Leave Woodville at o'clock A. M., and P. M., passing through Geneva and Wanskuck, thence down Charles and North Main Streets to Market Square.

Returning, leaves Market Square at A. M. and o'clock P. M.

SUNDAYS—Leave Woodville a. m. and p. m. Returning, leaves Providence a. m. and p. m.

JAMES E. HUTCHINSON, PROPRIETOR.

ODVILLE OMNIBUS,

The Omnibus was a large, horse-drawn conveyance that came before the street car. James Hutchinson was one of the local residents on Smithfield Road whose family had lived in the vicinity since the late eighteenth century.

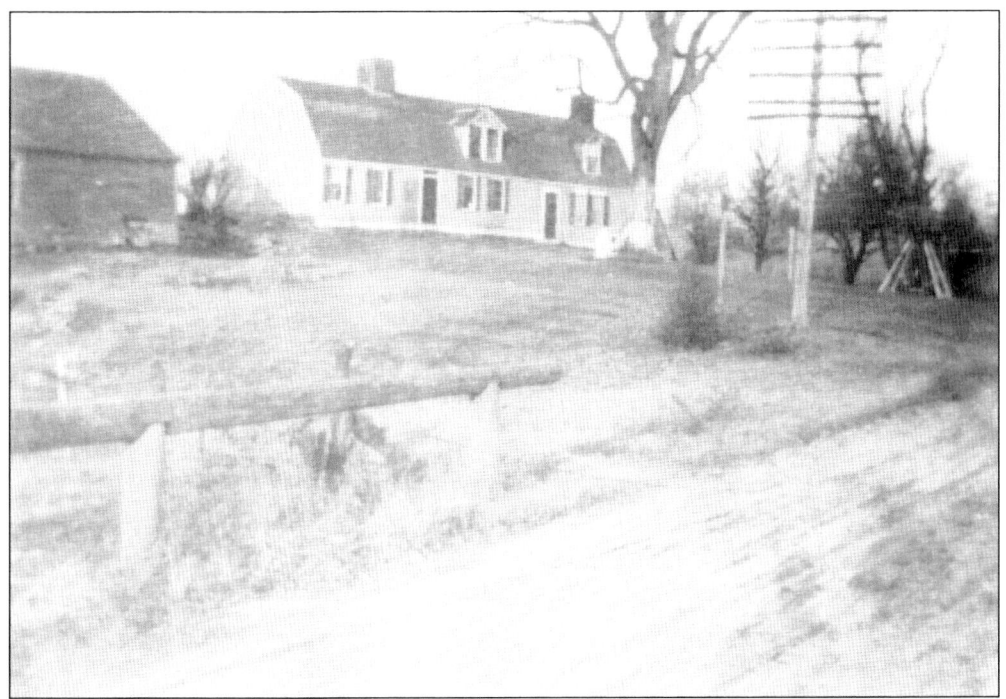

The Hezekiah Olney house was located at the corner of Mineral Spring Avenue and Terry Street. Hezekiah was a sixth generation descendant from Thomas Olney and was the brother of Captain Stephen Olney. He was born in 1761 and married Phebe Smith. This house was built between 1776 and 1780. Hezekiah died in 1820.

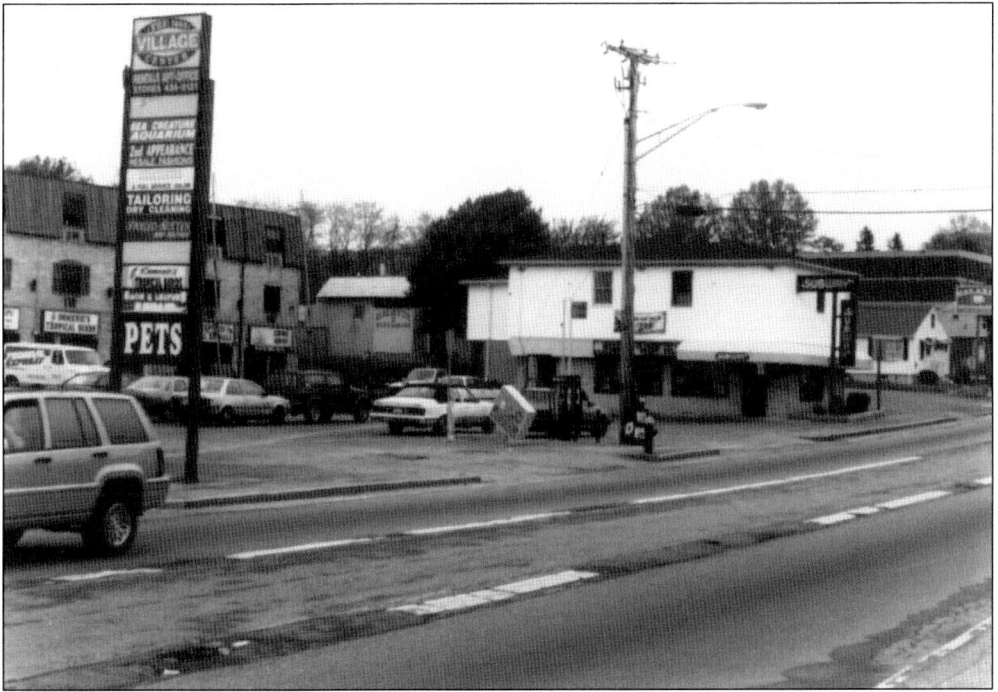

This is the site of the Hezekiah Olney house as it looks today.

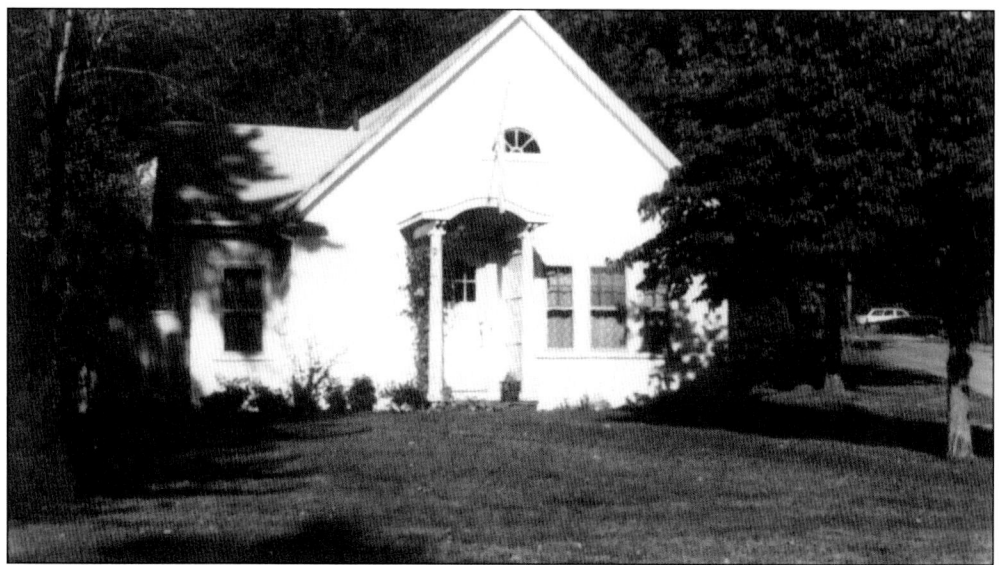

This home at 9 Cushing Street in Geneva was the site of the first fire station in this vicinity. It was used as early as 1916. It remained at this location until 1924.

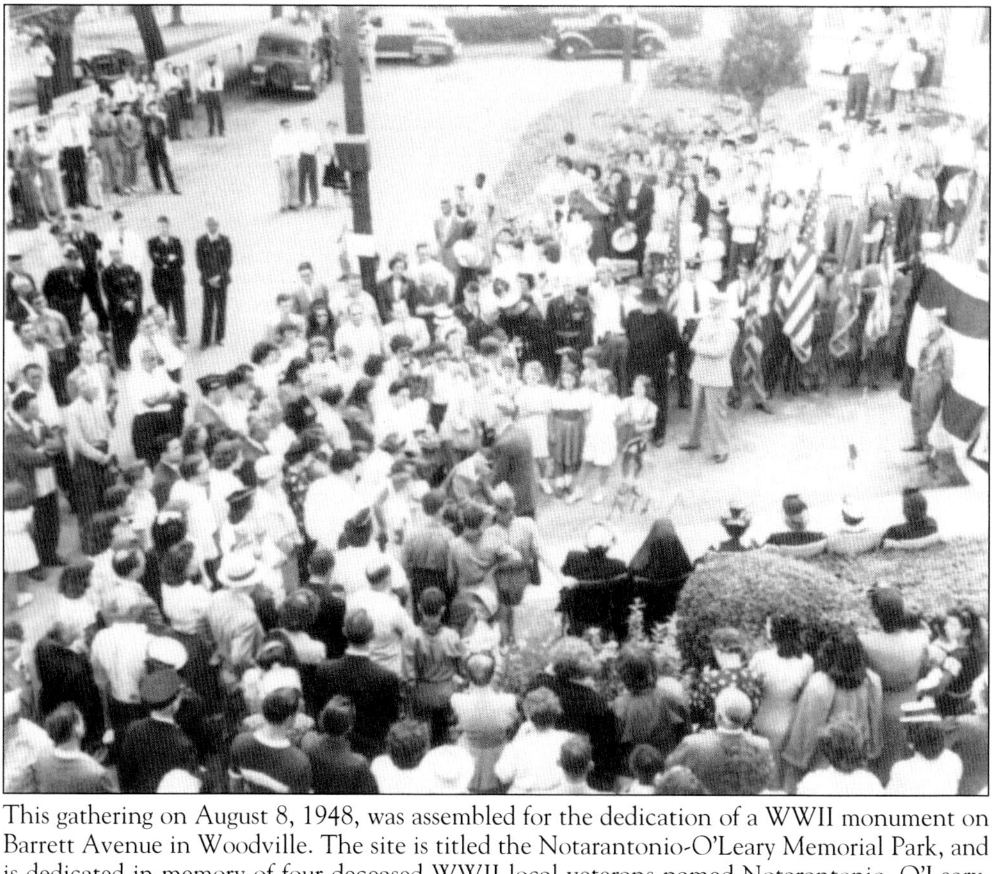

This gathering on August 8, 1948, was assembled for the dedication of a WWII monument on Barrett Avenue in Woodville. The site is titled the Notarantonio-O'Leary Memorial Park, and is dedicated in memory of four deceased WWII local veterans named Notarantonio, O'Leary, Ferreira, and Upton.

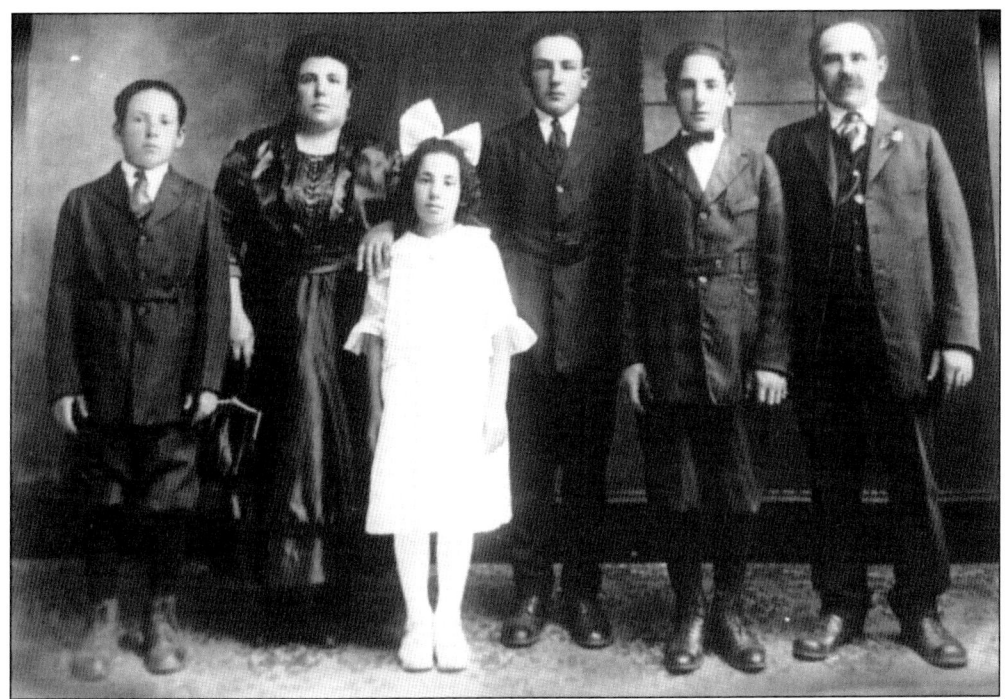

Among the numerous families to settle in the Woodville area, the Celona family became one of the most industrious. Giuseppe Celona built a home at 1420 Mineral Spring Avenue in 1920. Pictured here from left to right are: Anthony, Antonina, Josephine, John, Joseph Jr., and Giuseppe.

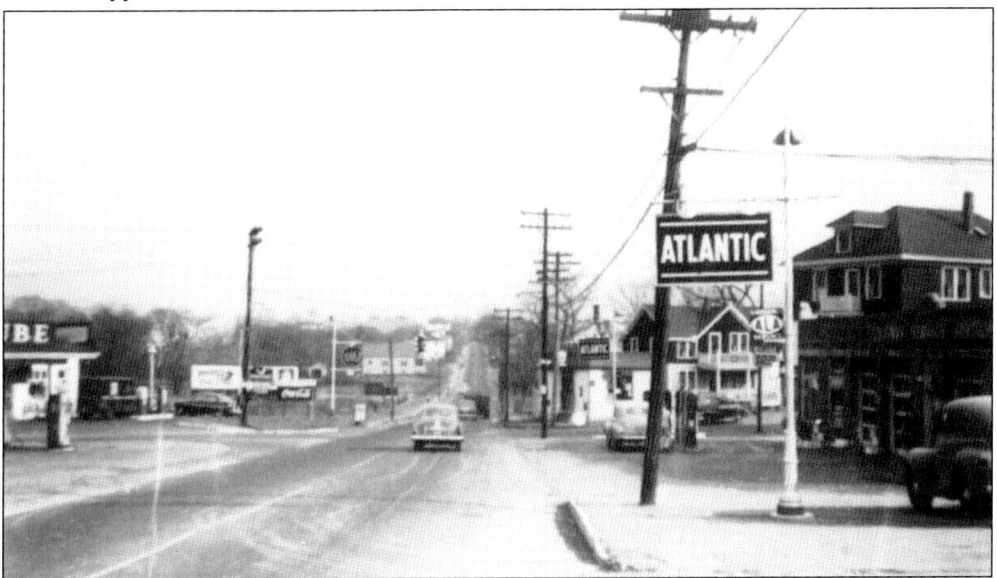

This view looks down Mineral Spring Avenue toward Pawtucket in 1952. The white variety store at the southeast corner of Douglas and Mineral Spring Avenues was opened in the 1920s by Henry Brown and Samuel Gursky. In 1947, Joe Celona Jr. bought the business. On the northeast corner is the white tile Gulf station still present today. The northwest corner had Morrissey's Oil Service and the southwest corner had Celona's gas station.

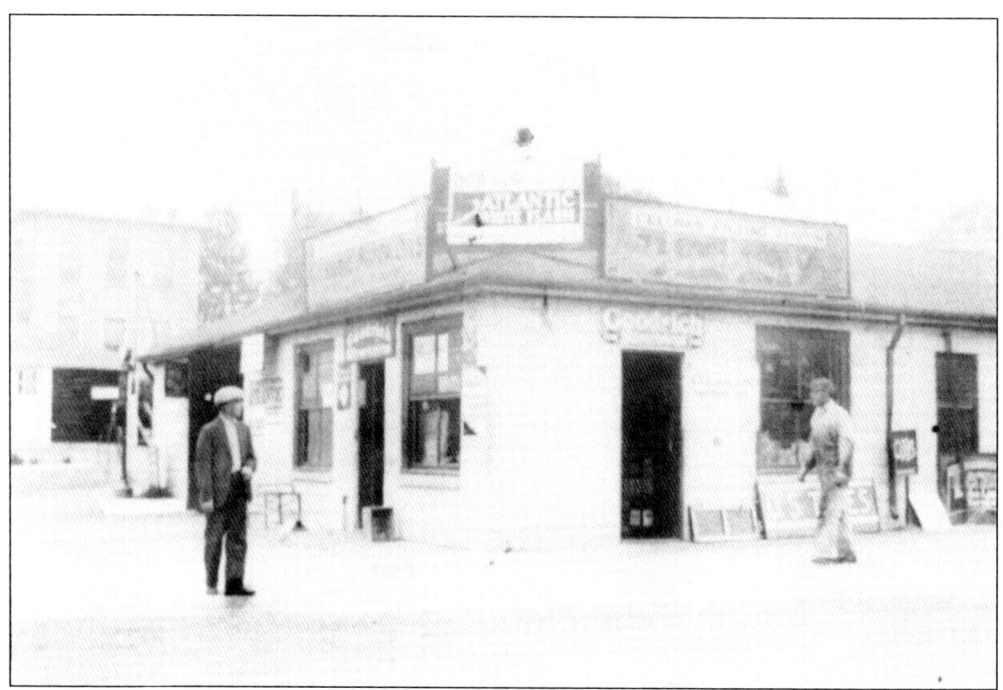

In 1924, Giuseppe Celona built a gas station on the southwest corner of Douglas and Mineral Spring Avenues. The business opened on July 4, 1924, and sold four different brands of gasoline. The first gas was sold to the driver of a Cunningham's Ice Delivery truck. To the right is Joe Celona Jr.

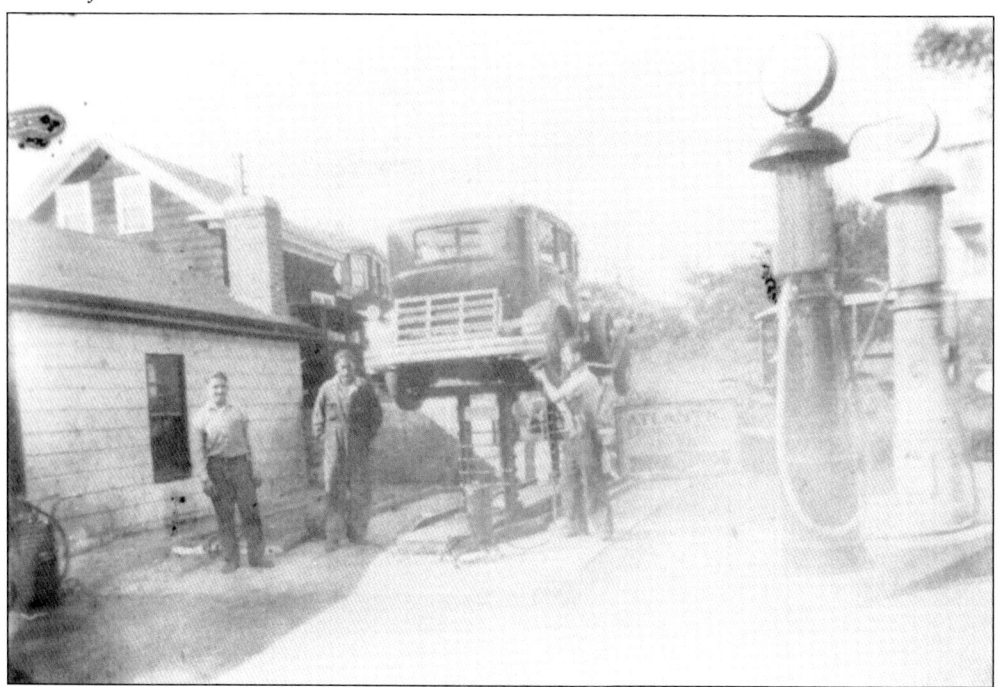

Employees do a grease job on an automobile at Celona's. Notice the old gasoline pumps. Persons from left to right are: Anthony Celona, Ernest Lippitt, and Joseph Celona Jr.

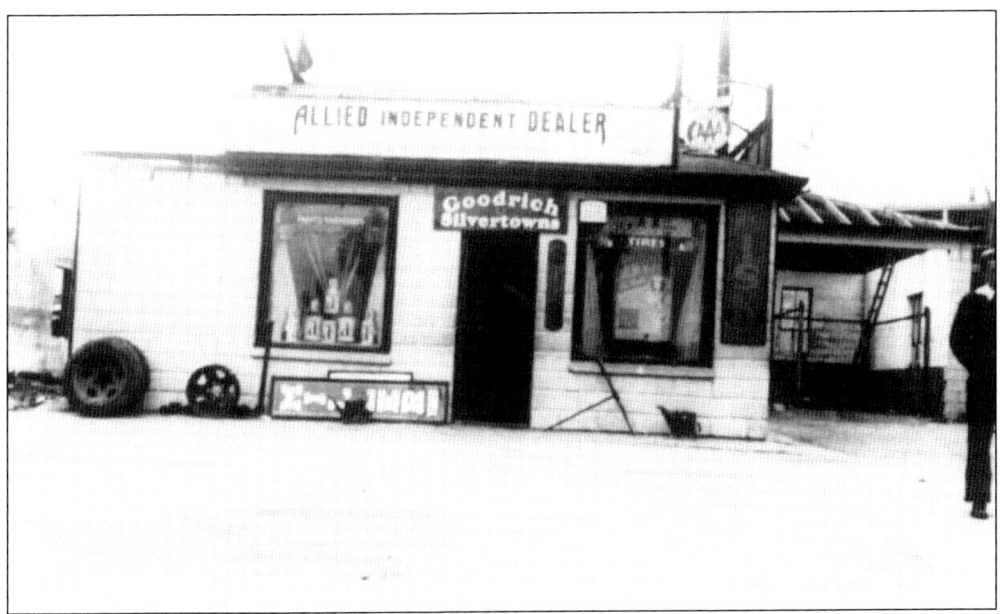

This photograph of Celona's station was taken in 1937 just before the demolition. Part of the complex included a barbershop in back. The buildings were demolished to make way for a modern station.

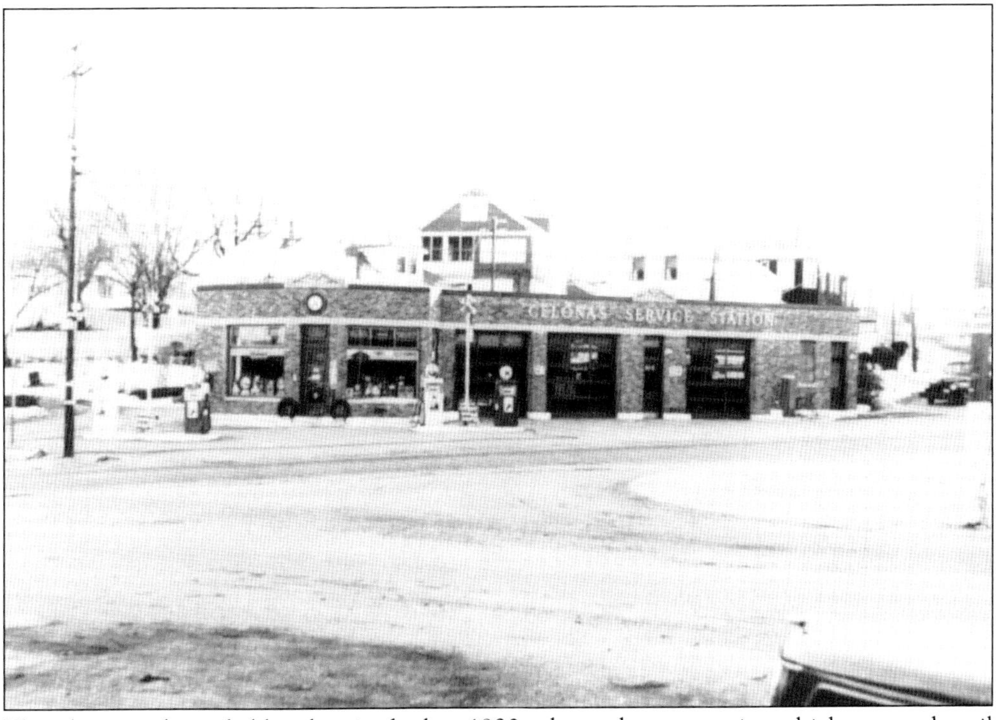

This photograph, probably taken in the late 1930s, shows the new station which was used until Joseph Celona Jr. retired. In 1972, the station was sold to Al Fotarsky.

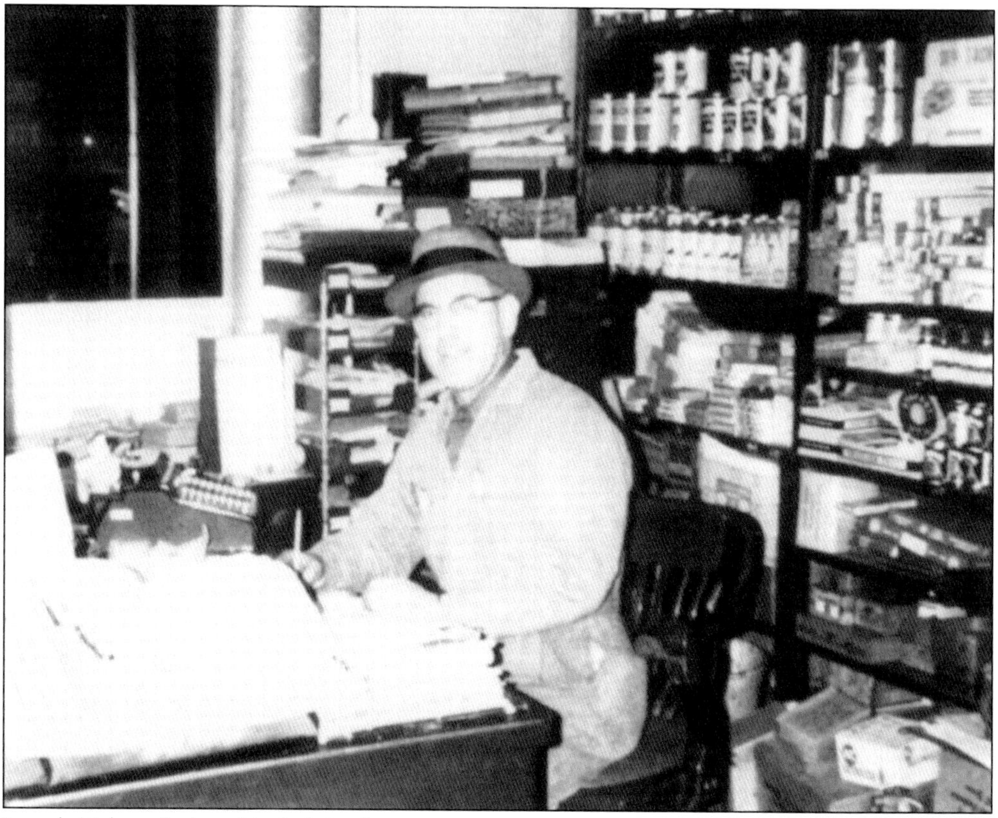

Joseph Celona Jr. is at his desk in the station.

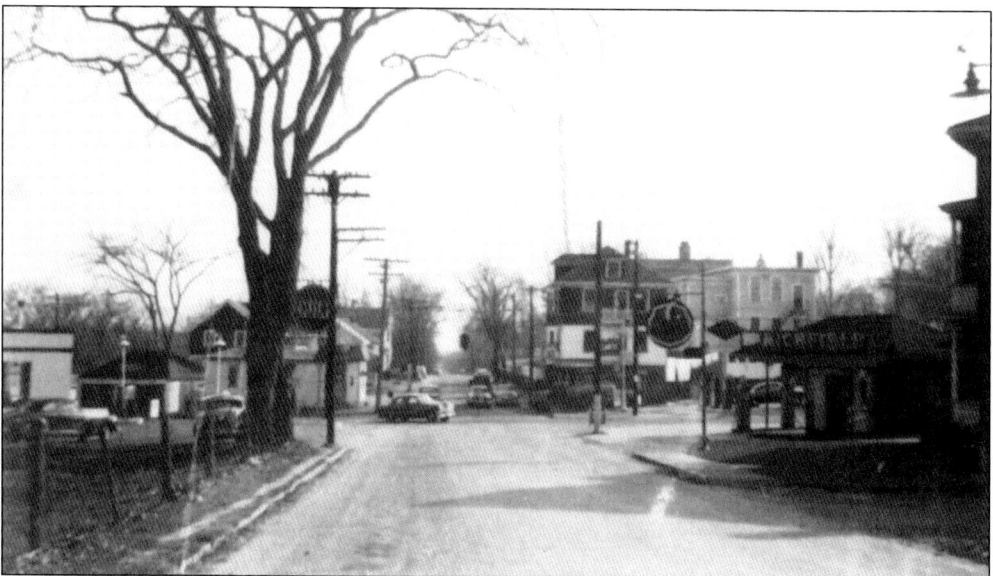

The four corners at Woodville are shown c. 1940s. The white tile Gulf station is to the left and Brown and Gursky's store is across the Mineral Spring Pike. The old Woodville School, built in the 1890s, can be seen in the distance on the right. Celona's station and the Richfield station, adjacent to Notarantonio's, are seen on the near right.

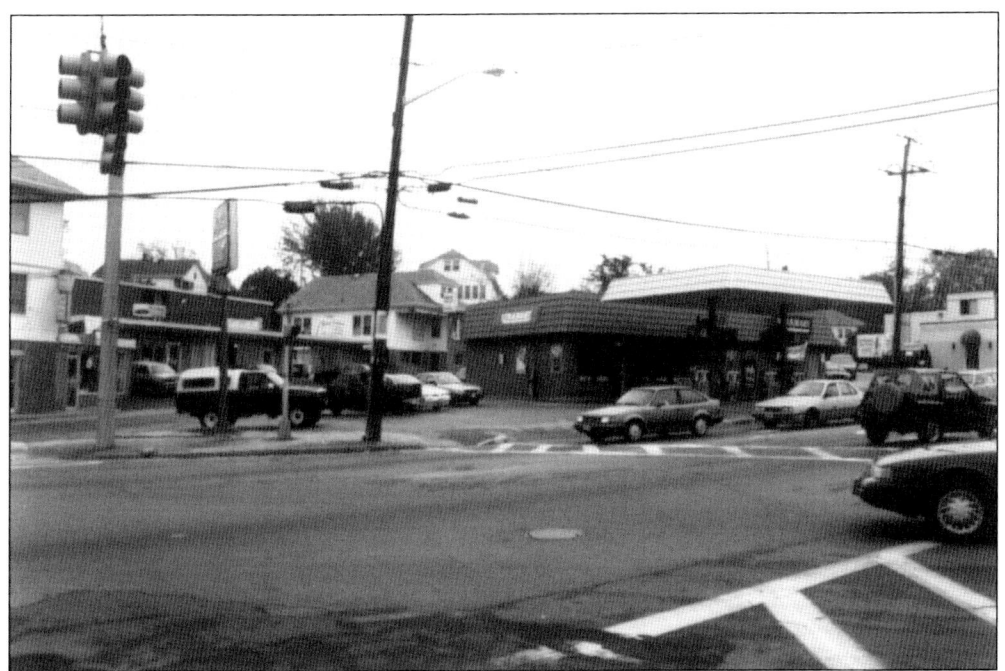

The site of Celona's station is shown as it appears today.

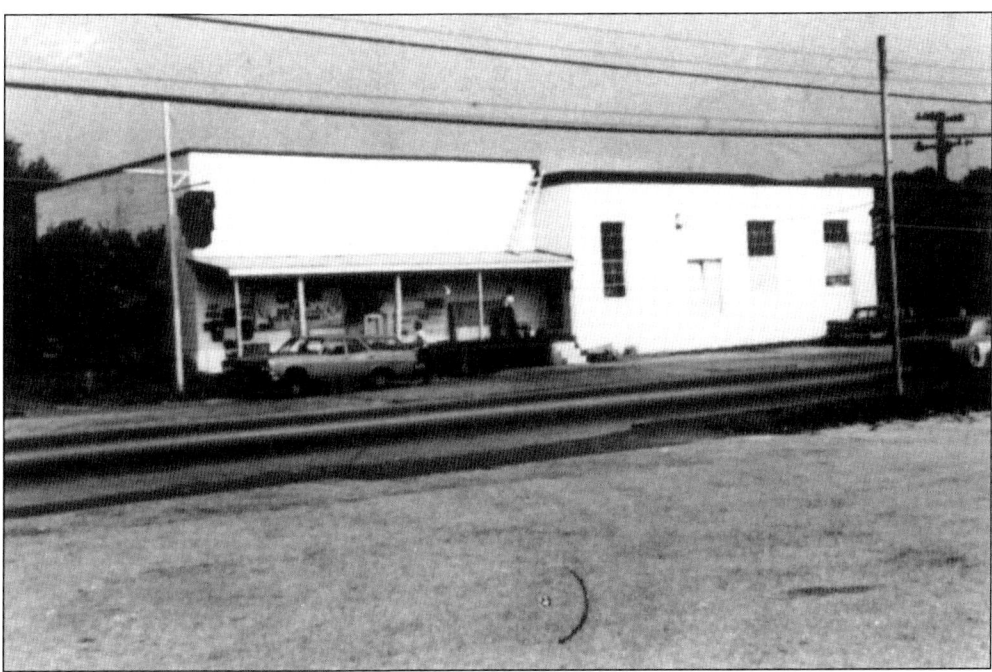

Giuseppe Celona started an ice company in 1910 by damming a brook and harvesting ice naturally. During the summer, he drained the pond and raised vegetables to sell to peddlers and from his own vegetable stand. In 1924, he built an artificial ice producing plant. The building in the photograph was erected in 1932.

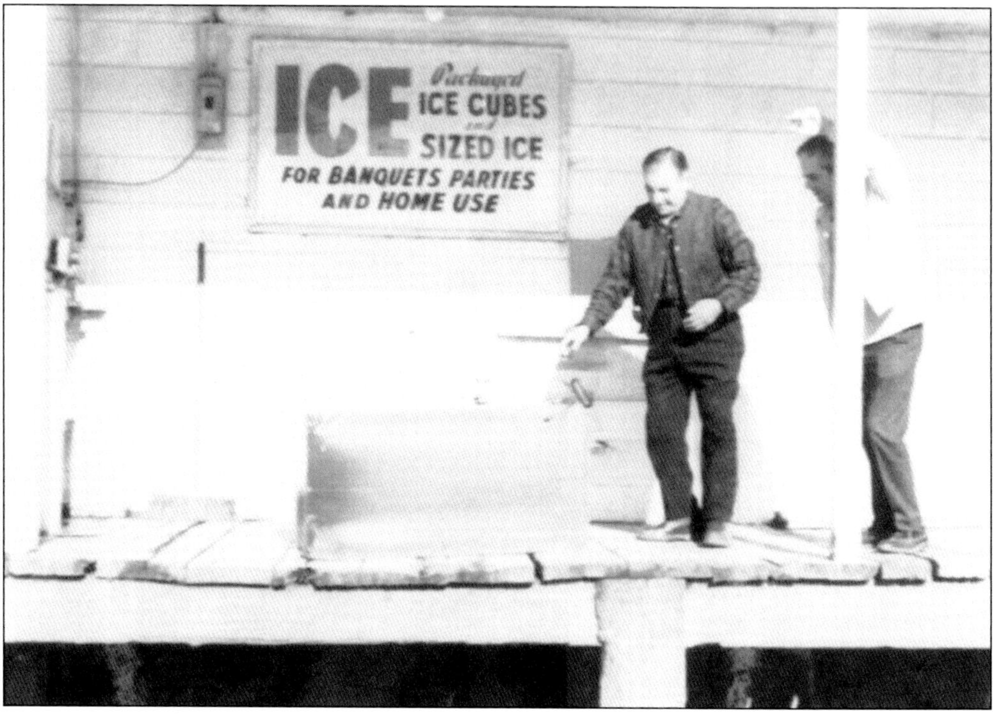

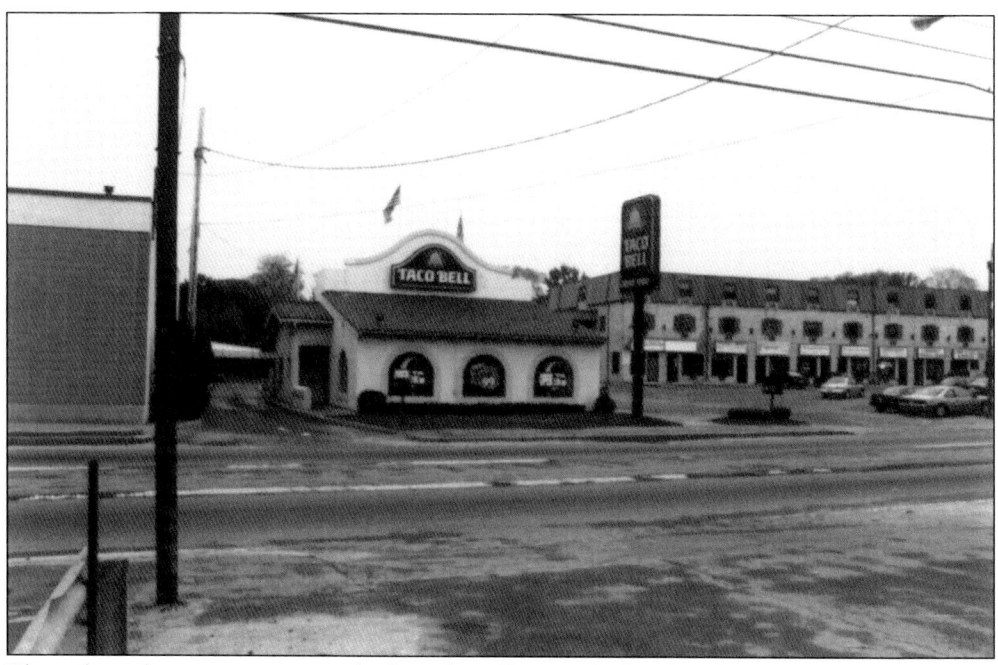

Here we see Anthony Bucci to the left, a longtime employee of the Celona family business. The customer is unknown.

This is how the ice company site looks today. The Hezekiah Olney house on Terry Street and Mineral Spring Avenue would have appeared on the right in this view, but it is no longer in existence.

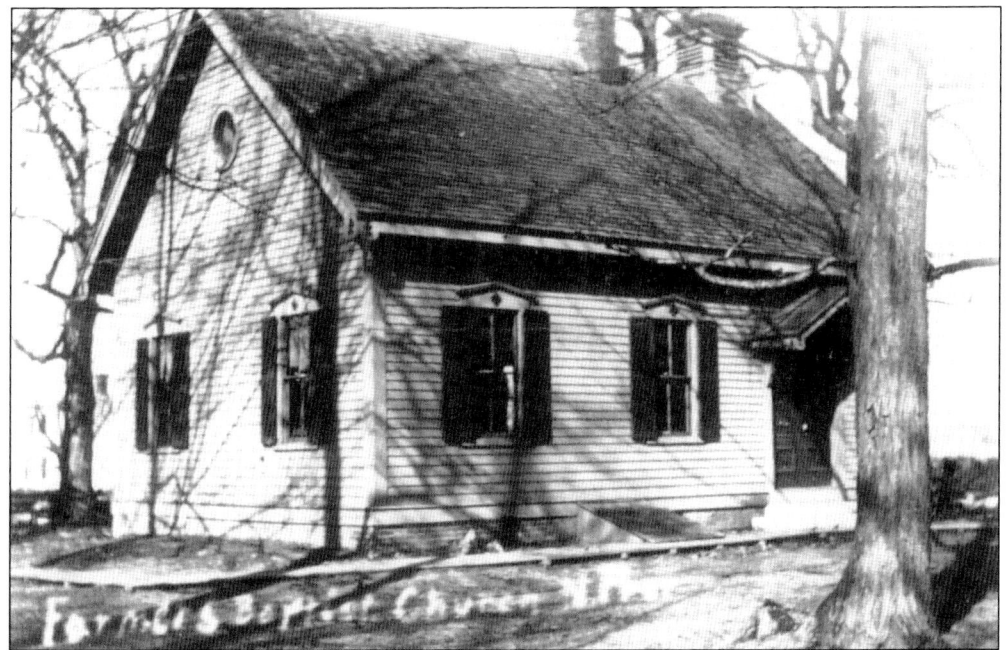

This is the 1884 Farmers' Chapel on Angell Road, now the residence of Mr. and Mrs. Norman Turner.

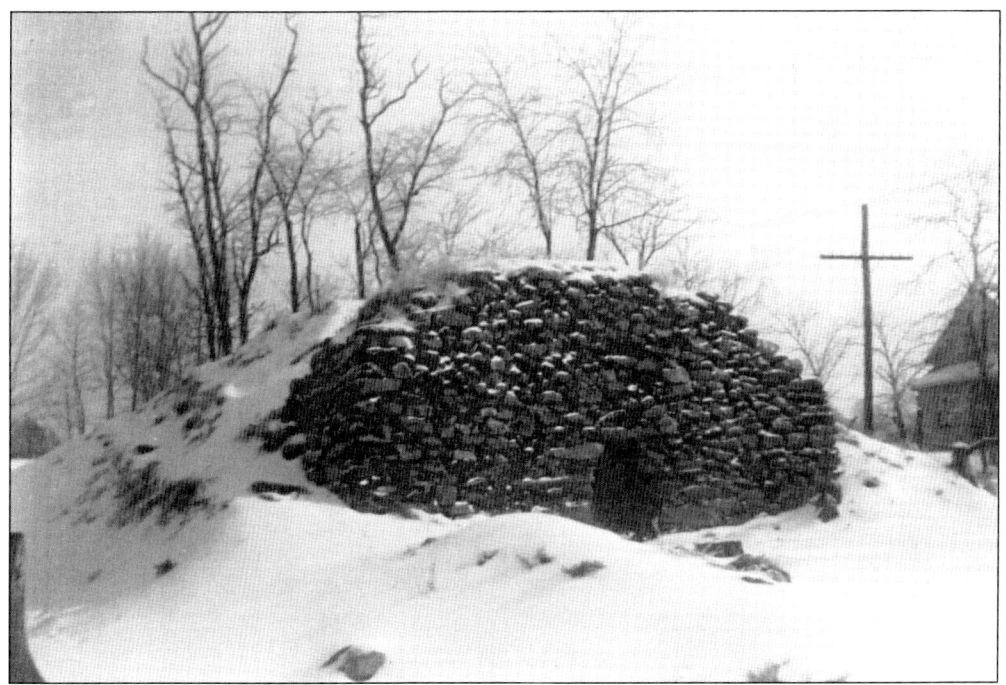

This photograph shows the eighteenth-century lime kiln on upper Smithfield Road. Houses are now built on the site.

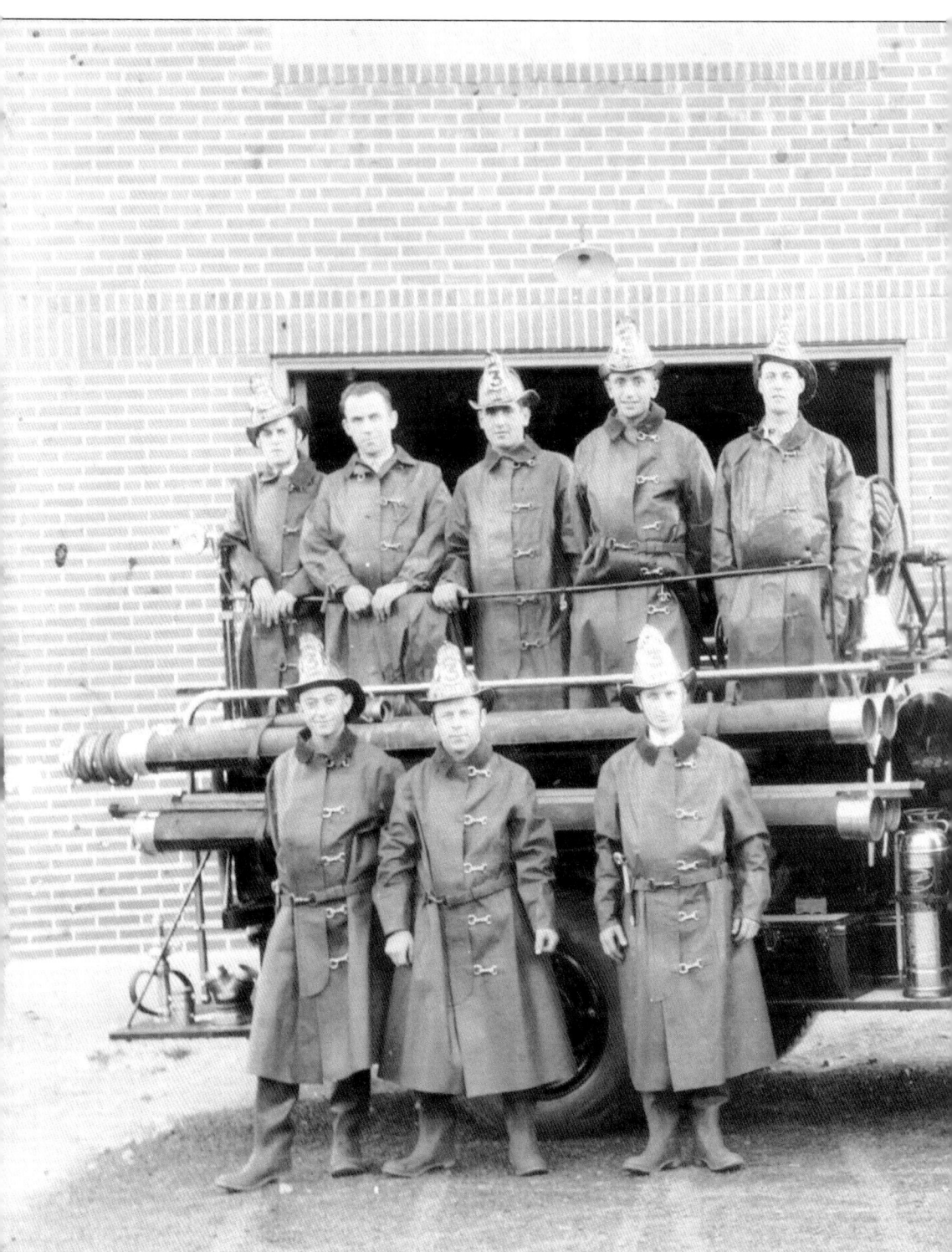

The Geneva Volunteer Fire Company is pictured here c. 1927 at their new station on Douglas Avenue adjacent to Cushing Street. From left to right are: (front row) John Bargamian, Arthur

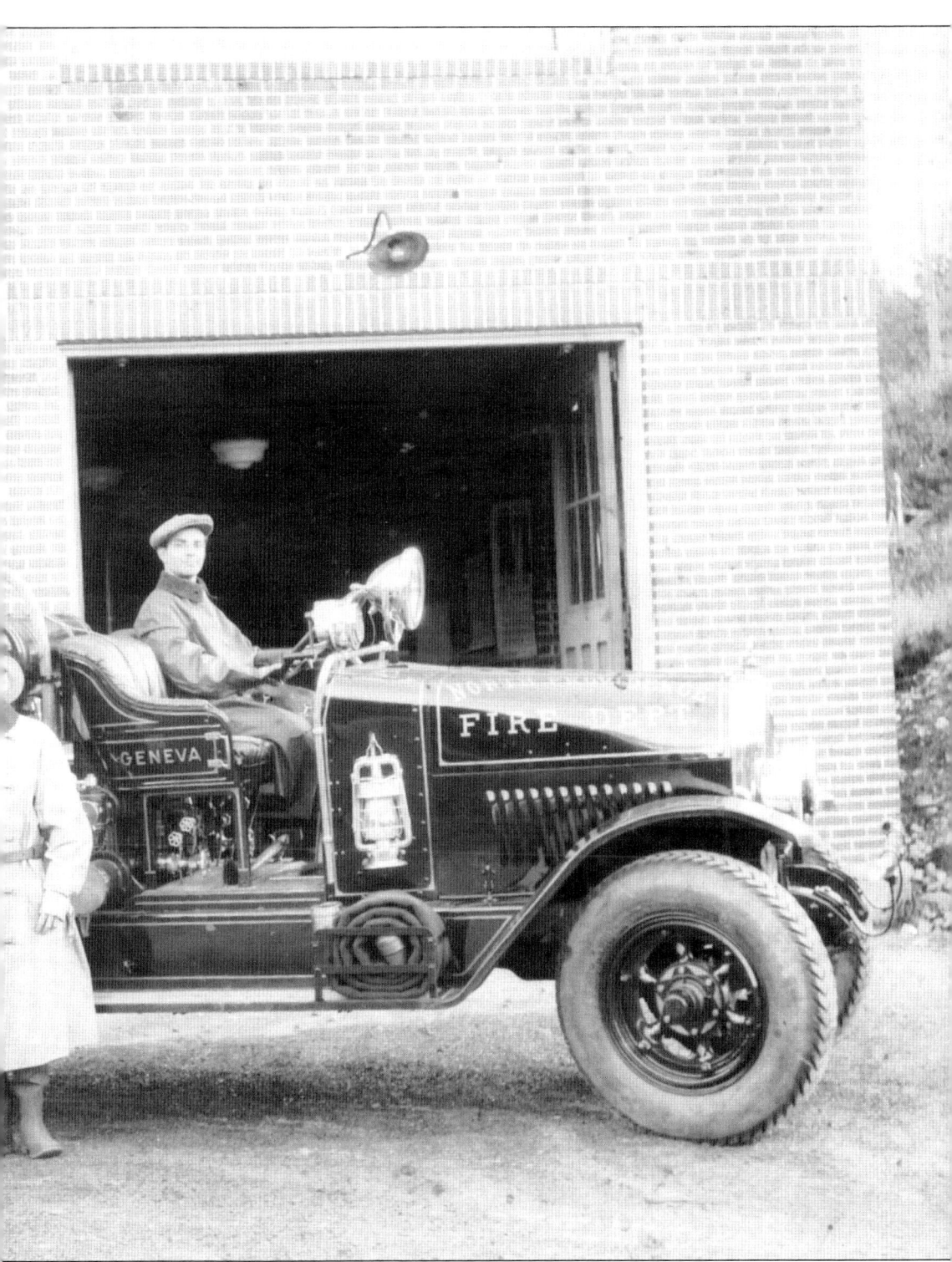

Taylor, Bugar Brothers, Captain Allen, and Joseph Capobianco (driver); (back row) Walter Morrissey, ? Taylor, Joseph Celona Jr., Hatchedor Bargamian, and Eugene Benjamin.

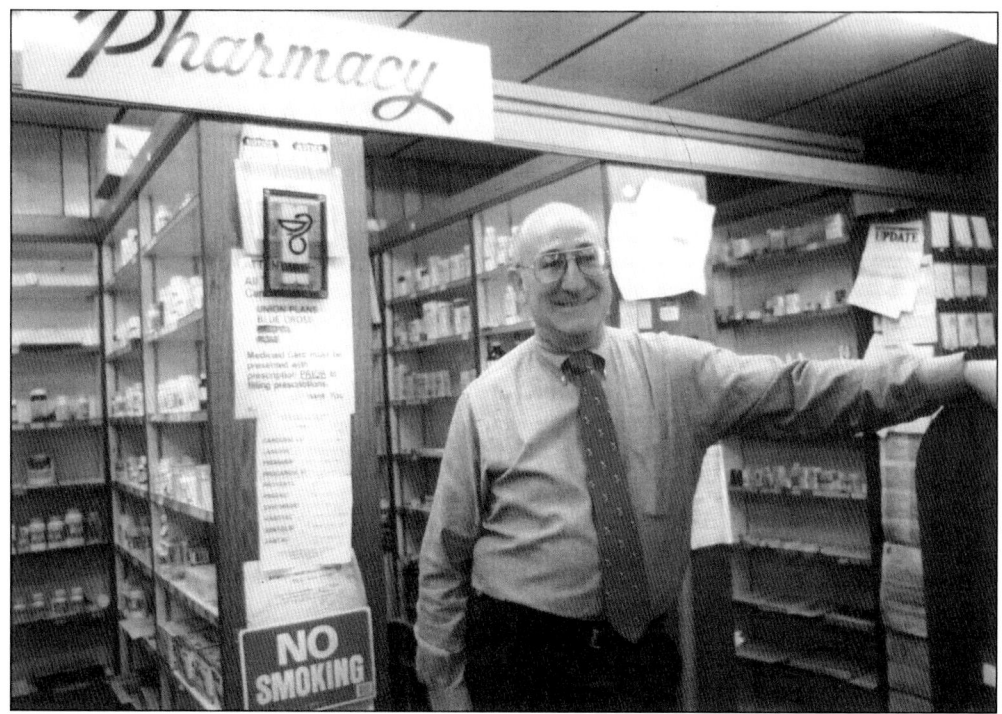

Eugene Pistacchio is behind the counter during the last weeks of operation of the Community Drug Store, the last of the Centerdale independent pharmacies. The Community Drug Store closed at the beginning of January 1996. This photograph was taken in December of 1995.

ACKNOWLEDGMENTS

We have been collecting historic photographs of North Providence since the 1970s. The purchase of our 1861 home provided a catalyst for our interest in North Providence history. Over the years, we have had the opportunity to meet many interesting people who provided us with priceless information. This is the first time that a history of all of North Providence has been attempted. We would like to acknowledge and thank the following people: William Achille, Sidney Angell, Donald Asselin, Carol Ashcroft (nee Dick), Carlton Baker, Gertrude Baron, Henry Batalon, Robert L. Black, Richard Brillon, Deborah Burton (dec.), Beulah Callaghan, Robert Carnavale, Joseph Celona Jr., Harold Darby, Eileen Dick, Florence Draper, Elizabeth Greene Dufresne, Deborah Imondi, Mildred Longo, Hugh McCarron, Betty and George O'Reilly, Veronica Owen, the *Observer* newspaper, Gilbert Plante, Steven Salisbury, Ann and Ella Santilli, Hope Senecal, Patricia and Michael Smith, Herbert Sweet, the descendants of William Tilley, Grace Van Wye, Beatrice Ward, and William M. Woodward.